The Boundary of Existence

The Wreck of the USS Saginaw and the Most Desperate Voyage in Naval History

R.J.Jones

Immersion Imagery

Published by Immersion Imagery

New South Wales, Australia

Cover Design: Immersion Imagery

Paperback ISBN: 978 1 7646431 0 8

Hardcover ISBN: 978 1 7646431 1 5

First Edition: April 2026

Email: immimagery@gmail.com

Contents

A Note from the Author

The wreck of the USS Saginaw first appeared as a standard maritime tragedy. A ship strikes a reef. Men scramble for survival. History moves on. Research revealed a saga of endurance that defies easy categorization. Civil War veterans faced a new kind of enemy. They navigated a fifteen-hundred-mile voyage in an open boat. Discipline held ninety-three men together on a desolate strip of sand for months.

The narrative pauses at intervals to look backward toward the wrecks of the whalers Gledstanes (1837) and Parker (1842). This atoll possesses an ancient identity. The Hawaiians know it as Hōlanikū, or "The Boundary of Existence." The place functions as a character. It sits as a sacred threshold between the living and the dead. It served as a literal graveyard for American ships. The Saginaw was one of many vessels claimed by these breakers. The ghosts of those earlier wrecks determined the fate of the Saginaw men. They provided a warning the officers arrived too late to heed, and a legacy of endurance that defined the limits of what a crew could suffer.

Three primary accounts guided the reconstruction of this history. Paymaster George H. Read wrote The Last Cruise of the Saginaw. His book provides a window into the mind of a nineteenth-century officer. He observed the disintegration of his world with wit and literacy. His voice offered the intimate details that breathe life into the historical record. He captured the taste of raw albatross and the texture of a rotting uniform.

Lieutenant-Commander Montgomery Sicard provided the perspective of command. His official reports and personal correspondence reveal the crushing weight of responsibility and the technical precision required to keep a crew alive in the face of certain death. Coxswain William Halford offered the visceral reality of the sailor. His "unvarnished" account of the gig's voyage provides the grit and physical bone-strain of the thousand-mile pull toward Hawaii.

This book remains a work of non-fiction. The dates, the geography, the technical specifications of the ship, and the acts of the crew come from naval archives, court of inquiry transcripts, and archaeological reports. Where the record remains silent, the known practices of the U.S. Navy in 1870 bridge the gap.

The ocean remains the most indifferent force on earth. The story of the Saginaw shows what happens when human ambition collides with that indifference. It proves the lengths to which people go to survive.

Dramatis Personae

U.S.S. SAGINAW (4th Rate)
October 1870
Complement: 93 Souls

OFFICERS OF THE WARDROOM

Lieutenant Commander Montgomery Sicard, U.S.N. Commanding Officer. A veteran of the Civil War steam navy. He rules through silence and precise orders. The weight of ninety-three lives rests on his shoulders. The decision to inspect Ocean Island remains his alone.

Lieutenant John G. Talbot, U.S.N. Executive Officer. Second-in-command. Sailors regard him as the finest seaman aboard. He maintains morale through action. He volunteers first for the relief expedition.

Paymaster George H. Read, U.S.N. Logistics Officer. The ship's victualer. He tracks the physical and psychological disintegration of the crew. His journal preserves the micro-textures of their survival.

Passed Assistant Surgeon George H. Frank, U.S.N. Medical Officer. He treats lacerations and starvation in a camp.

Passed Assistant Engineer James Butterworth, U.S.N. Chief Engineer. He manages the aging steam engines. On the island, he fashions the condenser from a boiler and speaking-tubes to provide the camp with fresh water.

Passed Assistant Engineer Henry C. Blye, U.S.N. Supervisor of Dredging. An officer detailed to oversee the contractor's work.

JUNIOR OFFICERS (STEERAGE)

Ensign J.K. Cogswell, U.S.N. Watch Officer. He assumes the duties of Executive Officer after the gig departs for Hawaii.

Second Assistant Engineer Herschel Main, U.S.N. Engineer. A technical wizard. He builds a working sextant from zinc scraps and a broken mirror to navigate the open ocean.

THE SHIP'S COMPANY

Solomon Graves Rating: Cabin Cook. He renders the oily meat of the albatross into the crew's daily ration.

William Halford Rating: Coxswain. A sailor of massive physical strength. He serves as the engine of the open-boat voyage and survives as its lone witness.

Peter Francis Rating: Quartermaster. A seasoned helmsman. He steers the gig through heavy seas.

John Andrews Rating: Seaman. A civilian diver who joins the Navy on the reef to escape the island.

James Muir Rating: Seaman. A specialist in ship's stores. He volunteers for the boat crew to force a rescue.

SUPERNUMERARIES (CIVILIANS)

Mr. George W. Townsend Contractor. Head of the dredging party. A man of industry whose machines remain at the bottom of the lagoon.

Mr. A.M. Bailey Foreman. A pious man. His pocket Bible provides a spiritual anchor for the crew.

THE RECOVERY EXPEDITION

Captain Thomas Long. Master of the Hawaiian government steamer *Kilauea*. A veteran mariner of the Pacific. Tasked by the Hawaiian King and the American Minister to find the missing men. He navigates the treacherous currents of the Northwestern Hawaiian Islands to effect the final rescue at Ocean Island.

For Sharon,
My true north.

"The charts are a century out of step... and I'll not leave these waters until I've ensured the safety of those who follow us."
Lieutenant-Commander Montgomery Sicard

The Boundary of Existence

The Wreck of the USS Saginaw and the Most Desperate Voyage in Naval History

Part 1

THE WRECK

Chapter 1

High noon offered no sanctuary. The sun hung as a molten weight directly above the Midway Islands, two parched slivers of sand lost in three thousand miles of empty, sapphire-dark sea. The world felt flattened, reduced to a blinding white glare and the vertical, crushing heat of the horse latitudes.

The USS *Saginaw* occupied the center of this stillness, her black hull a target for the radiating heat. Dry, crisp air rose from the island, burning exposed skin and leaching moisture from the lungs. This parched atmosphere stood in stark contrast to the heavy, rotting swelter of the Mexican coast they had left seven months ago. From the quarterdeck, the horizon crowded the ship, drawing a tight circle around the wood. Unbroken light fused the sea and sky into a silver mist, ending the world at the ship's rail.

A thin finger of shade cast by the mainmast swung across the deck with the ship's roll. Paymaster George Read adjusted his cap. Perspiration pooled beneath the wool band and slicked his fingers. The visor failed to check the secondary assault of the glare, a brilliant, upward radiation that bounced off the water and seared the retinas. The light pierced the eyes and settled behind the forehead as a throbbing ache.

To starboard, the lagoon lay as a flat, hammered expanse of turquoise, walled off from the deep Pacific by the churning white line of the outer reef. Black figures scurried over the white coral. To spare these men of Mr. Townsend's work party the searing distortion of the reef-glare, Read had issued the crew wire-mesh goggles. The contraptions transformed the men into a legion of faceless, steel-eyed insects, picking at the crust like scavengers on a sun-bleached bone.

The *Saginaw* swung heavily around her anchor chains, a tethered watchdog for a construction project that felt increasingly like a folly. For seven months, they had burned through the Navy's appropriation, attempting to blast a channel through a reef that proved harder than flint. The stone broke their drills. The sea remained indifferent to the violence.

A dull *crump* rolled across the water. A plume of white spray geysered into the air near the cut, hanging suspended for a heartbeat before collapsing back into the surf. Another blast. Another yard of coral pulverized.

Read leaned against the rail. The iron stung his palm. The Pacific Mail Steamship Company wanted a coaling station here, a midway point for their steamers running from San Francisco to the Orient. To fulfill this corporate ambition, the *Saginaw*, a veteran of the blockade, now served as a laboring tender for a glorified dredging operation. She bore the weary aspect of a soldier forced into a drayman's harness. As the first vessel ever birthed from the ways at Mare Island, her timbers of California laurel and oak carried the pedigree of the Pacific coast, yet eleven years of service had hollowed her out.

The ship carried the scars of a decade spent in the service of a restless empire. Before the rebellion, she had patrolled the humid, treacherous reaches of the East China Sea, her paddlewheels churning through the silt of the Yangtze as she hunted pirates and protected the merchant houses of Shanghai. When the war came, she had been summoned home to the Pacific Squadron to guard the coast against Confederate raiders that never arrived. She had spent the years of the blockade pacing the shoreline like a caged wolf, her boilers straining to maintain a readiness for a battle that remained a thousand leagues to the east.

Now, a fourth-rate side-wheel gunboat, she carried her history in the gouges of her deck and the permanent soot-stain on her funnel. Salt scoured her black hull. Her rigging, though taut, held the brittle texture of hemp that had surrendered its tar to the sun. Unlike the tall-masted clippers of the San Francisco docks, the *Saginaw* was a squat, symmetrical anomaly, a "double-ender." She was sharply pointed at both bow and stern, with rudders at either end, designed to navigate the narrow, muddy reaches of Confederate rivers without the need to turn. Midships, her hull widened into massive, rectangular sponsons. These iron cheeks housed the paddlewheels, their blades now locked and furred with a thick, parasitic growth of green algae.

Dominating the forward and aft decks, the Parrott rifled pivot guns sat under canvas covers, their black iron muzzles pointing toward the horizon like blind sentinels. These were the same muzzles that had once commanded respect in foreign ports, their heavy reinforcing bands at the breeches giving them a brutish, top-heavy appearance. Along the sides, the 24-pounder broadside howitzers occupied their ports, their brass fittings dulled by a film of salt. These were tools of war, designed for the scream of grape and canister, now relegated to the role of ornamental weights. Between her two schooner-rigged masts, the single funnel rose like a soot-stained factory chimney. It threw a slab of heat-soaked shadow across the midships deck, a dark patch that trapped the stagnant air against the wood.

A marine leaned into this sliver of shade, his shoulder inches from the radiating iron. He wiped his forehead with a rag, his blue wool uniform darkened by sweat and flecked with the black grit drifting from the flue. The men moved with the lethargy of prisoners. The novelty of the albatross colonies and the aimless scouring of the tide-line for shells had worn off weeks ago. With the island's secrets exhausted, the world had shrunk to the grinding monotony of the ration schedule: salt beef, salt pork, hardtack, and rice, all of it underscored by the sour, metallic tang of the ship's own stagnant water tanks.

Exhaustion had settled into Read's bones. Seven months of staring at a ring of sand. Seven months of the same faces in the wardroom, the same stories retold until they lost all flavor, the same complaints about the flies and the delay. He tapped his foot on the deck. Scuttlebutt suggested the money had run out. Townsend had blasted his cut, but it was barely fifteen feet wide, hardly enough for a China steamer to navigate in a swell.

"Hot work for the contractor's men, Paymaster."

Read turned. Lieutenant Commander Montgomery Sicard stood near the companionway. The Captain remained buttoned to the chin in his frock coat. He was a man of rigid discipline, his beard trimmed to a sharp point, his eyes constantly scanning the rig as if expecting a sudden squall in a cloudless sky.

"Indeed, Captain," Read replied, straightening his posture. "I imagine they will be glad to see the Golden Gate again. As will we all."

Sicard nodded, his expression unreadable. "The work is concluding. Mr. Townsend informs me he has reached the limit of his appropriation. We embark his party tomorrow."

The words hung in the hot air, sweet and sharp. Tomorrow.

"Then we are for San Francisco, sir?"

"We are for home, Mr. Read. Once we clear the channel." Sicard paused, his gaze fixing on the white line of breakers that marked the edge of the atoll. "Though I intend to make a detour. Ocean Island lies some fifty miles to the west. The charts are unreliable, and it is my duty to fix its position before we depart these waters for good."

"A detour, sir?" Read asked. The word felt heavy, a sudden anchor dropped into his rising spirits.

Sicard did not turn. "A brief one. A mere matter of a day's steaming to verify the reef's extent. The charts are a century out of step, Mr. Read, and I'll not leave these waters until I've ensured the safety of those who follow us. Once the position is fixed, we shall set our course for the coast."

Read suppressed a sigh. Ocean Island. Another sand spit. Another reef. But it was a small price to pay for the promise of the northerly winds.

"A wise precaution, sir."

Sicard touched the brim of his cap and moved forward to inspect the windlass.

Home. The word summoned a cascade of sensory memories. The smell of damp fog in the San Francisco streets. The bite of a cold apple. The sound of carriage wheels on cobblestones. The taste of fresh beef that had not been cured in brine for three years.

Below decks, the ship was a stifling oven. The oscillating engines, unique marvels of engineering when they were installed, were cold iron beasts now, silent and brooding. The coal bunkers were dangerously light; they had burned much of their supply condensing water for the contractor's men.

They would be sailing home, relying on the *Saginaw's* schooner rig, using the steam only when absolutely necessary.

High above the mainmast, a frigate bird circled, its forked tail twitching against the trade wind. The bird was free to leave. It could ride the thermals north, away from this blinding white purgatory.

The boatswain's whistle chirped, cutting through the lethargy. The watch was changing. Men shuffled up from the berth deck, blinking in the glare. Their bare feet slapped against the wood. They looked gaunt. The "coast fever" they had picked up in Mexico still lingered in the blood of half the crew, resurfacing as shakes and sweats whenever the constitution flagged.

Townsend's boat pushed off from the reef, the oars dipping in ragged unison. The blasting was done for the day. The silence that followed was heavy, filled only by the omnipresent roar of the ocean crashing against the barrier reef.

Read walked to the side. A shark, six feet of grey muscle, cruised along the hull, visible for a moment before vanishing under the paddlewheel sponson. The *Saginaw* tugged gently at her cable, swinging her bow toward the pass. The iron rusted, the wood bleached, the men withered, but the ship endured.

Read took a deep breath of the salt air. It smelled of dead fish and exposed reef, a low-tide stench that permeated the uniform wool. But underneath it, faintly, was the scent of the open sea. He turned and headed for the wardroom hatch.

That night, the *Saginaw* slept uneasily. Her timbers creaked with the restless energy of a horse sensing the open gate. When the sun finally burned through the mist, it did not rise on another day of lethargic dredging, but on the friction of escape. The boatswain's pipe chirped forward. The steam winch rattled to life, the chain clanking against the iron hawsepipe as the slack was taken up.

***

The deck of the *Saginaw* vibrated with the thud of heavy boots and the screech of block and tackle.

Paymaster George Read stood near the gangway, his ledger tucked under his arm, though he had long since ceased to make entries. The time for accounting was over; the time for loading was at hand. Alongside the port beam, the flat-bottomed scow bobbed in the chop, laden with the detritus of Mr. Townsend's failed enterprise.

It was a scrapyard in miniature. Rusted piping, coils of thick hemp hawser, crates of blasting powder, and the heavy, awkward bulk of the diving apparatus were piled in a heap. The contractor's men, skin burned to the color of mahogany and peeling in ragged strips, worked the falls with a frantic energy that bordered on violence. They slung a steam boiler, its iron flanks scarred by salt, and signaled the winch.

"Heave round!"

The ropes complained, stretching taut before the boiler lifted from the scow, swinging precariously over the gunwale before settling onto the *Saginaw's* deck with a hollow clang that shuddered through the timbers.

Read watched the transfer with a mixture of relief and disdain. This iron junk was the only tangible result of fifty thousand dollars and half a year of their lives. A channel too shallow for commerce and a pile of scrap metal. But as the last crate thumped down, the mood on deck shifted as if the weight of the cargo had tipped a scale.

"All secure for sea, sir!" The shout came from the boatswain, his voice cracking with an uncharacteristic buoyancy.

Then came the moment every man aboard had fantasized about since crossing the equator.

"Hoist the pennant." A small bundle rose quickly to the main truck, fouling momentarily on the crosstrees before a sharp tug broke the stop. The bunting unrolled, catching the stiff trade wind.

The homeward-bound pennant, a slender ribbon of red, white, and blue, streamed out from the masthead, snapping and undulating like a living thing. It stretched past the mizzen, past the taffrail, trailing its swallow-tail tip into the wake far astern. It was a mathematical declaration of their exile, one foot of length for every man aboard, plus a generous allowance for the sheer joy of leaving.

A cheer erupted from the waist of the ship. It was not the disciplined hurrah of a dress inspection, but a raw, throaty roar that rose from the bellies of ninety-three men. Captain Sicard permitted himself a tight, grim smile before turning his attention back to the binnacle. Even the marine guard, usually stoic as statues, exchanged glances that spoke of soft beds and fresh bread.

"San Francisco," Read murmured, the syllables tasting like sweet wine.

The transformation of the crew was telling. An hour ago, they had been the walking dead, gaunt, yellow-eyed victims of the tropics, moving with sluggish indifference. Now, they scrambled up the ratlines with the agility of monkeys. The lethargy of the lagoon evaporated, burned off by the friction of anticipation.

"Anchor's aweigh, sir!"

The cry from the forecastle signaled the severance of their final tie to the coral. The heavy chain rumbled through the hawsepipe, bringing up the mud of the lagoon floor, the last piece of Midway they would ever touch.

"Ahead slow."

The deck lurched. For the first time in months, the *Saginaw* was under her own power. The great paddlewheels, housed in their sponsons like the haunches of a beast, began to turn. *Thump-whoosh. Thump-whoosh.* The sound was a heartbeat, driving the blood back into the ship's veins.

Read walked to the taffrail. The water churned white and frothy as the blades bit in, pushing the gunboat toward the narrow cut in the reef. The turquoise prison of the lagoon began to recede. The white sand of the islands, blinding in the afternoon sun, looked suddenly small, almost benign, now that they were no longer condemned to it.

He looked at the men gathered near the pivot gun. Coxswain Halford was there, coiling a line with precise, powerful movements, his broad back soaked in sweat. Lieutenant Talbot stood near the wheel, his posture relaxed, the tension of the last few weeks draining from his shoulders. They were talking, not of coral or blasting powder, but of the Golden Gate.

"I'll have a steak as big as a hatch cover," one sailor said, his voice carrying over the wind. "And a beer so cold it cracks my teeth."

"You'll have the bellyache, more like," Halford retorted, though there was no bite in it. "Salt pork and beans for you, lad, until you get your land legs."

Laughter. Actual laughter. It sounded foreign against the backdrop of the surf.

The *Saginaw* cleared the channel, her bow dipping into the long, rolling swell of the open Pacific. The motion was different here, deeper, slower, more powerful than the chop of the lagoon. The ship sighed as she took the strain, her timbers adjusting to the sea.

Read gripped the rail. The trade wind rushed over the deck, cool and clean, stripping away the smell of the stagnant lagoon water and the coal smoke. Above, the immense length of the homeward-bound pennant whipped in the sky, pointing the way east. Pointing home.

He did not look back at the atoll. He fixed his eyes on the horizon, where the sea met the sky in a hard, blue line. Somewhere beyond that curve lay the world of the living.

"Course west by north, sir," the quartermaster called out.

Read frowned slightly. *West*. Away from San Francisco.

He remembered Sicard's order. *Ocean Island*. A detour. Fifty miles to check a chart and scan a reef. A day's steaming, perhaps two. A nuisance, nothing more.

The ship heeled to port as the helm went over, the paddlewheels thrashing a new, labored rhythm against the swell. The fresh trade wind, which had felt so clean a moment ago, was now a headwind whistling through the rigging. Read turned his collar up against the spray and turned his back on the horizon. He moved to the companionway and stepped into the hatch. As his head dipped below the coaming, the clean air vanished, replaced by the solid, suffocating blanket of coal dust, damp wool and the lingering odor of salt beef that had been boiled two days prior.

***

Read descended the ladder into the wardroom country, his boots finding the brass-shod steps by muscle memory. The transition from the glare of the Pacific to the gloom of the officers' quarters was always jarring. Here, the *Saginaw* ceased to be a ship sailing under the open sky and became a burrow, a wooden tunnel driven through the ocean.

The wardroom was the vessel's brain and its sanctuary. It was a narrow, rectangular space painted in cream and faux-mahogany, designed to maintain the illusion of a gentleman's club amidst the squalor of a gunboat. A long table, bolted to the deck, dominated the center. Above it, a swinging lamp described erratic arcs in the air, casting sliding shadows against the bulkheads.

Read moved to his stateroom door, sliding the louvers open to catch the faint draft from the wind-sail rigged on deck. The space was coffin-tight. His bunk, built over a drawer of uniforms, left barely enough room to turn around. On the small desk, his ledgers were stacked with military precision, held in place by a heavy brass weight to counter the ship's roll.

The vibration here was constant. It hummed in the wood of the desk and rattled the water pitcher in its rack. The *Saginaw* fought the sea rather than riding it, a beast struggling against the elements.

He stepped back into the common area. Lieutenant Talbot was there, seated at the table, polishing the lens of a sextant with a scrap of velvet. The executive officer looked up, his face pale in the half-light.

"The glass is falling, Paymaster," Talbot said quietly, not breaking his rhythm. "We shall have a lumpy night of it."

"Better a lumpy night moving east than a calm one at anchor," Read replied. He steadied himself against a stanchion as the deck canted sharply to port. The ship had a wicked roll, a consequence of her shallow draft and the heavy guns carried high on the spar deck.

Read made his way forward, passing through the bulkhead that separated the officers' country from the machinery. This was the heart of the beast.

The engine room hatch was open, a gaping mouth breathing up a concoction of hot oil and steam. Read paused at the coaming, looking down into the iron pit. The *Saginaw* was driven by two oscillating engines, technological marvels when they were bolted in during the war, now temperamental veterans.

The scene below was a vision of organized violence. The entire cylinders rocked on trunnions, swaying back and forth to align with the crank. It gave the engine room a disorienting, living rhythm, as if the ship were chewing the sea.

A fireman, stripped to the waist and black with coal dust, moved across the grating with a long-spouted oil can. He dodged the swing of a crank arm with the indifference of a man who had made the same move a thousand times. The heat rising from the pit was breathless, carrying the metallic tang of friction. Somewhere deep in the bowels, a shovel scraped against the iron floor of a coal bunker, the sound of the ship being fed. It was a hungry sound. The coal bunkers were dangerously light, hollowed out by months of condensing water for the contractor's men. Read stared into the gloom, feeling the heat of the firebox against his face. A steamship in 1870 was a tethered beast, its range dictated entirely by the cubic footage of its bunkers. Without the black dust, the *Saginaw* was just a clumsy, heavy-hulled schooner dragging two massive, dead paddlewheels through the sea, a slave to the trade winds she was built to defy.

Read pressed on, ducking his head to pass under the hammock hooks of the berth deck.

If the wardroom was the brain, and the engine room the heart, this was the gut. The enlisted men's quarters ran the length of the forward hull, a cavernous, low-ceilinged tunnel that smelled of three score unwashed men. The air here was thick, almost chewable.

It was the dog watches, and the space was a hive of activity. Men sat on their sea chests, mending clothes or carving scraps of whalebone. Others lay in the shadows, trying to sleep before the mid-watch, their arms thrown over their eyes. The space was suffocatingly crowded. The *Saginaw* was built for a crew of fifty; she now carried ninety-three.

Read navigated the narrow aisle between the mess tables. A group of sailors looked up as he passed, touching their knuckles to their foreheads in silent salute. They looked hard-used. Their duck trousers were stained with rust and tar, their faces gaunt from months of salt rations and tropical sun.

The passage narrowed near the chain lockers, where the air grew heavy with the scent of bilge water. Near the iron grating of the brig, the wardroom steward sat on the deck, his back against the oak bulkhead. Double irons fused his wrists, the metal rings having worn the skin of his forearms to a dull, bruised gray.

"Steward," Read said, pausing.

The man looked up, his expression unreadable in the dim, flickering light. The shackles clinked with a leaden, hollow sound as he shifted his weight. "Mr. Read, sir."

"Is the water reaching you? The heat in this hole is enough to boil a man."

"It finds its way, sir," the steward replied. His voice remained steady, lacking the tremor of a man in disgrace. "I reckon the San Francisco air will be a finer tonic than the water in this bucket."

Read glanced at the shackles. "The Captain's discipline is a hard master, Steward. But the voyage is short. Hold your patience."

"I have plenty of that, sir. A man in irons learns to wait on the clock."

Read nodded and moved past the brig.

He reached the forward storeroom, the domain of his own department. The door to the bread room was secured with a heavy padlock, a necessary precaution not against thieves, but against the ship's other inhabitants.

As he unlocked the hasp, a grey shape the size of a kitten scurried across his boot and vanished behind a barrel of flour.

Rats.

They were the *Saginaw's* true owners. They had come aboard in San Francisco, perhaps, or multiplied during the long, idle months in the Mexican ports. Now, they were a legion. They infested the bilges, nested in the cable tiers, and waged a nightly war for the provisions. They gnawed on the leather of the pump washers; they squealed in the bulkheads while he tried to sleep.

He lifted the lid of a hardtack crate. The biscuits were there, stacked in neat rows, but the tell-tale sawdust of gnawed edges dusted the bottom of the box. He sighed, dropping the lid with a clatter that sent two more shadows darting into the gloom.

"Bold as brass, ain't they, sir?"

Read turned. Coxswain Halford stood nearby, holding a lantern. The big sailor's face was a map of weather-beaten creases, his eyes dark and unblinking.

"They are getting worse, Halford," Read said, wiping his hands on his trousers. "If we do not make San Francisco soon, they'll be navigating the ship."

Halford chuckled, a low rumble in his chest. "Let 'em have the run of the bilges, sir. Long as the jagged end of the reef stays under the keel, I can live with the rats."

"The Captain has set our course for Ocean Island," Read said. He did not look at the sailor, instead fixing his gaze on the flickering lantern. "A matter of the charts, I understand."

Halford's smile didn't reach his eyes. He nodded slowly, the light casting deep shadows into the weathered creases of his face. "Aye. I heard the word passed. A bad spot, that. The *Parker* left her bones there. But the Captain knows his business."

The ship pitched heavily, the bow dropping into a trough with a shudder that ran the length of the keel. The timbers creaked, a chorus of complaints from the oak knees and drift bolts.

"She's complaining," Read murmured.

"She's old, sir," Halford said, patting a beam as one might pat a horse. "And she's carrying a lot of top-hamper with that diving gear on deck. But she's a good sea-boat. She'll get us home."

Read left the berth deck, climbing the forward ladder to escape the stifling atmosphere. He emerged onto the forecastle, into the clean rush of the trade wind.

The sky was a deepening purple, the stars beginning to prick through the canopy. The ocean was a vast, heaving wilderness of black water, capped with white foam where the wind tore at the crests.

Here, the industrial nature of the *Saginaw* was most visible. The massive paddle-boxes jutted out from the hull like fortifications, breaking the clean lines of the ship. Inside them, the great wheels churned the sea, throwing up cataracts of spray that hissed against the planking.

On the foredeck, the clutter of the mission was lashed down with geometric precision. The contractor's boiler, a rusted iron cylinder, sat like a tombstone near the pivot gun. Coils of hose, crates of copper fittings, and the diving bell itself, an alien, windowed sphere, were wedged between the cannons. The ship was a freighter, a warship, and a salvage vessel all at once, and she groaned under the confusion of purposes.

Read walked to the rail, looking aft. The sparks from the funnel streamed downwind, a fiery wake in the sky. The homeward-bound pennant was invisible in the dark, but he knew it was there, streaming out towards the east.

He felt the vibration of the paddles through the soles of his boots. *Thump-splash, thump-splash.* It was a fragile sound against the immense silence of the Pacific. A thousand miles to the south lay Hawaii; two thousand miles to the east, America. To the west... nothing. Just the reef they were hunting.

A rat ran along the scuppers, pausing to sniff the air before disappearing into the chain locker.

Read shivered, though the wind was warm. The ship felt heavy tonight. Heavy with iron, heavy with men, and heavy with the miles yet to go. He turned his back on the darkness of the west and looked toward the stern light, burning steady and yellow against the night.

"One day," he whispered to himself. "One day to check the reef. Then home."

He tapped the rail three times, a superstition he had picked up from the men, and headed back toward the warmth of the wardroom.

Chapter 2

The silence of the cabin was a deception. Outside the painted bulkheads, the *Saginaw* was a cacophony of straining timber and rushing water, but here, in the sanctuary of command, the only sound was the rhythmic ticking of the chronometer in its velvet-lined box. Lieutenant Commander Montgomery Sicard sat at his desk, his back straight, his hands resting flat on the green baize surface. He did not lean. Even in private, the habit of posture was a discipline he refused to relax.

He was thirty-four years old, young for the command of a fourth-rate steamer, yet the face reflected in the darkened glass of the stern port was etched with the lines of a man who had aged prematurely under the sun of the blockade squadrons. His eyes were grey and unblinking, accustomed to scanning horizons for the smudge of coal smoke that betrayed a runner. Now, they scanned a different sort of enemy: a chart of the North Pacific that was largely, dangerously blank.

He adjusted the wick of the gimbaled lamp, the flame casting long, swinging shadows that danced with the roll of the ship. The *Saginaw* was laboring slightly, her motion stiffened by the deck load of the contractor's machinery. Every creak of the joinery was a language he understood, a constant report on the vessel's health. She was tired. The boilers were scaling, the copper sheathing was fouled, and the bunkers were nearly swept clean. She was a relic of the transition age, a hybrid trapped between the romance of sail and the tyranny of coal. With her fuel low, she was a cripple, her autonomy measured in mere hours of steam. To turn back west was to burn dust he could ill afford.

Sicard picked up the packet of orders from the Navy Department, the red wax seal long since broken. He knew the text by heart, yet he read it again, seeking the precise boundaries of his authority. *Proceed to San Francisco.* The directive was clear. The desire to obey it, to turn the prow east and let the trade winds drive them straight for the Golden Gate, tugged at the muscles of his chest like a taut hawser. He could picture the harbor, the forest of masts, the cold fog rolling over the hills. He could taste the fresh lamb and the sweet water.

But the chart commanded his attention more than the letter.

He smoothed the heavy paper. Midway was behind them, a known quantity. Ahead lay the vast, blue emptiness leading to California. But there, fifty miles to the west, directly upwind, lay the smudge of ink labeled "Ocean Island."

The cartography was an embarrassment. The reef was marked, but its contours were vague, sketched in by the hurried observations of passing merchantmen or the terrified reports of survivors. It was a void in the hydrography of the Pacific, a trap waiting in the dark. Sicard knew the history. The British whaler *Gledstanes* had broken her back there in thirty-seven. The American ship *Parker* had followed five years later. It was a graveyard, a jagged crescent of coral that sat low in the water, invisible until the breakers were already under the keel.

He took his dividers and walked the points across the paper. Fifty miles. At their current speed, steaming against the trade wind, it was a deviation of perhaps twelve hours. A day lost.

A day against the seven months they had already wasted in the lagoon. The crew would hate him for it. He knew the mood on the berth deck; he could feel the vibration of their eagerness in the very planks under his feet. To turn the ship's head west, back toward the setting sun and the emptiness of Asia, would be seen as an act of cruelty.

Standing up, the low deckhead forcing him to stoop, he began to pace the small carpet, three steps, turn, three steps, wrestling with the knowledge that while sailing for San Francisco would obey his orders to the letter, saving him from any court of inquiry, it might damn him in his own conscience. He would bring the ship home, discharge the contractor's men, and receive the commendation of the Department for a job completed.

But what if there were men on that reef?

The thought was a cold splinter in his mind. If another ship had struck Ocean Island in the last year, a whaler, perhaps, or a China trader blown off course, the survivors would be clinging to that sand spit, watching the horizon with eyes burned blind by the sun. If the *Saginaw* passed fifty miles to the east, steaming blithely for home, she would be their last hope, and she would never know it. They would die of thirst, or exposure, or madness, while he sat in the club in San Francisco drinking claret.

Sicard stopped pacing. He looked at the dividers, still resting on the chart. The distance was trivial.

The Navy Regulations were a guide, but the unwritten law of the sea was a commandment. *Succor to the distressed*. It was not optional. To leave a known hazard unexamined, when he was the only representative of the United States government within a thousand miles, would be a dereliction of the highest order. It would be a failure not of obedience, but of character.

He exhaled slowly. The isolation of command was never more acute than in these moments. He could not consult Talbot; the executive officer was a fine sailor, but the burden of the choice belonged to the Captain alone. If he delayed their return and ran the ship into a gale, the blame was his. If they burned too much coal fighting the headwind, the blame was his.

But if he saved a life, the duty was satisfied.

He buttoned his frock coat, smoothing the wool over his chest. He checked his appearance in the mirror, impeccable, as always. The men must see no hesitation, no doubt. They must see only the inevitable progression of orders.

He reached for his cap, setting it squarely on his head. The decision was made. The *Saginaw* would not run for home. Not yet. She would turn her back on the east and drive her blunt nose into the teeth of the wind. She would do her duty.

Sicard opened the cabin door and stepped out into the humid night. The air was thick and tropical, contrasting sharply with the mental chill that had settled over him. He climbed the companionway to the poop deck, his boots ringing on the brass treads.

The officer of the deck, Master's Mate Hershberger, was at the rail, watching the phosphorescence in the wake. He straightened as Sicard emerged.

"A fine night, Captain," Hershberger said, touching his cap.

"It is, Mr. Hershberger," Sicard replied, his voice level and devoid of warmth. "Have the course changed. Steer West by North." Hershberger blinked, his hand freezing halfway down from the salute. He looked at the compass, then back to the Captain, the hesitation lasting only the space of a heartbeat. "West by North. Aye, aye, sir."

"You have the deck, Mr. Hershberger."

"I have the deck, sir."

Sicard walked to the binnacle, watching as the helmsman spun the wheel. The *Saginaw* hesitated, her momentum carrying her east for a moment longer, before the rudder bit. The bow swung slowly, heavily, traversing the dark horizon until it pointed back toward the empty quarter of the ocean. The wind, which had been on the quarter, now howled through the rigging from dead ahead, singing a mournful note in the taut wire stays.

The ship pitched, digging into the head sea. The easy roll was gone, replaced by a jarring, persistent slam as they fought the Pacific.

The vibration shuddered down through the keel, traveling from the exposed violence of the bridge to the enclosed gloom of the officers' country. With every plunge of the bow, the vibration rattled the crockery in the pantry, carrying the news of the course change through the bulkheads and into the silence of the wardroom.

***

Paymaster George Read sat at the wardroom table, a cup of lukewarm coffee cradled in his hands. The swinging lamp overhead described a wild arc, the shadows of the officers swaying in counterpoint. The mood, so buoyant only hours ago at the sight of the homeward-bound pennant, had soured into a thick, resentful silence.

"Fifty miles," grumbled Passed Assistant Engineer Blye. He was staring at his hands, the knuckles ingrained with the permanent grease of his trade. "Fifty miles to windward. That is two days added to the run, easy. Two days more of salt beef and weevils."

"The Captain is thorough," Lieutenant Talbot said from the head of the table. He spoke without looking up from his book, his tone mild but carrying the subtle warning of the executive officer. "If there are poor devils on Ocean Island, Mr. Blye, you would not begrudge them a rescue, I trust."

"I begrudge the coal," Blye muttered, though quiet enough to avoid a direct reprimand. "We are burning good dust to chase ghosts."

Read said nothing. He watched the coffee tremble in his cup. The same irritation gnawing at his own patience, the desperate, childish desire to just *go home*, but he suppressed it. The logic of the detour was sound, even if the reality was miserable.

Opposite him, Dr. Frank, the ship's surgeon, was not part of the gripe session. He was peeling an orange with surgical precision, but his hands were shaking. The zest came away in jagged, uneven strips.

"It is a graveyard," Frank said suddenly. His voice was too loud in the small space.

Read looked up. The surgeon's face was pale, slick with a sheen of sweat that the heat of the lamp could not entirely explain.

"The charts call it a hazard, Doctor," Read said gently. "Not a graveyard."

"I feel it," Frank insisted, dropping the knife. It clattered onto the plate. "I have felt it since we turned the helm. There is something wrong with this night. We are steaming into the abyss, gentlemen. I tell you, I have a heaviness here." He pressed a hand to his chest. "We should have run east. We should have run east and never looked back."

The silence in the wardroom deepened. Sailors were a superstitious lot, but officers usually hid it better. To hear the surgeon, a man of science who sawed through bones and stitched flesh without blinking, speak of "feelings" and "heaviness" was deeply unsettling.

Talbot closed his book with a snap. "The barometer is stable, Doctor. The ship is sound. Your nerves are frayed by the tropics. I suggest a dose of your own brandy and a turn in your bunk."

Frank looked at the Executive Officer, his eyes wide and unblinking. "I shall not sleep tonight, Mr. Talbot. I do not think any of us should sleep."

He stood up abruptly, his chair scraping against the deck, and retreated into his stateroom, sliding the door shut with a force that vibrated the bulkhead.

Read picked up the coffee pot. It was light, nearly empty. He shook it, listening to the dregs slosh against the tin. "Steward," he called out, his voice sounding flat in the humid air. "Fresh pot. And mind the grounds this time." It was a petty complaint, but it was the only thing in the room he could control.

Read exchanged a glance with Blye. The engineer raised an eyebrow, tapping his temple with a greasy finger.

The atmosphere in the room had curdled. The air used up, recycled through ninety lungs and flavored with the anxiety that Frank had just uncorked. Read drained his coffee, the dregs bitter on his tongue, and stood.

"I believe I will take the air," he said.

He climbed the ladder to the spar deck.

There was no moon, and the cloud cover was thick, blotting out the stars. The ocean was not a visual reality; it was a sound, a vast, rushing hiss of water that seemed to come from everywhere and nowhere.

The *Saginaw* was moving with agonizing slowness. The familiar, energetic thumping of the paddlewheels had slowed to a lethargic heartbeat. *Chunk... swish. Chunk... swish.*

Read moved aft, his eyes adjusting slowly until the shapes of the rigging stood out as deeper blacks against the night sky. He found the Officer of the Deck, Master's Mate Hershberger, leaning over the taffrail.

"We are barely making way, Mr. Hershberger," Read observed.

"Three knots, Paymaster," Hershberger replied, his voice low. "Captain's orders. We are under slow bells. He does not want to overrun the reckoning in the dark."

"Is the visibility that poor?"

"Can you see the bow?"

Read looked forward. The forecastle was swallowed by the gloom. The outline of the pivot gun was a vague lump, and beyond that, the world simply ended. There was no horizon. The sea and the sky were welded together in a wall of slate.

"If the reef is low," Hershberger said, "we won't see the breakers until we are in them. Hence the speed. We are feeling our way, sir. Like a blind man in a strange room."

Read gripped the rail. The ship pitched again, a long, slow heave that lifted his stomach. The wind was fresh, stripping the heat from his skin, but it brought no comfort. It smelled of nothing, no land, no spice, just the cold, sterile scent of deep water.

Dr. Frank's words echoed in his mind.

He looked over the side. The wake was a faint phosphorescent smear, fading quickly into the dark. They were alone. The fifty thousand dollars, the blasting, the albatrosses of Midway, it all seemed a lifetime ago. There was only this: the rhythmic complaint of the old wooden hull, the slow beat of the paddles, and the sensation of moving inexorably toward a danger they could not see.

A sharp hiss of steam form the relief valve made him jump.

"Nervous night," Hershberger muttered, shifting his weight.

"Yes," Read agreed. He turned his face to the west, straining to see the bowsprit. There was nothing but the wet, heavy air, and the hiss of the ocean rushing past the hull, waiting for them in the dark.

Chapter 3

The geography of the North Pacific is a study in isolation, but Kure Atoll is something more malevolent: a trap.

Located at the extreme northwestern tip of the Hawaiian archipelago, it sits 1,200 miles from the nearest center of civilization in Honolulu. It is the final punctuation mark of a volcanic chain that began forming millions of years ago, a geological senior citizen long since subsided beneath the waves and worn down by time, leaving only a calcium carbonate skeleton to mark its grave.

To the mariners of the nineteenth century, the atoll was a phantom. Charts placed it erratically, sometimes miles from its true position, sometimes missing it entirely. A low-lying whisper of sand and coral, invisible at night until the white line of breakers roared out of the darkness. For the wooden ships that plied the trade routes between the Sandwich Islands and Japan, Kure was a hazard to be given a wide berth.

But the Pacific currents are deceitful, and the winds of the northern trades unforgiving. By 1870, the atoll had already earned a grim epithet among the whaling fleets: the Graveyard.

The first stone in this cemetery was laid on a dark night in July 1837. The British whaler *Gledstanes* beat west, her hold filled with 1,200 barrels of sperm oil, the fruit of a long and brutal season on the Japan grounds. Captain John Brown was a prudent man. He knew of the reef's existence, it had been sighted by the Russians years earlier, and he had posted lookouts.

But Kure respects no vigilance.

The ocean that night was rough, the sky obscured by a thick blanket of cloud that blotted out the stars. The *Gledstanes* moved at seven knots, a considerable speed for a bluff-bowed whaler driven by a stiff breeze.

There was no warning. No shallowing of the water. No shift in the color of the sea. Just the terrifying cry from the forecastle, "Breakers ahead!", followed instantly by the splintering crunch of oak on limestone.

The ship was impaled. The coral heads of the high-energy surf zone act like a coarse rasp against a wooden hull. The *Gledstanes* drove hard onto the reef, the impact snapping her masts and shredding her copper sheathing. The surf, sensing the intrusion, began its work immediately. Massive rollers, energized by thousands of miles of fetch, lifted the 400-ton hull and slammed it repeatedly against the coral pavement.

In the chaos of the surf zone, the discipline of the Merchant Navy held. Brown ordered the boats lowered. A desperate evolution, performed in pitch blackness on a deck disintegrating beneath their feet. The men fought the tangle of rigging and the roar of the breakers, launching three whaleboats into the lee of the wreck.

They waited for dawn in the open boats, shivering in the spray, listening to their ship die.

When the sun finally rose, it revealed a bleak salvation. A few miles away, across the turquoise lagoon, lay a spit of white sand, scrubbed clean by the wind and populated only by seabirds and monk seals. Dry land, but barely.

The crew of the *Gledstanes* landed on what is now Green Island. Alive, but erased from the world. In 1837, there was no radio, no scheduled patrol, no expectation of rescue. They were frail sparks of life on a geological anomaly. To wait for a passing ship was to choose a slow death by dehydration or madness.

Captain Brown surveyed his domain. He had his men, a few casks of water scavenged from the wreck, and the tools of their trade. Whalemen are, by necessity, the most resourceful mechanics of the sea. They repair iron and wood in the middle of the ocean, far from any chandlery. Brown looked at the wreck of the *Gledstanes*, rapidly breaking up on the reef, and saw not a tragedy, but a lumber yard.

"We shall build our way out," he decided.

For five months, the island became a shipyard. The men rowed back out to the reef daily, a dangerous commute through the shark-infested lagoon. They dove into the surf to salvage what the ocean would yield. They floated timber, planks, and spars back to the beach. They recovered the carpenter's chest, a prize more valuable than the 1,200 barrels of oil now slicking the reef.

On the white sand, under a sun that blistered the skin, a new vessel began to take shape. Not a whaleboat open to the elements, but a proper schooner, thirty-eight feet long. They laid her keel from the splintered remains of the *Gledstanes'* mainmast. Her ribs were fashioned from the futtocks of the mother ship, steam-bent over fires fed by driftwood. Her planking was a patchwork of salvaged deck boards, fastened with nails pulled from the wreck and straightened on coral anvils.

The labor was Herculean. Lacking a forge, they used simple fires to work the iron. Lacking oakum for caulking, they picked apart old rope and mixed it with lime burned from coral and oil rendered from monk seals. The camp smelled of rotting kelp, burning fat, and the tang of sweat.

Discipline was the mortar that held the project together. On a desert island, the social contract usually dissolves into anarchy within weeks. Brown maintained the hierarchy of the quarterdeck. Watches were kept. Rations measured to the ounce. The men worked not for wages, but for the promise of life.

By December, the vessel was finished. A Franken-ship, a rough-hewn child of the wreck, scarred and ugly, but she floated. They named her, with a lack of subtlety that befitted their desperation, the *Deliverance.*

Captain Brown, the Chief Mate, and eight men boarded the tiny schooner. They left the rest of the crew, some twenty souls, on the island with a promise to return. A gamble of the highest order. The *Deliverance* had to sail 1,200 miles upwind to Honolulu, through winter gales, in a boat held together by scavenged nails and seal oil.

They launched her into the lagoon, her hull scraping over the sand. She took the swells of the open ocean with a stiffness that worried the captain, but she held. For weeks, they battled the northeast trades, the little schooner leaking, the men constantly bailing, their eyes fixed on the eastern horizon.

They made it.

The *Deliverance* sailed into Honolulu harbor, a ghost ship crewed by scarecrows. The sight of the ragged vessel, built from the bones of a wreck, caused a sensation on the waterfront. The British Consul immediately dispatched a vessel to Kure to rescue the remaining crew.

Every man of the *Gledstanes* survived. The story became a legend in the Pacific fleet, a testament to the tenacity of whalemen. But the island remained. The *Deliverance* had escaped, but the *Gledstanes* was gone, her iron anchors and trypots left to rust in the surf.

***

Five years after the *Gledstanes* survivors sailed their jury-rigged schooner into history, the reef was silent. The huts they had built on Green Island stood empty, bleaching under the relentless sun, their thatched roofs slowly unraveling in the trade winds. The island had returned to its primitive state, populated only by the screaming terns, the lumbering monk seals, and a single, feral resident left behind by the British crew: a dog.

A creature of the wreck, a living ghost that had learned to survive on the raw flesh of seabirds and the brackish water found in coral hollows. For five years, it paced the white perimeter of the island, the sole witness to the isolation of the North Pacific.

Then came the storm of September 1842.

The American whaler *Parker* was not merely passing; she was hunting. Cruising the Japan grounds, she was a vessel of New Bedford, a city that built ships to withstand ice, blubber, and the violence of the whale. But she was not built for the coral saw-teeth of the Leeward Islands.

The gale began in the afternoon, a thickening of the horizon that quickly escalated into full fury. By midnight, the *Parker* fought for her life. The sea was a confusion of black valleys and white crests, the wind tearing the tops off the waves and hurling them across the deck as a blinding spray. Visibility dropped to zero. The horizon was gone. The line between air and water vanished.

At two in the morning, the lookout screamed. It was the same cry that had doomed the *Gledstanes*, but this time it was swallowed by the roar of the gale.

The *Parker* struck while rising on a swell. A massive comber lifted the ship and drove her hard onto the reef, the impact shattering the rudder and snapping the keel. In an instant, the orderly world of the ship, the watches, the course headings, the hierarchy, was replaced by a chaotic struggle against drowning.

The hull breached. Water flooded the hold, mixing with the whale oil to create a slick, suffocating soup. The masts went over the side, a tangle of spars and rigging beating against the hull like a flail.

For the men of the *Parker*, there was no orderly lowering of boats. The *Gledstanes* had wrecked in manageable weather; the *Parker* wrecked in hell. Men washed overboard in the darkness, their cries extinguished instantly. Others clung to the shrouds, lashed by the sea, waiting for a dawn that seemed an eternity away.

When the sun finally broke through the gray scud of the storm, the devastation was evident. The ship was a broken vertebrae of timber and iron, rapidly disintegrating in the high surf. But just as with their British predecessors, the survivors saw the white sand of Green Island across the lagoon.

They made the crossing on rafts of lashed spars and swimming. They washed ashore battered, half-drowned, and stripped of everything but their lives. Twenty-six men, cast up on the same stage where the *Gledstanes* drama had played out.

As they stumbled up the beach, coughing the salt water from their lungs, they found they were not entering a wilderness. They were entering a ghost town.

The huts were there. Crude, weathering structures of driftwood and canvas, standing in a silent row. A surreal discovery. To be shipwrecked at the end of the earth is a horror; to find a village waiting for you is a madness. They walked among the structures, touching the rough wood, finding the discarded refuse of the previous tenants, a rusted nail, a broken bottle, a piece of hardened leather.

And then, a dog appeared.

It watched them from the scrub, wild-eyed and matted, a creature that had forgotten the sound of a human voice. It did not wag its tail. It did not bark. It assessed them with the cold, predatory gaze of an animal that had clawed out a living on the edge of existence.

For the survivors of the *Parker*, the initial relief of finding land quickly soured into a grim reality. The *Gledstanes* men had been lucky; they had saved tools, provisions, and timber. The *Parker* men had nothing. The wreck had broken up too fast. No adzes to build a boat, no casks of water, no hardtack. They were truly marooned.

The island offered life, but it demanded a price. The water they dug for in the sand was brackish and foul. The birds were plentiful, but catching them required an expenditure of energy the starving men could ill afford. The monk seals, those docile giants of the beach, became their primary larder. The men learned to kill them with clubs, bludgeoning the animals as they slept, drinking the warm blood to slake their thirst, eating the oily meat until their pores oozed the smell of rancid fat.

The weeks turned into months. The discipline that had saved the *Gledstanes* crew began to fray under the pressure of deprivation. No boat-building here, only the endless, circular routine of survival. Wake. Hunt. Kill. Eat. Sleep.

And the dog.

The animal remained on the periphery, a constant reminder of the island's previous captives. A link to the civilized world, a pet that had once slept on a hearth rug in England or sat by a sailor's feet in a galley. But on Kure, hunger dictates morality. As the hunger deepened, the dog ceased to be a mascot; it became fifteen pounds of protein. The ribs showing through the animal's matted coat mirrored their own.

The taboo against eating the companion of man is ancient, but the reef strips away such niceties, leaving only the raw, grinding realities of survival.

They caught it. The details of the act were not recorded in the ship's log, some shames are too deep for ink, but the result was etched into the history of the reef. They killed the last survivor of the *Gledstanes* to feed the survivors of the *Parker*. A meal of desperation, a consumption of the past to sustain the present.

The *Parker* crew remained on the island for nearly eight months. They were eventually rescued not by their own ingenuity, but by the chance arrival of the ship *James Stewart*. They left the island as they had found it: a graveyard of ambitions, littered with the bones of ships and the ghosts of difficult choices.

When the USS *Saginaw* turned her bow toward this same reef twenty-eight years later, the huts of the *Gledstanes* were gone, reclaimed by the storms. The bones of the dog were buried in the shifting sands. But the precedent had been set.

Kure Atoll was not merely a hazard to navigation. It was a crucible. A place where the veneer of civilization was stripped away by the salt wind, leaving only the raw, brutal machinery of survival.

The *Saginaw* was steaming toward a place where men had eaten their best friend to live another day.

***

To the hydrographers of the United States Navy in 1870, the location was merely a coordinate: 28 degrees, 25 minutes North; 178 degrees, 20 minutes West. A navigational hazard to be triangulated, sounded, and marked on a chart with the cool, detached precision of the Victorian age. Ocean Island, a generic label for a geological nuisance that required a wide berth and a vigilant lookout.

To the whaling captains of New Bedford, it was simply the "Graveyard," a place defined by its capacity to destroy profit and shatter oak.

But long before the first chronometer ticked on the deck of a Western ship, long before the first iron nail rusted in the Pacific salt, the atoll was known by a name carrying a vibration far heavier than a simple warning.

Hōlanikū.

In the vast, oceanic cosmogony of the Hawaiian people, the archipelago is not merely a chain of volcanic accidents; it is a narrative of life and death, written in stone and magma. The inhabited islands in the southeast, where the earth still bleeds fire and the peaks pierce the clouds, belong to the *Ao*, the realm of light, consciousness, and the living. Here, the sun rises, and the god *Kāne* presides over the vibrant, waking world.

But the islands are not static. They move, drifting slowly to the northwest on the Pacific Plate, and as they move, they age. They erode, subside, and sink, returning to the abyssal womb from which they were born.

This northwest trajectory is the path of the setting sun. The path into *Pō*, the primordial darkness, the realm of the gods, the ancestors, and the night.

For a thousand years, it was understood the human soul traveled this geographic line. When the breath left the body, the spirit did not ascend to a cloud-filled heaven but began a literal journey northwest. It moved from island to island, leaping from specific promontories, stripping away the heavy attachments of the human world, passing from the high islands to the low islands, entering a zone of increasing spiritual density and physical desolation.

Hōlanikū stands at the extreme limit of this progression.

The oldest sibling in the chain, a geological relic that has existed for nearly thirty million years. It is the final punctuation mark before the Emperor Seamounts and the endless, empty void of the North Pacific. Its name translates, in its most profound sense, as "bringing forth heaven" or the "boundary of existence." The point where the physical world dissolves into the metaphysical. A threshold between the known and the unknowable. The back wall of the world.

The geography of the atoll supports this mythology with an eerie precision. *Hōlanikū* is a spectral presence. It sits incredibly low in the water, a phantom ring of calcium carbonate that barely breaks the surface of the swells. From the deck of a ship, it is invisible until one is dangerously close. No mountain to guide the navigator, no tree line to break the horizon. Only the violent white line of the surf crashing against a barrier that separates the deep, dark blue of the open ocean from the brilliant turquoise of the lagoon.

Inside that ring, a sanctuary of stillness surrounded by the chaotic energy of the Pacific. The island is a cacophony of life, home to millions of seabirds, terns, boobies, albatrosses, frigates, whose sheer numbers darken the sky. In the Hawaiian worldview, these birds are not merely animals. They are *kinolau*, the physical body forms of deities. The Great Frigatebird is a manifestation of the war god Kū; the albatross carries the spirit of Lono.

To step onto the sand of *Hōlanikū* is to step into a crowded room of gods, a place where the veil between the material and the spiritual is worn paper-thin. This was not a place for the living to linger. It was a place of transition. To go there in the flesh, to anchor a ship in the lagoon and walk the beaches, was to trespass in the garden of ghosts. A realm reserved for the *'aumākua*, the ancestral guardians, and the spirits passing into the infinite.

When Captain Sicard stood on the quarterdeck of the *Saginaw*, adjusting his sextant and issuing his orders, he believed he was performing a simple geometric exercise. He calculated coal consumption, drift, and speed. He viewed the ocean as a neutral medium, a friction-less surface to be traversed by the industrial might of steam and the discipline of sail. He saw the "West by North" heading as a logical detour to verify a chart.

He did not know he was guiding his ship out of the realm of men.

The *Saginaw* was a vessel of the Industrial Revolution, a machine of iron, brass, and fire. She smelled of coal smoke and grease, the scents of the modern age. But as she turned her blunt prow away from the sunrise and drove into the teeth of the trade winds, she crossed a spiritual event horizon.

She moved against the natural flow of life, sailing purposefully toward the *Pō*.

The "heaviness" that Dr. Frank, the ship's surgeon, felt in the wardroom, the inexplicable dread that had sent a man of science trembling into his bunk, was perhaps an instinctive, primal reaction to this transgression. The human animal, no matter how civilized or rational, retains a vestigial sense of territory. It knows when it enters a place where it does not belong.

The crew of the *Saginaw* were not just sailors fighting a headwind; they were interlopers knocking on the door of the afterlife.

As the night of October 29th deepened, the ship steamed slowly, blindly, toward this ancient boundary, bringing the noise and arrogance of the nineteenth century into a silence that had lasted for millions of years.

Chapter 4

The darkness on the bridge was an oppressive shroud, a suffocating blanket of humid air that pressed against the eyes and made the ears ring with the strain of listening. It was three o'clock in the morning. The USS *Saginaw* moved through the water with the tentative, groping motion of a man walking in a pitch-black room, her paddlewheels turning at a dead slow cadence. *Thump-swash. Thump-swash.*

Captain Montgomery Sicard stood by the binnacle, his body tense, vibrating in sympathy with the low rumble of the oscillating engines. He had not left the deck since the order to change course. His uniform was damp with the salt spray that occasionally whipped over the hurricane deck, but he did not feel the chill. His entire consciousness was projected forward, past the bowsprit, into the impenetrable void ahead.

The ship was making barely three knots. It was a prudent speed, a cautious speed. According to his calculations, the reef of Ocean Island should be at least ten miles to the west. They were feeling their way toward it, intending to sight the breakers at dawn.

He checked the compass card again. West by North. The needle trembled slightly, glowing faint yellow in the binnacle light.

"Keep a sharp lookout forward," Sicard said, his voice low but cutting through the wind.

"Aye, aye, sir," the response drifted back from the forecastle, swallowed instantly by the hiss of the sea.

Sicard gripped the rail. He did not like this darkness. It was lacking even the faint delineation of a horizon line to separate the black water from the black sky. The ocean was a soundscape of confused noises, the slap of waves against the sponsons, the creak of the mainyard, the groan of the rudder pintles. Every splash sounded like a breaker; every shift in the wind sounded like the roar of surf.

He pulled his watch from his vest. 3:20 AM. The night felt endless.

"Breakers! Breakers ahead!"

The scream came from the cathead, raw and terrified, shattering the hypnotic rhythm of the engines.

Sicard did not think. He did not process the fear that spiked cold in his chest. Instead, he ceased to exist as a commander. For three fatal seconds, the connection between his will and his voice severed. His vision tunneled down to the illuminated compass card floating in the binnacle, shivering violently in its gimbals. *West by North*. The geometry was precise; the math had been verified. The reef could not be here. It was a cartographic impossibility. The roar coming over the bow was the sound of a collapsing mountain. His mind frantically re-ran the dead reckoning, seeking an error in the log to explain the white water, while his body stood frozen in a vacuum of disbelief. He gripped the teak rail, knuckles white, watching the foam rise above the bowsprit.

"Captain?"

The voice was Talbot's, breathless and close at his ear. It snapped Sicard's head up. He looked at his executive officer, and for a terrifying heartbeat, the face registered as a stranger's, just flesh and bone waiting to be crushed. Then the shame hit him, hot and sharp, jump-starting the stalled engine of his discipline.

The drill took over, the years of command hardening his voice into a weapon of authority. He leaped to the break of the hurricane deck.

"Stop the engines!" he roared.

The bell clanged in the engine room, a sharp, frantic metal sound rising from the bowels of the ship. The rhythmic thumping ceased instantly, replaced by the hiss of escaping steam.

Sicard strained his eyes against the dark. There. A line of white phosphorescence, jagged and terrifyingly high, stretched across the entire forward horizon. It was right under the bow.

"Back the engines!" Sicard shouted, leaning over the rail, his voice cracking with the force of the command. "Back her! Back her hard!"

"Hard a-starboard!"

The Quartermaster spun the wheel, the spokes blurring in the dim light. The bell clanged again, two sharp strikes. Below decks, the engineers threw the heavy levers. The great pistons shuddered, halted, and then began to drive the crankshaft in reverse.

The paddlewheels bit into the water, churning a chaotic maelstrom of foam against the ship's forward momentum. The *Saginaw* shuddered, a deep, structural complaint as the torque fought the inertia of four hundred tons of oak and iron.

It was too slow.

The white line was rushing toward them. The roar of the surf, masked until this moment by the wind and the engines, suddenly rose to a deafening thunder.

Sicard gripped the stanchion, his knuckles white. He watched the bowsprit stab into the darkness, aiming straight for the center of the fury. The ship was slowing, the drag shuddered through the hull, but the ocean was not a static surface. A massive swell lifted the stern, pushing the vessel forward, driving her down the face of the wave like a surfboard.

"She won't answer!" the helmsman shouted. With the engines backing, the rudder had lost its bite. The ship was a dead weight, sliding downhill.

Sicard watched the inevitable unfold with a strange, detached clarity. The first roller curled over the reef, a wall of glowing green water. Dark teeth of coral heads bared themselves in the trough.

"Hold fast!"

The *Saginaw* slammed into the coral with a tectonic concussion that snapped the head back and stopped the breath in Sicard's throat. The impact threw him violently against the binnacle. The sound was hideous, the shriek of copper sheathing being ripped from the hull, the snap of oak timbers shattering under intolerable pressure.

The foremast whipped forward like a fly rod, the stays singing under the tension before holding. The ship shuddered, pinned for a second on the limestone, and then the ocean delivered the second blow.

A towering breaker crashed over the stern, sweeping the length of the deck in a deluge of white water. The *Saginaw* was lifted bodily, her iron keel grinding across the reef with a noise like a thousand millstones. She dropped again, harder this time, a bone-breaking smash that tore the rudder post free and sent the wheel spinning wild.

Steam roared from the funnel, a white geyser venting into the night as the safety valves blew. The engine room was chaos.

Sicard scrambled to his feet, water streaming from his frock coat. The deck was canted at a crazy angle, heaving and pounding with every surge of the surf.

"Clear away the boats!" he bellowed, though he knew it was a futile command against the thunder.

He looked forward. The stem-post buried into the limestone, but the Pacific refused to let the wreck rest. A succession of rollers caught the stern and heaved it shoreward. The hull ground against the reef with the scream of tortured oak until the ship lay beam-on to the breakers. The heavy engines and iron boilers pinned the midships to the highest point of the coral, a dead weight that held the center fast while the bow and stern dangled over deep water. The *Saginaw* spanned the gap like a bridge with no pilings. Gravity and the surge fought over the unsupported ends; the keel arched, and every timber shrieked against its iron bolts.

***

For Paymaster George Read it began with a shock that felt less like a collision and more like an execution. The impact threw him forward, his shoulder slamming against the wooden partition of his berth. The air in the stateroom, previously silent save for the hum of the ventilation, was instantly filled with a resonant thud. The sound vibrated in his teeth, a dull, heavy impact that telegraphed through the keel as the ship's spine shattered.

Then came the trembling.

The *Saginaw* shuddered. It was a terrifying, mortal convulsion, as if the vessel were a living creature recoiling from a lethal wound.

Read lay frozen for a heartbeat, his mind struggling to bridge the gap between the dreamless dark and this new, violent awake. *A collision*, he thought. *We have struck a steamer.*

But then the grinding began, a low, tearing sound, the noise of oak planking being shredded against something harder than itself. It came from beneath the floorboards, a continuous, agonizing scream of wood and copper.

The realization hit. He scrambled out of the bunk, his bare feet hitting the deck. The floor was no longer level. The ship had taken a sudden, sickening list to starboard, pitching him sideways against the desk. The ledger he had been working on hours before slid off the surface and crashed into the bulkhead.

He groped in the black air, his hands sweeping frantically for the matches he kept by the basin. His fingers brushed the box, but his hands were shaking so badly he fumbled it. The matches scattered across the tilting deck.

"Calm," he whispered, the word lost in the rising cacophony. "Calm."

He abandoned the light. He needed clothes.

His fingers scrabbled across the slant of the desk and closed not on the matchbox, but on cold, heavy crystal. The inkstand. A manic, bureaucratic compulsion seized him. He jammed the glass block into his pocket, the weight banging absurdly against his hip as the deck lurched. He groped for the pens, his mind shrinking to the terrified logic of a clerk: he must preserve the ability to write, even as the water rose to dissolve the words. He made it halfway to the door before the ship slammed down on the reef again, jarring his neck. The shock shattered the delusion. He was hoarding fluid while the Pacific poured in to drown them. He cursed, a raw sound in the dark.

The discipline of the service, drilled into him over years of routine, asserted itself over the panic. He was the Paymaster. He was the custodian of the government's funds and the ship's papers. If the ship was lost, his duty was not to the rigging or the boats, but to the iron safe bolted to the deck of his office.

He found his trousers by touch, hopping on one leg to pull them on as the ship lurched violently again. A second impact, harder than the first. The *Saginaw* was being lifted and dropped. The sensation was nauseating, a vertical heave followed by a pile-driving smash that compressed the spine and threatened to dislocate the knees.

He found his coat. He patted the pockets. The heavy brass ring of keys was there.

He felt his way to the door, the angle of the deck fighting him. The louvers were jammed. He shoved the panel hard, the wood groaning in protest, and stumbled out into the wardroom country.

The space was a cavern of noise. The comfortable gentlemen's club of the officers' mess had been transformed into the inside of a drum. Above, on the spar deck, a stampede was underway. The thud of heavy boots running aft, the dragging of chains, and the unintelligible shouting of commands filtered down through the planking.

But under it all was a new sound, a high-pitched, deafening hiss that sounded like the earth itself was screaming.

Steam. The boilers were being vented.

Read groped his way along the bulkhead, using the stanchions to pull himself uphill against the list. He passed the door of the Chief Engineer's room. It was open. Someone was cursing in the dark, a low, repetitive litany of profanity.

"Blye?" Read called out.

"She's done!" the voice answered from the gloom. "Bottom's out! God damn it, the bottom's out!"

Read did not stop. He reached the ladder leading to the steerage hatch. The air here was thick with dust, coal dust, shaken loose from the bunkers, and the dry, choking powder of old paint flaking from the overheads. He coughed, tasting the grit, and began to climb.

Gravity and the heaving deck conspired to drag him back down the rungs. The ship was rolling wildly now, pivoting on the rock that had impaled her. As he reached the top of the ladder, a deluge of salt water cascaded down the hatchway, drenching him instantly. It was warm, tropical water, but it felt cold with the shock.

He emerged onto the deck and stopped.

The scene before him was a vision of the apocalypse painted in shades of black and white.

The night was still pitch dark, but the ocean was illuminated by its own violence. The *Saginaw* was surrounded by a boiling cauldron of luminous foam. The breakers were heaving walls of ink-black glass, towering ten, perhaps fifteen feet above the bulwarks. They glowed with a spectral, milky light as they curled and crashed, their energy exploding against the reef with a roar that drowned out the escaping steam.

The ship was broadside to the sea. A massive roller materialized out of the darkness. It moved with the tectonic, inexorable weight of the deep ocean. It hit the *Saginaw* on the port quarter, a solid hammer-blow of water.

The ship groaned. The mainmast whipped like a sapling in a gale. A sheet of white water swept the entire length of the deck, burying the pivot gun and smashing the gig against its davits.

Read clung to the hatch coaming, the water rushing past his waist, tugging at him with the strength of a undertow. Debris swirled in the flood; buckets, coils of line, pieces of the contractor's machinery that had broken loose from their lashings.

"Clear away the boats!"

The voice belonged to Captain Sicard. He was standing near the break of the poop deck, a dark silhouette against the white spray. He was shouting through a trumpet, but the wind tore the words away as soon as they left his lips.

Read scrambled aft, fighting the water and the angle of the deck. He saw men, shadows really, working frantically at the boat falls. The discipline was ragged but holding. There was no screaming, only the grunts of effort and the sharp, panicked commands of the boatswain.

He reached the spot where the cutter was lashed. Coxswain Halford was there, a knife in his hand, hacking at a line that had fouled the block.

"Bad business, Mr. Read!" Halford shouted, not looking up. The sailor's face was illuminated by a sudden flash of lightning, no, not lightning.

Someone had lit a blue light on the bridge. The eerie, chemical glare washed the deck in a corpse-like pallor.

"Are we fast?" Read yelled back, leaning close to the sailor's ear.

"Hard and fast!" Halford roared. "She's bilged! The rocks are eating her alive!"

As if to confirm the diagnosis, the ship lifted again. This time, the impact was followed by a tearing sound so loud it sickened the stomach. The funnel guys snapped with the report of pistol shots. The tall smokestack tottered, swayed for a breathless second, and then crashed over the side, taking a section of the bulwark with it. A cloud of steam and soot erupted from the broken uptake, blinding them for a moment in a hot, choking fog.

Read wiped his eyes, smearing the soot and salt spray across his face, and looked over the side. The reef was right there. The coral heads bared themselves in the trough of the wave, jagged black teeth waiting for the next bite. We are not just wrecked, he thought with a strange, detached clarity.

He remembered the money. The papers.

He turned back toward the companionway, but the deck pitched violently, throwing him to his knees. He slid across the wet planking, his hands scrabbling for purchase on the slick wood. His fingers found a ring-bolt, and he held on, the water rushing over his head, filling his nose and mouth with the taste of the Pacific.

He spat the water out, gasping for air. The "frightful thud" that had woken him seemed like a polite knock compared to this. The *Saginaw* was not fighting the storm; she was losing. The ocean was taking her apart, piece by piece, and they were trapped in the wreckage.

Read looked up at the rigging. The stars were gone.

The sky was a void, merging seamlessly with the black violence of the water. The structure beneath their feet had ceased to be a platform for navigation; it had become a killing floor, slick with foam and canted at a lethal angle.

***

William Halford wrapped his arm around the fife rail of the mainmast and held on as the Atlantic Ocean, no, the Pacific, he had to remember where the hell he was, tried to wash him into the scuppers.

The *Saginaw* was dying. Halford had seen ships die before, but usually they went down fighting, plunging into the deep with their dignity intact. This was different. This was a mauling. The ship was being chewed to pieces.

He blinked the brine from his lashes, the salt stinging his eyes. The waist of the ship was a confused tangle of water and wreckage. The seas were coming over the port beam, green and solid, hitting the deckhouses with the force of a sledgehammer. But the sound that cut through the gale was not the wind. It was the death rattle of the engines.

From the open hatch of the fireroom, a cloud of steam billowed out, thick and white, smelling of sulfur and wet iron. The sea had breached the hull. The fires were drowning.

Halford let go of the rail and scrambled toward the hatch. He didn't know why, habit, perhaps. A fireman clawed his way up the ladder, his face a mask of soot and terror.

"Water's over the grate bars!" the man screamed, his voice thin against the roar of the surf.

The rhythmic vibration of the machinery, the heartbeat that had thumped under their feet for seven months, stopped dead. The *Saginaw* was now just wood and copper, motionless on the rock, waiting for the waves to finish the job.

"Bear a hand with the launch!"

The shout came from the Boatswain. Halford turned. The large launch, the heaviest boat they carried, was sitting in its chocks on the main deck. It was their best hope. It could carry thirty men and provisions.

Halford threw himself at the falls, joining a knot of men struggling to lift the heavy boat. They heaved, their boots slipping on the wet planking. The boat lifted, swinging wildly in the gale.

"Steady!" Halford roared. "Fend her off!"

A massive comber, black and white-capped, rose up out of the darkness. It hit the ship just as the boat swung outboard. The wave caught the launch, lifting the two-ton vessel like a toy, and smashed it back against the side of the ship.

The sound was sickening, the crunch of seasoned oak snapping into kindling. The launch disintegrated. Planks, thwarts, and oars were instantly sucked away into the boiling foam.

Then came a groaning crash that vibrated through the soles of Halford's feet, distinct from the screaming of the timber. The diving bell, that massive, windowed iron sphere lashed near the pivot gun, tore free. The ship heaved, the bell trundled across the deck like a runaway planet, crushing the port bulwarks with a shrieking tear of copper and oak before plunging over the side.

It vanished instantly into the dark water. There was no splash, just a heavy, final thunk as it hit the reef. The fifty-thousand-dollar folly, the entire reason they had rotted in the lagoon for seven months, was gone in a heartbeat.

Halford stared at the empty davits. The port cutter was gone. The launch was gone. They were losing the means to leave.

"The gig!" he shouted to the man next to him. "Check the gig!"

But before he could move aft, the ship gave a lurch that threw every man to the deck. It wasn't the roll of a wave. It was a structural failure. A screech of tearing metal, the copper sheathing ripping apart, echoed from the bow.

Halford looked forward. The darkness was lit by the eerie blue flare of a signal light someone had managed to ignite on the quarterdeck. In that ghostly chemical glare, the unthinkable.

The bow of the *Saginaw* was moving independently of the stern.

The ship had broken her back. The forward section, weighed down by the heavy Parrott gun and the anchor chains, sagged into the dark. Iron bolts shrieked as they sheared. The forward third of the vessel tore free, dipping and twisting in the surf before dropping into the deep water on the ocean side of the reef. The forecastle and the crew's quarters vanished. Halford didn't think about who was still below; there was no time for the dead. He threw his weight against the mainmast shrouds as the *Saginaw*, suddenly lightened by the loss of her bow, bucked like a spurred horse. The midships were now an open wound, defenseless against the surge.

A mass of black water boarded the waist, heavy as a falling house. It crushed the remaining bulwarks and snatched a private of the Marine Guard. He was gone, swept into the boiling blackness. The ocean held him for a heartbeat, a dark speck in the maelstrom, before the following surge rose. A monolithic surge curled over the stern and hurled the private back over the rail. He slammed onto the deck planks, a bruised heap of blue wool and salt water. Brine poured from his mouth as his fingers clawed at the wet wood. Halford looked past the gasping Marine toward the source of a new, high-pitched scream, not of a man, but of the ship itself. The boiler pipes had ruptured, venting a white ghost of pressure that masked the center of the vessel. Through the hiss, a different sound emerged. It came from above, in the gloom of the starboard paddle box.

On the hurricane deck, the wardroom steward sat on a hatch cover. He did not join the scramble for the boats. His wrists were heavy with irons, the metal rings clinking a dull, rhythmic accompaniment against the cedar as the ship groaned. A thin, melodic tune rose above the roar, the notes recognizable and steady.

"All roun' de little farm I wandered," he sang softly, the words barely carrying over the crashing surf. *"When I was young."*

He stared into the darkness, his melody unbroken by the tilting deck or the spray raking his face.

"Way down upon de Swanee Ribber," he continued, his voice a flat, haunting contrast to the shriek of tearing iron. *"Far, far away."*

He sat like a statue in the shadows, his eyes fixed on the white water where the bow had vanished.

"Aft!" Captain Sicard's voice cut through the chaos. He was standing by the mizzen rigging, remarkably calm, though his frock coat was soaked. "All hands aft! Lay aft!"

Halford scrambled up the incline of the deck. The ship was pivoting on the reef, the stern swinging toward the coral shelf. They were stuck fast, but the pounding was tearing the remaining hull apart beneath them. The deck planks were starting to spring, the caulking spewing out like entrails.

"We cannot lower the remaining boats," Sicard shouted, gesturing to the boiling surf that surrounded the stern. "The rocks will stove them in. We must bridge the gap."

He pointed to the mainmast. It was swaying dangerously, the stays slack as the hull twisted.

"Cut away the mainmast," Sicard ordered. "Fell it onto the reef."

It was a desperate gamble. If the mast fell wrong, it would crush the men huddled on the quarterdeck. If it fell short, it would be swept away. It had to fall exactly onto the ledge of the reef, creating a bridge from the wreck to the coral.

"Axes!" Halford yelled. "Bring the axes!"

Two men appeared with fire axes. They attacked the shrouds first, the heavy wire rigging pinging as it parted. Then they turned the blades on the pine mast itself.

Halford grabbed an axe from a tiring sailor. He swung with a grunt, the steel biting deep into the wood. The chips flew, stinging his face. The ship shuddered with every wave, threatening to throw him off his feet, but he planted his boots wide and kept swinging. *Chop. Chop. Chop.* It was the only thing he could control in a world gone mad.

"Stand clear!"

The mast whined. It leaned, hesitated, and then fell.

It crashed over the starboard rail, the top hamper smashing into the white water. The tip of the mast slammed onto the coral shelf, gouging a furrow in the limestone, but it held. It was a bridge. A slippery, precarious, sea-washed bridge, but a bridge nonetheless.

"Go!" Sicard ordered. "Make for the reef!"

Halford didn't hesitate. He was a coxswain; his job was to lead. He climbed onto the horizontal spar.

The wood was slick with spray and rain. The angle was steep. Beneath him, the ocean surged through the gap between the ship and the reef, a meat-grinder of jagged rock and churning water. If he slipped, he would be shredded.

He crawled on his hands and knees, gripping the wood until his fingernails ached. The mast bobbed and scraped against the coral with every wave. A rat, terrified and wet, scurried over his hand, digging its claws into his skin before vanishing toward the shore. Even the vermin were abandoning the ship.

Halford reached the crosstrees. The surf was breaking right over the mast here, threatening to wash him off. He timed the waves. *One... two... now.*

He lunged forward, jumping from the spar to the solid rock.

He landed hard.

It was not rock. It was a field of knives.

The reef was composed of living coral, sharp as broken glass. Halford's boots skidded, and he went down on his knees. The coral sliced through his duck trousers and into the flesh. The sting, hot and immediate, but he scrambled up, ignoring the blood running down his shins.

He turned back to the ship. The scene was a nightmare. The *Saginaw* was a dark, broken shape against the night, lit only by the dying blue flare. Men were crawling along the mast like ants on a twig. Some were slipping, hanging by their arms while others hauled them back up.

"Keep moving!" Halford bellowed, his voice raw. "Don't stop! Get off the timber!"

A wave crashed over the reef, hitting Halford at the knees. The water was warm, but the wind was freezing. He staggered back, trying to find a foothold that didn't cut him. There was no dry land here. They were standing in the surf zone, shin-deep in water, on a platform of razor-blades, surrounded by the deafening roar of the Pacific.

Paymaster Read stumbling along the mast, clutching a bundle to his chest. The officer looked like a ghost, his face pale and eyes wide. He slipped near the end, his boots sliding off the rounded wood.

Halford lunged forward, grabbing Read by the collar of his coat and hauling him onto the coral.

"Steady, sir," Halford grunted.

"The papers," Read gasped, holding up the sodden package. "I have the papers."

"To hell with the papers," Halford spat, looking back at the wreck. "We need water. We need food."

The ship groaned again, a terrible, rending sound that signaled the end. The stern section was settling. The ocean was claiming the last of the *Saginaw*.

"She's going!" someone screamed.

Halford watched as the quarterdeck dipped lower. The sea washed over the poop, extinguishing the last lantern. Darkness swallowed the wreck. Now, there was only the sound, the grinding, the smashing, the roaring.

They were ninety-three men standing on a sharp, submerged reef in the middle of the night, a thousand miles from nowhere. They had no ship. They had no shelter. They were wet, bleeding, and shivering.

Halford looked down at his feet. The water swirling around his boots was pink with blood, his own, and the blood of the shipmates crowding around him.

"Move inland!" Sicard's voice came from the darkness, still commanding, though breathless. "Move toward the lagoon! Find high ground!"

Halford turned away from the wreck. He began to pick his way across the sharp terrain, every step a calculation of pain, moving toward the sound of calmer water.

But the darkness hid no sanctuary. The water merely deepened, forcing the retreat to halt in the swirling current of the lagoon edge. There was nowhere else to go. The survivors clustered together in the waist-deep surge, shivering as the adrenaline leached out of their blood, waiting for the sun to illuminate their prison. When the light finally broke the horizon, it revealed the grey, jagged reality of their footing.

***

Paymaster George Read stood thigh-deep in the water, his arms wrapped around his chest to contain the shivering that had racked his body for three hours. He was not alone. Around him, huddled in a miserable, shivering phalanx, stood the ninety-three officers and men of the USS *Saginaw*. They were a pathetic assembly. Some were half-naked, stripped to their under-drawers in the panic of the night. Others wore the remnants of uniforms that were soaked, torn, and stained with the grease of the engine room.

But it was the water around their legs that held Read's attention. As the grey light of morning began to seep into the eastern sky, the foam swirling about their knees took on a sickening, rusty hue. It was blood. The reef they stood upon was not a flat shelf of rock; it was a vast field of staghorn coral. In the darkness, the men had stumbled and fallen, cutting their feet and shins to ribbons. Now, in the growing light, the salt water stung the open wounds with a ferocity that made strong men weep silently.

Read looked down at his own trousers. They were shredded at the hems, the fabric dark with blood. The sting, a constant, burning reminder of their fragility, but he forced his eyes upward.

The sun was rising.

It broke the horizon with a brilliant orange that illuminated the scene with the clarity of a stage set. To the east, the Pacific Ocean stretched away in an unbroken plain of blue, rolling in with the majesty of a force that had destroyed them without malice.

To the west lay the wreck.

Read stared at the thing that had been his home. The *Saginaw* was unrecognizable. The ship had broken in two. The forward section, the forecastle, the berth deck, the heavy guns, had vanished entirely, swallowed by the deep water on the ocean side of the reef. Only the after section remained. It lay high on the coral ledge, beaten and canted at a forty-five-degree angle.

The massive paddle-box on the port side was smashed, the iron framework twisted like wire. The funnel was gone. The planking of the hull was sprung, gaping open like the ribs of a slaughtered animal, revealing the dark, wet interior of the wardroom where he had sat drinking coffee only hours before. The sea broke over the stern, sending cataracts of white water cascading through the skylights, washing away the books, the instruments, and the memories of their voyage.

Sicard stood isolated from the huddled crew, his boots shifting in the coral grit. His gaze was locked on the exposed ribs of the stern, staring into the dark, wet cavity where his cabin had been. Read followed the look.

The desk, the chronometers, the chart where the dividers had pricked out the fatal geometry of *West by North*, it was all gone, pulverized against the limestone.

The Captain's hand drifted to his throat. He clawed at the gold lace of his collar, scratching at the rank insignia as if the bullion had suddenly grown hot against his skin. For a heartbeat, the rigid spine snapped. His shoulders dropped, and the wet frock coat seemed to hang empty, the man inside shrinking under a burden that possessed no mass but infinite weight. He looked at the water washing over his boots, a man measuring the depth of his own ruin.

"God help us," whispered Dr. Frank. The surgeon was standing next to Read, clutching a small canvas bag of instruments. His eyes fixed on the gap where the forward hull used to be. "The forward officers... the men..."

"They are here, Doctor," Read said, his voice rasping in his throat. "We are all here. By some miracle, we are all here."

It was true. A muster taken in the dark, shouted over the roar of the surf, had confirmed it. Every man had made it to the reef. It was a statistical impossibility, a defiance of the odds that seemed almost cruel. The ocean had spared their lives, but it had taken everything else.

Read turned his back on the wreck. He looked across the lagoon.

The contrast was jarring. While the ocean side of the reef was a maelstrom of violence and noise, the lagoon was a sheet of polished turquoise, calm and serene. And there, perhaps three miles away, lay their destination.

Ocean Island.

A low, flat spit of white sand, rising no more than twenty feet above the tide. Covered in a dense, scrubby vegetation that looked grey-green in the morning light. There were no palm trees swaying in the wind, no waterfalls, no signs of comfort. It looked desolate, scorched, and utterly lonely.

"A small strip of terra firma," Read murmured.

"It is land, Paymaster," said Captain Sicard.

Read started. He had not realized the Captain was beside him. Sicard stood straight, despite the footing. He had lost his cap, and his frock coat was torn at the shoulder, but his bearing remained rigid. He was staring at the island with a hard, assessing gaze.

"Yes, sir. It is land."

"The men cannot stay here," Sicard said, his voice devoid of emotion. "The tide will rise. We must move the sick and the injured to the island immediately. We have the gig?"

"The gig is stove, sir. The launch and the first cutter are gone. But we have the second cutter and the dinghy."

Sicard nodded, accepting the inventory of disaster. "We shall wade, then. We shall float the supplies we can salvage and wade to the beach. It will be a long walk."

Read looked at the distance. Three miles. Three miles of wading through a lagoon that was undoubtedly patrolled by sharks, dragging whatever flotsam they could pull from the wreck, under a sun that was already beginning to heat the air.

He looked back at the men. They were in a state of shock. The adrenaline of the crash had faded, replaced by the cold reality of their predicament. They were castaways.

Yesterday, they were representatives of the United States Government, backed by the industrial might of the steam engine and the authority of the flag. Today, they were ninety-three mortal creatures clinging to a rock, stripped of their technology, their hierarchy, and their dignity.

A sailor near the front of the group bent down and picked something out of the water. It was a piece of salt pork, a chunk of ration that had washed out of the broken hold. He looked at it for a moment, then wiped the brine off on his shirt and bit into it raw.

The sight turned Read's stomach, yet it also clarified the situation. The civilization of the wardroom, the napkins, the silver, the conversation, was gone.

"Mr. Read," Sicard said, turning to him. "Secure the provisions. Whatever washes up. Hardtack, pork, water. Especially water. Post a guard. Nothing is to be consumed without order."

"Aye, sir."

"And the papers?"

"I have them, sir. And the funds."

Sicard looked at the sodden bundle Read was clutching. A grim smile touched the Captain's lips, though it did not reach his eyes. "The funds will be of little use here, Paymaster. There is no market on that sandbar. But keep them. It is government property."

The Captain turned away, shouting orders to the Boatswain to organize a salvage party.

Read remained standing in the bloody water. He watched the sun climb higher, burning the mist off the lagoon. The heat was coming. He could feel it on the back of his neck. The salt drying on his skin began to itch.

He looked once more at the *Saginaw*. A wave crashed into the open stern, sending a spray of white water high into the air. A heavy timber, perhaps a part of the keel, floated free and drifted into the lagoon.

It was over. The career of the USS *Saginaw* had ended on a nameless reef in the middle of nowhere. But for George Read, and for the shivering men around him, the ordeal had only just begun. He adjusted his grip on the wet ledger, took a step forward, and winced as the coral sliced his foot again. He began the long, painful limp toward the island.

Part 2

THE ISLAND AND THE GIG

Chapter 5

The migration from the reef to the island was a three-mile procession through a beautiful, turquoise purgatory. It began with a descent; the men had to slide off the high, hammered shelf of the outer reef and drop into the lagoon. The water here was deceptively calm, a shocking azure in the morning light that hid the treacherous topography of the bottom.

It was a stumbling, submarine march across a field of submerged knives. The floor of the lagoon was a maze of coral heads, staghorn and cauliflower formations that rose from the sand like petrified briar patches. For the men who had lost their boots in the night, every step was a calculation of agony. They moved in a ragged column, wading chest-deep, feeling with their lacerated toes for a patch of soft sand, only to find the razor-edge of a coral shelf. The salt water, initially a cool relief, soon became a torture, stinging the fresh cuts on their shins and feet until the nerves screamed with a dull, rhythmic throb.

The stove gig, kept afloat by its air tanks but swamped to the gunwales, served as a life-raft for the non-swimmers and a barge for the few precious casks of water they had salvaged. Fifty men surrounded the boat, their hands gripping the gunwale, half-towing and half-supporting themselves. When the lagoon floor dropped away into sudden, dark blue channels, they kicked frantically, their legs dangling in the void, eyes scanning the clear water for the grey shapes of the sharks that patrolled the atoll.

"Close up!" Halford roared from the front of the line. "Keep the spacing tight!"

Read felt a displacement of water against his thigh, a heavy, muscular push of current that wasn't the tide. He looked down. Through the distortion of the surface, a grey shape glided between him and the man ahead. It was a Galapagos shark, perhaps eight feet long. It moved with an arrogant, sinuous lethargy, indifferent to the intrusion.

It circled the legs of a stumbling coal-heaver. The boy froze, his eyes wide, clutching a crate of hardtack to his chest. The shark nudged the boy's calf with its snout, a wet, sandpaper bump of curiosity.

"Don't splash," Halford warned, his voice low and hard. "Don't thrash. Just walk. If you run, you trigger them."

The shark turned, its pectoral fin slicing the surface tension, and slid away into the deep blue channel. Read didn't breathe until the grey shadow dissolved into the gloom. He looked down at his own shaking hands. The illusion of their dominance was gone; they were just meat in a larder.

The shark did not return, but the fear remained, making the rest of the journey a torture of anticipation. The progress was agonizingly slow. It took hours to cross the lagoon. The sun rose higher, hammering down on heads unprotected by hats, burning the salt-crusted skin. The wake behind the column dissipating ribbons of pink, the collective blood of ninety-three men washing away into the current. By the time the water shallowed to the waist, then the knee, the men were no longer marching; they were staggering, their bodies drained, fueled only by the desperate gravity of the dry land ahead.

They crawled up the incline of the beach on hands and knees, collapsing the moment they reached the high-tide line.

***

The sun over *Hōlanikū* flayed. By mid-morning, the white coral sand of the beach was a blinding reflector, throwing the tropical heat back into the faces of the ninety-three men huddled above the high-tide line.

Paymaster George Read sat on a hummock of coarse grass, scraping the salt crust from his eyebrows. His uniform was stiff with dried brine, transforming the wool into a coarse, abrasive armor that chafed at the neck and wrists. Around him, the crew of the late USS *Saginaw* lay in a stupor of exhaustion. They looked less like sailors and more like the victims of a massacre who had forgotten to die. Their feet were wrapped in bloody rags, eyes hollow, fixed on the middle distance or staring back across the water at the black, broken tooth of the shipwreck on the horizon.

Read's gaze shifted to the steward. The man stood apart, his wrists still locked in the heavy iron bands, his posture rigid despite the fatigue. The key lay somewhere in the debris of the wardroom, buried under ten fathoms of water. Read signaled to a boatswain's mate named Miller.

"Miller. Bring a sledge and a chisel. Get those irons off him."

Miller approached, his own movements heavy and leaden. He placed a steadying hand on the steward's shoulder, guiding him toward a flat spar of driftwood that had washed up near the grass. The steward knelt and rested his bound wrists on the timber. He looked away as Miller positioned the chisel. The hammer fell, a sharp, metallic crack that echoed against the silent dunes. The chisel bit into the soft iron, spitting a single spark. With a second blow, the shackles snapped and hissed into the sand. The steward stood slowly, rubbing the deep, gray indentations where the metal had chewed into his skin. He gave Miller a single, curt nod.

The beach itself was a scene of surreal devastation. The tide had brought in the harvest of the disaster, depositing a "promiscuous mass" of flotsam along the waterline. It was a chaotic jumble that defied the logic of the quarterdeck. A crate of soaked hardtack sat atop a coil of rigging next to a fine officer's frock coat, its arms spread wide in the sand like a discarded skin. Splintered spars and empty casks littered the limestone. A sextant case lay nearby with the lid torn off; its precision lenses were shattered, rendering the instrument a useless piece of brass junk.

To Read's accountant eyes, this garbage dump was a tragedy of inventory. Every item represented a line in his ledger that was now void. The order and hierarchy of the ship had been vomited onto the sand in a wet, tangled heap.

"Mr. Read."

The voice was calm, quiet, and utterly incongruous with the surroundings. Read scrambled to his feet, wincing as his lacerated soles pressed into the sand.

Captain Montgomery Sicard stood nearby. He was battered, his uniform soaked and torn at the shoulder, salt drying white in the creases of his frock coat. But unlike the men collapsing in the sand, he was standing.

"We must establish the camp, Paymaster," Sicard said. "And we must secure the provisions. The sun will spoil the meat if we do not get it under cover."

"Aye, sir. The men are... they are spent, Captain."

"They are alive," Sicard corrected. "And they are still in the United States Navy. We shall remind them of that fact."

Sicard turned to the Executive Officer, Lieutenant Talbot, who was dozing fitfully against a piece of driftwood.

"Mr. Talbot. Beat to quarters."

Talbot blinked, confused for a moment, before the habit of obedience snapped his spine straight. "Aye, aye, sir."

The boatswain's mate, a burly man named O'Connell, stepped forward. He placed a silver whistle to his cracked lips. The call was shrill and piercing, cutting through the sound of the wind and the distant roar of the reef. *Tweet-tweeeeeeee-tweet.*

The effect was galvanic. The huddled shapes on the sand stirred. Heads lifted. The instinct drilled into them by years of service overrode the shock of the wreck. Slowly, painfully, the men stood up. They formed ranks on the uneven sand, shuffling into their divisions. The lines were ragged, the uniforms torn, the faces gaunt, but they stood.

Sicard walked to the center of the formation. He waited until the last cough had died away, until the only sound was the hiss of the surf.

"Men," Sicard began. His voice was not loud, but it carried the hard edge of command. "The ship is gone. We have lost our vessel, but we have not lost our duty. We are castaways, but we are not savages. We are a ship's company, and we will conduct ourselves as such."

He paced slowly down the line, looking each man in the eye.

"Our situation is grave," he continued. "We are a thousand miles from Honolulu. We have limited water and limited food. But we have discipline. If we maintain it, we shall survive. If we lose it, we shall die here."

Read watched the faces of the crew. The fear was still there, but something else was creeping in, relief. They were being told what to do. The burden of survival was being lifted from their individual shoulders and placed back on the collective structure of the Navy. The chaos of the "promiscuous mass" on the beach was being ordered.

"Mr. Talbot," Sicard ordered. "Divide the men into gangs. I want a salvage party to return to the reef immediately. Anything that floats must be saved. We need lumber, copper, and canvas."

"Aye, sir."

"Mr. Read," Sicard turned to him. "You will take charge of the provisions. Secure everything edible. Post a sentry. Establish a daily ration. We are on short allowance as of this moment. One quarter ration of pork, one quarter ration of biscuit."

"Understood, Captain."

"The Carpenter will organize a gang to build shelter. We will not sleep in the open tonight. Use the sails and the oars. Build a tent for the sick first."

The orders flew, precise and practical. The paralysis of the morning broke. The men moved, not with the sluggishness of despair, but with the purpose of labor.

Read walked toward the pile of debris, his mind already organizing the task. A barrel of salt beef, half-buried in the sand. He signaled two marines.

"You there. Dig that out. Roll it to the high ground behind the scrub. And handle it gently; if the hoops spring, we lose the brine and the meat rots."

As he worked, dragging a heavy tarp over a pile of wet hardtack, Read glanced back at Sicard. The Captain was standing by the water's edge, looking out at the distant wreck of the *Saginaw*. It was a humiliating sight for a commander.

But as Read watched, he realized the truth. The *Saginaw* was just wood and iron. The real ship, the hierarchy, the chain of command, the shared will, had been carried ashore. It was alive and functioning on this desolate strip of sand.

A sailor near Read, a young landsman who had been weeping only an hour before, wiped his nose and heaved a crate of tinned mutton onto his shoulder.

"Where do you want this, Paymaster?" the boy asked.

"Over there," Read said, pointing to the designated storehouse area. "Stack it square. We'll count it by sundown."

The sun beat down, raising blisters on their necks. The flies, sensing the damp wool and the exposed meat, began to swarm. The smell of the lagoon, sulfurous and fishy, was overpowering.

The sheer density of men and refuse on the narrow strip of sand was becoming suffocating. Read wiped his hands on his trousers, needing to escape the immediate chaos to assess the true dimensions of their confinement. He signaled to a Corporal of Marines and two barefoot landsmen standing nearby.

"With me," Read ordered. "We need to find a secure cache for the dry stores inland."

They turned their backs on the sea and trudged up the slope.

***

The transition from the white sand of the shore to the interior was abrupt. The ground rose slightly, forming a low dune that acted as a windbreak. Beyond it, the vegetation took hold. It was a tangled, impenetrable thicket of *Scaevola*, naupaka, the Hawaiians called it, a hardy shrub with waxy leaves and twisted branches that grew chest-high.

"Watch your step," Read warned, pushing a branch aside. "The ground is honeycombed."

The island was a thin crust of guano and sand held together by root systems, perforated everywhere by the burrows of bonin petrels. With every third step, a boot punched through the surface, sinking into a hollow cavity. The air here was stagnant, stripped of the cooling trade wind by the brush, and thick with the ammonia reek of bird droppings.

But it was the birds themselves that unnerved him.

They were everywhere. Great Laysan albatrosses sat on their nests, regarding the intruders with a placid, fearless gaze. They did not fly. They did not flee. They simply watched, turning their heads in unison as the men passed. To walk through the colony was to wade through a sea of white feathers and clacking beaks.

"They have no fear," Read observed, stopping to look down at a Great Frigatebird nesting on a low branch. The bird watched him, its red throat pouch inflating slowly. It did not flinch when his shadow fell across it.

"They do not know us, sir," the Corporal said, reaching out to tap the bird's beak with his rifle barrel. "They ain't learned to be afraid yet."

Read shivered, though the sun was blazing. It wasn't just innocence; it was authority. He remembered the charts, the Hawaiian name for this place: *Hōlanikū*. He had read that the natives considered these birds the physical bodies of the gods.

He looked at the thousands of nesting pairs stretching to the horizon. They weren't stepping into a larder; they were trespassing in a temple. And they were about to turn it into a slaughterhouse.

"Do not harm them," Read said instinctively, knocking the barrel aside. "We may need them later."

It was a reminder that this place had evolved in a vacuum, entirely innocent of the violence of men.

They pushed deeper, perhaps three hundred yards from the beach. The roar of the surf faded to a dull, omnipresent vibration in the soles of their feet. The lagoon was invisible now, hidden by the scrub. They were in the center of the atoll, a flat, grey-green saucer of vegetation baking under the vertical sun.

Read stopped, having stubbed his toe against something unyielding in the soft coral sand. A grey, weathered shape protruded from the base of a naupaka bush, a piece of timber bleached to the color of bone by decades of exposure, yet possessing a regularity that nature did not manufacture.

"Halt," Read said.

He knelt in the sand, ignoring the protest of his lacerated feet. He began to dig with his hands. The sand was warm and dry, pouring back into the hole as fast as he scooped it out.

The object revealed itself slowly. It was a heavy timber, perhaps eight inches square, hewn from solid oak. It was embedded deep in the island's geology, anchored by the roots of the scrub that had grown over it.

Read brushed the sand from the surface. The grain was deep and furrowed, the soft wood worn away by wind and rain, leaving the hard ridges standing in relief. He traced the line of it until his fingers found a hole. A trunnel hole. The wooden peg that had once secured this beam was long gone, rotted away to dust.

"Is it from a ship, sir?" the landsman asked. He looked back toward the beach where the *Saginaw* lay broken, a dark, oily ruin against the horizon, then back to the timber at their feet.

"Yes," Read said softly. He didn't look up from the furrowed grain. "But not ours. This is old."

He dug further, following the timber until he found the end. It had been severed. Not broken by the violence of a crash, but cut. The marks of an axe were still visible, though softened by time. The cut was jagged, desperate. And near the end, the wood was black. Charred.

Read sat back on his heels.

"The *Gledstanes*," he murmured. "Or perhaps the *Parker*."

"Sir?"

"Whalers," Read said, his voice distant. "Wrecked here decades ago. They would have scavenged the old ribs to build their fires."

The birds nesting in the shade of the bushes were sitting on top of a history of despair.

"They were here," Read said, standing up and dusting the sand from his hands. "Right where we are standing. They waited here for months."

The Corporal looked at the charred wood with a new expression, not curiosity, but dread. "Did they get off, Paymaster?"

"Eventually," Read lied. He knew the history; he knew they were rescued. But he also knew the *Parker* crew had eaten the *Gledstanes* dog. He knew the degradation that came with the waiting. He did not share that.

He looked at the timber again. It was dry as tinder.

"Mark this spot, Corporal," Read ordered, his voice returning to its official cadence. "There is iron here. Bolts, fasteners. And the wood itself.

We will need fuel. If we are to boil water, we will need every scrap of burnable material this island holds."

"Aye, sir."

Read turned back toward the beach. The discovery had shifted the atmosphere. The island was no longer a blank slate, a *terra incognita* to be mapped and conquered. It was a palimpsest, a manuscript that had been written over before.

As they retraced their steps through the bird colony, Read felt the weight of the "Graveyard" pressing on him. The albatrosses watched them go, indifferent witnesses to the cycle. The *Gledstanes* had come, and her bones were buried in the sand. The *Parker* had come, and burned the *Gledstanes*. Now the *Saginaw* was here.

He pushed through the final barrier of brush and emerged back onto the dunes. Below him, the beach was a hive of activity. Men were dragging wet canvas, stacking boxes, and erecting makeshift tents. It looked industrious. It looked hopeful.

But Read's hand still felt the texture of the dry, charred oak. He knew what lay beneath the sand. He knew that if no ship came, the men working below would eventually become part of the island's geology, just like the timber he had found.

"Let us move," Read said, stepping down the slope. "The Captain needs a report."

***

Read stood near the water's edge, watching the fishing party return. They moved slowly, wading through the shallows, dragging a seine net they had fashioned from a rescued trysail. Their silhouettes were ragged, but their voices carried a note of triumph that had been absent since the wreck.

"Haul away, lads! Keep the lead-line down!"

The net came up onto the sand, a heavy, dripping bundle. As the mesh was opened, a spill of living jewels tumbled onto the beach.

Read stepped closer, mesmerized by the colors. The fish were magnificent. There were parrotfish with scales of iridescent blue and green, their beaks hard and white like porcelain. There were wrasse painted in violent stripes of neon orange and black, and surgeonfish that gleamed with a slick, metallic gunmetal. Compared to the grey salt pork and the weevil-ridden biscuit that had been their diet for seven months, this catch looked like salvation.

"A fine haul, Mr. Read," said Quartermaster Peter Francis, gripping a large, struggling parrotfish by the tail. "Fresh mess for the wardroom tonight. And enough for the berth deck too, I reckon."

The men crowded around, their eyes fixed on the fish with a predatory intensity. The hunger was already there, a sharp, gnawing presence in the gut that the short rations of the morning had failed to quell.

Dr. Frank pushed through the circle. The surgeon looked haggard, his uniform shirt stained with sweat, his medical bag still clutched in his hand as if it were a talisman. He looked down at the vibrant pile, and his face tightened.

"Do not celebrate yet," Frank warned, his voice thin.

"Doctor?" Read asked, looking up. "Surely fresh protein is indicated."

"The color, Paymaster," Frank said, pointing a finger at the catch. "In these latitudes, the beauty is often a warning. The poison of the reef concentrates in the flesh. Ciguatera. I saw it in the West Indies. "Their constitutions cannot take another shock," Frank added, his voice dropping to a harsh whisper. "The 'coast fever' is resurfacing, Paymaster. If we feed them poison on top of the ague, we will empty the camp in a week."

A silence fell over the group. The fish flopped on the sand, their brilliant colors suddenly looking garish, toxic.

"We must test it," Sicard's voice cut in. The Captain had approached unnoticed. "Cook a portion of the liver. Feed it to the..."

"I'll try it, Captain," Francis volunteered, though his voice lacked its earlier enthusiasm. "I've eaten reef fish in the Fijis. These look right enough."

"No," Sicard ordered. "We cannot risk a man. Segregate the catch. Keep the deep-water species if you can identify them. Discard the yellow ones.

Discard the toadfish. The rest... boil it. Boil it until the flesh falls apart. And pray."

The joy of the harvest evaporated. The men sorted the fish with sullen caution, tossing the most vibrant specimens back into the lagoon where they floated for a moment, stunned, before darting away. The remaining catch was carried up the beach to the fires, but the anticipation was gone.

Sicard stood by the surf line. His face was a mask of rigid calculation. He turned to the dunes where the monk seals lay sleeping in the heat.

"Mr. Read, take a detail to the north beach. Secure a seal. We need meat that is safe."

"Aye, sir," Read replied, though his stomach turned at the thought.

He took Halford and two coal-heavers. They trudged north, their boots sinking into the hot, granular coral. Ahead, a dark shape broke the pristine whiteness of the beach.

It was a female monk seal, heavy with winter fat, dozing near the waterline. As the shadow of the men fell across the sand, she didn't flinch. She didn't scramble for the water. She simply rolled onto her side, exposing her pale belly to the sun, and watched them approach with large, liquid eyes. She blinked slowly, trusting the isolation of her world.

"Strike her," Halford ordered the coal-heaver. "Hard. Back of the head."

The man, a young coal-heaver named Lynch, stepped into the animal's personal space. He held a heavy club of driftwood, a piece of the ship's railing that still held an iron bolt. He raised it above his head.

He froze. The seal looked up at him. Her whiskers twitched, sniffing the air near his boots. Her face was undeniably dog-like, a wet nose, a broad forehead, an expression of mild, bovine curiosity. She let out a soft huff of breath.

Lynch lowered the club an inch. His hands were shaking. He looked at Halford, his face pale beneath the sunburn. "She... she ain't running, Coxswain. She's just looking at me."

"She doesn't know what you are," Halford said, his voice low and hard. "Teach her. Swing."

Lynch swallowed dryly. He tightened his grip until his knuckles turned yellow. He squeezed his eyes shut for a fraction of a second, steeling himself against the betrayal. Then he swung.

It was a glancing blow. The club hit the seal's shoulder with a dull *thud*.

The animal screamed, a high, human-sounding wail of confusion and pain. She thrashed, rearing up, her heavy body undulating in a panic that threw sand into the men's faces. Lynch froze, horrified by the noise.

"Again!" Halford roared, stepping in. "Hit her again! Don't let her suffer!"

Lynch swung wildly. *Thump. Thump.* The blows landed on the neck, the jaw, the back of the head. It wasn't a clean kill; it was a bludgeoning. The seal barked and snapped, blood spraying from her nose, turning the white sand into a red slurry. It took five strikes before she finally slumped, a massive tremor rolling through her blubber as the life left her.

"Bleed her," Halford said, breathing hard. He snatched the knife from his belt and slashed the throat. The smell hit Read instantly, a hot, iron-rich reek of copper and lamp oil.

The remaining seals did not flee. One mate returned to its fallen companion, nosing the cooling body and moaning in a voice so human it made the sailors hesitate. Halford alone didn't wait. He plunged his hands into the incision, working the skin loose from the fat.

Read turned away, pressing his hand to his mouth. Behind him, the sound of the skin being peeled from the carcass, a slick, wet tearing noise, continued relentlessly.

***

As the light failed, the heat of the day finally broke. The temperature dropped, and a damp chill settled over the low scrub of the island. The men retreated to the makeshift shelters they had erected, low tents made of salvaged canvas and propped up with oars and driftwood.

Read crawled into the shelter designated for the officers. It was a cramped, triangular tunnel of canvas, the floor covered with a layer of pulled grass and a heavy tarpaulin. It smelled of wet wool, unwashed bodies, and the lingering reek of the guano-rich soil.

He lay down, using his ledger as a pillow. His body ached with a profound, bone-deep exhaustion. The cuts on his feet throbbed in time with his heartbeat. He closed his eyes, listening to the murmur of the men in the adjacent tents and the distant, rhythmic boom of the surf on the outer reef.

Sleep was a heavy curtain waiting to fall. He welcomed it. He needed to escape the reality of the sand, the thirst, and the uncertainty. But more than that, he needed to escape the memory of his own hands.

A rustling started in the brush outside the tent, too specific for the wind, sounding like dry leaves dragged over sandpaper. *Scritch-scratch. Scritch-scratch.*

Then came the squeaking. High-pitched, communicative chirps that seemed to surround the camp.

Read opened his eyes. The interior of the tent was pitch black, through the open flap, the dying cooking fire glowed faintly. Shadows were moving across the light. Small, erratic shadows.

"What is that?" Lieutenant Talbot whispered from the darkness beside him.

Before Read could answer, the invasion began.

A dark shape scurried over Read's boot. Then another. Then a weight landed on his chest, light but muscular, scrabbling for purchase on his coat.

Read sat up with a shout, batting the thing away. His hand struck soft fur and hard muscle. The creature squeaked in protest and bit him, a sharp, needle-like pinch on the knuckle, before leaping into the darkness.

"Lights!" someone yelled from the enlisted men's tents. "Show a light!"

A lantern flared to life in the neighboring shelter, and the scream that followed was one of pure horror.

"Rats! There are thousands of them!"

Read fumbled for his own matchbox, his heart hammering against his ribs. He struck a light, the sulfur flaring blue then yellow.

The sight that greeted him was the stuff of delirium. The floor was moving. Dozens of rats, small, grey-brown Polynesian rats, lean and feral, were swarming over the bedding. They were not scurrying in panic; they were exploring with a terrifying, fearless curiosity. They ran over the legs of the officers, sniffed at the boots, and gnawed at the canvas edges of the tent.

Outside, the ground seemed to undulate. The light of the lantern revealed a carpet of vermin emerging from the scrub. They flowed like water, pouring out of the holes in the guano crust, drawn by the smell of the cooked fish and the presence of the intruders.

"Get out!" Talbot roared, grabbing a piece of driftwood and swinging it wildly. *Thwack.* He connected with a rat, sending it flying against the canvas, but three more took its place.

Read scrambled backward, kicking out at the sea of grey fur. The rats were relentless. They were not afraid of the men. They were the masters of *Hōlanikū*, the apex scavengers of a closed ecosystem, and they regarded the crew of the *Saginaw* not as threats, but as a new source of protein.

A rat ran up Read's sleeve, its claws sharp through the wool. He shook his arm violently, flinging the beast away. It landed on its feet and immediately turned back, its black eyes glittering in the lamplight, its whiskers twitching.

"The provisions!" Read gasped, the realization hitting him harder than the fear. "They are after food!"

He scrambled out of the tent, followed by the other officers. The scene in the camp was chaotic. Men were running from their shelters, beating the ground with oars, stomping with their bare feet, cursing and screaming. The lantern light swung wildly, illuminating brief vignettes of the war: a sailor shaking a rat off his leg; a marine stabbing at the sand with his bayonet; a pile of hardtack boxes swarming with grey bodies.

"Guard the stores!" Sicard's voice rose above the din. "Form a perimeter around the food!"

Read rushed to the supply cache. The canvas tarp he had so carefully arranged earlier was moving. It rippled as if something was boiling underneath. He grabbed the corner and threw it back.

A dozen rats scattered, squealing, their mouths full of biscuit. They had chewed through the wood of the crates in hours.

"Beat them back!" Read yelled, grabbing a shovel. He brought the blade down, severing a rat in two, but the blood only seemed to excite the others.

For an hour, the battle raged. It was a grotesque, undignified war. The pride of the Navy fought with sticks and stones against an enemy that numbered in the thousands. The air was filled with the sound of crunching bones, the high-pitched shrieks of the dying animals, and the breathless cursing of the men.

But for every rat they killed, ten more emerged from the darkness. The island was vomiting them forth.

Eventually, exhaustion won. The men could not fight the tide forever. They retreated to their tents, wrapping themselves in their blankets like mummies, tucking their trousers into their socks and pulling their coats over their heads.

Read lay in the dark, sweating under the heavy wool, listening. The scratching never stopped. The weight of them running over his legs. The wet, tearing sound of teeth gnawing on leather. He felt a small, cold nose press against the fabric near his ear, sniffing for the flesh beneath.

He gripped the handle of his shovel in the dark, his knuckles white. He closed his eyes, but he could not close his ears. The squeaking was everywhere. It was the sound of their own grave being dug, one tiny scratch at a time.

"God," he whispered into the stifling wool of his coat. "Let morning come."

He squeezed his eyes shut, the sound was inescapable, the wet, tearing noise of thousands of teeth working against canvas, leather, and wood.

Chapter 6

The ledger lay open on the crate that served as his desk, the pages curling in the humid heat. Captain Montgomery Sicard stared at the columns of figures, his mind performing the grim arithmetic of survival. It was a calculation that refused to balance.

On the credit side: three small casks of fresh water salvaged from the wreck, plus the contents of the breakers from the gig. Total volume: perhaps sixty gallons.

On the debit side: ninety-three men.

Sicard rubbed his temples, feeling the grit of sand and dried salt that seemed permanently etched into his skin. The Navy standard ration was one gallon per man per day for cooking and drinking. That was a luxury of the past. Even at a survival ration of one pint a day, a torture in this tropical furnace, the supply would last less than a week.

He looked up. The canvas of the tent hung limp and heavy. The air inside was stifling, smelling of wet wool, ammonia from the guano soil, and the unwashed bodies of his officers. Outside, The sun was a heavy hammer, beating down on the white sand with an intensity that made the air shimmy.

Sicard stood, ducking his head to clear the ridgepole. He had to inspect the wells.

He emerged into the blinding glare of the camp. The men were moving with the lethargic economy of the dehydrated. There was no unnecessary conversation, no skylarking. They sat in the shade of the naupaka bushes, their mouths open, panting like the dogs they had no water to give.

Private O'Neil shifted as the shadow of the Captain fell over him. He made a sluggish, half-hearted attempt to rise to attention, but his knees, jellied by the heat and the lack of fluid, buckled. He slid back into the sand without raising his hand to his brow.

Sicard stopped dead. It was a hairline fracture in the porcelain of their discipline. If the salute went, the orders would follow, and then the rationing, and finally the civilization.

"On your feet, Private!" Sicard barked. The sound was shrill, cracking with a disproportionate, terrifying rage that silenced the rustle of the scrub. "You will stand! You will show the proper courtesy!"

O'Neil scrambled up, trembling, his eyes wide with the shock of the assault. He managed a shaky salute.

Sicard stepped in close, smelling the sour reek of the man's unwashed wool. He reached out and aggressively fastened the top button of the private's torn tunic, his fingers digging into the man's chest.

"We are not savages," Sicard hissed, his hands shaking as he smoothed the dirty cloth. "We maintain the form. If we lose the form, we lose everything."

The men stared, terrified not by the reprimand, but by the wild, desperate glitter in their Captain's eyes. He was not screaming at a marine; he was screaming at the anarchy waiting in the wings.

Sicard released the man. The fabric fell from his fingers. He stepped back, breathing hard through his nose, and adjusted his own cuffs with a sharp, automatic tug. He forced the tremor from his hands and turned his back on the private, staring out at the heat-shimmer of the dunes until the mask of command slid back into place.

"Mr. Talbot," Sicard called to his executive officer, who was supervising a work gang near the center of the island.

Talbot approached, his face flushed a dangerous crimson. "Sir."

"Report on the excavation."

"We have struck water in three places, Captain," Talbot said. He wiped his forehead with a rag that was stiff with grime. "At four feet, the sand becomes damp. At six feet, it fills."

"And the quality?"

Talbot hesitated. He licked his lips, which were cracked and bleeding. "It is... clear, sir."

"That is not what I asked, Mr. Talbot."

"It is potable, perhaps. But only just."

Sicard frowned. "Show me."

They walked inland, away from the ocean side, toward the center of the depressed basin that formed the island's interior. The heat here was magnified, trapped by the surrounding dunes. A group of marines was digging a pit, their shovels scraping rhythmically against the coral sand.

The hole was deep, a square cut into the geology of the atoll. At the bottom, a pool of water had gathered, seeping in from the sides. It looked cool. It looked inviting. To a man whose tongue felt like a piece of dry leather, it looked like salvation.

A marine corporal looked up, his eyes pleading. "It's filling fast, Captain."

Sicard descended the crude steps they had carved into the slope. He knelt by the muddy pool. He cupped his hand, dipping it into the water. It was cool to the touch.

He raised it to his lips and took a sip.

The taste hit him instantly, a sharp, metallic tang of magnesium and the unmistakable, nauseating heaviness of brine. It was not seawater, exactly; the sand had filtered out some of the particulate, and the rain had diluted it slightly. But it was not fresh. It was brackish, a purgative mixture that would do little to slake thirst and everything to destroy the bowels.

Sicard spat it out. The taste lingered, coating his palate with salt.

He looked up at the expectant faces of the men. They were watching him, desperate for him to declare it sweet, to grant them permission to drink.

"It is salt," Sicard said, his voice flat.

The disappointment was palpable. The marine corporal slumped against his shovel, his shoulders dropping.

"But, sir," the man rasped. "It's wetter than nothing. Maybe if we boil it..."

"If you drink this," Sicard said, standing up and brushing the wet sand from his knees, "you will be dead in three days. It will scour your stomach and dehydrate you faster than the sun. Fill it in."

"Fill it in, sir?"

"Fill it in," Sicard repeated, harder this time. "I will not have men sneaking down here in the night to poison themselves. We dig elsewhere."

He climbed out of the pit, his legs feeling heavy. He walked to the next site, fifty yards away. The result was the same. Clear, cool, and poisonous.

Sicard walked toward the windward beach, needing the breeze to clear the taste from his mouth. He stopped at the edge of the scrub, looking out at the endless Pacific.

He knew the science of it. An atoll was a sponge. The fresh water from the rain should sit as a lens on top of the heavier saltwater that permeated the coral foundation. The *Gledstanes* crew had found water here. The *Parker* crew had survived here. Therefore, the lens existed.

But where?

Perhaps the storm that wrecked them had washed the fresh lens away, mixing the layers. Perhaps the birds, with their millions of burrows, had contaminated the ground. Or perhaps the water the whalers found was gone, evaporated by thirty years of drought.

He looked back at the camp. Paymaster Read was issuing the midday ration. A quarter-pint of water. A gill. A few swallows.

Sicard watched a young marine receive his cup. The boy stared at the liquid for a long moment, as if praying to it, before drinking it in small, reverent sips. When the cup was empty, he ran his finger around the inside and licked the tin dry.

The burden of it pressed down on Sicard's chest, heavier than the heat. If they did not find sweet water within forty-eight hours, discipline would break. Thirst was a more primal force than duty. Men would begin to drink the lagoon water, or the blood of the birds, and the dysentery would finish what the reef had started.

He turned back to the island, his eyes scanning the depressions in the dunes, looking for the tell-tale green of sedge grass that might indicate a sweeter source. He would dig a hundred holes if he had to. He would turn the entire island over with a shovel.

"Mr. Talbot!" Sicard shouted, his voice cracking slightly with the dryness of his own throat.

"Sir?"

"Move the digging parties to the depression near the albatross colony. The vegetation is thicker there. And tell the Carpenter to bring the axe. If we find no water in the sand, we shall see if the roots of the pandanus hold any moisture."

He did not wait for an acknowledgment. He marched toward the new site, his boots sinking into the hot sand, his mind already calculating the next equation. Ninety-three men. Zero gallons.

The sun reached its zenith, turning the white sand into a blinding reflector. The digging yielded nothing but Thermic Fever and damp grit.

***

From the vantage point of the high dune, Paymaster George Read had watched the final leg of the transfer, his heart hammering against his ribs with a force that had nothing to do with exertion and everything to do with fear.

Out on the lagoon, the salvage cutter, manned by Coxswain Halford and the strongest swimmers, had towed the raft toward the beach. It was a terrifying piece of architecture: a crude platform of lashed spars supporting the massive, rust-streaked cylinder of the donkey boiler. The iron vessel sat dangerously upright, a top-heavy monolith that caused the raft to list drunkenly with every ripple of the current. It sat so low in the water that the lagoon lapped at the rusted rivets of the firebox door. One sudden shift, one loose lashing, and their only hope for hydration would plunge into the coral depths, lost forever.

But the water passage, fraught as it was, proved to be the easy part. The transition to land was a feat of brute, breathless engineering.

As the raft grounded in the shallows, fifty men, gaunt, sunburned, and dehydrated, waded out to meet it. They had no cranes, no davits, no steam winches to multiply their strength. They had only the raw leverage of their shoulders and the methods of the ancients.

They laid a track of "rollers" up the incline of the beach, short, round logs sawed from the wreckage of the mainmast.

"Heave... and... *heave!*"

The chant was a dry rasp in the throats of the crew, a rhythmic croak that barely carried over the surf. Ropes woven from salvaged running rigging were lashed around the boiler's belly. Twenty men pulled from the front, the coarse hemp biting into their blistered hands. Thirty more shoved from the rear, their bare feet digging deep trenches in the soft, yielding sand as they fought the inertia of three tons of dead iron.

The boiler moved inches at a time. It groaned as it rolled, crushing the wooden logs deep into the coral sand until they disappeared, forcing the men to dig them out and run them to the front of the line again. It was a punishing cycle of lift, drag, and push. Men slipped and fell, their faces buried in the hot sand, only to be hauled up by their mates and thrown back against the iron. The boiler was not just heavy; it was radiating a fever heat, having baked in the sun all morning, searing the skin of the sailors who pressed their shoulders against its flanks.

It took two hours to move the machine fifty yards. By the time they wrestled it to the clearing they had designated, the work gang had collapsed in the shade of the naupaka, chests heaving, too exhausted to even cheer.

Now, an hour later, the sun was directly overhead. There were no shadows left to hide in, the sand radiated the heat back up through the soles of their boots.

Paymaster George Read tongue swelling in his mouth, a sensation like a piece of dry cotton expanding to choke him. He moved slowly down the beach toward the area the men had christened "The Foundry."

Here, the atmosphere was different. While the rest of the camp lay in a stupor of exhaustion, sheltering from the noon glare, this patch of sand was a hive of frantic, industrial energy.

Second Assistant Engineer Herschel Main stood in the center of the chaos. He was stripped to the waist, his skin burned a violent red, his canvas trousers stiff with a mixture of coal dust, salt, and grease. He looked less like a naval officer and more like a blacksmith in hell.

"Easy with the flange!" Main roared at a group of firemen who were wrestling a heavy iron cylinder across the sand to mate it with the boiler. "If you crack that casting, we are all dead men."

Read approached the object of their labor. It was the *Saginaw's* donkey boiler, a vertical steam vessel that had once powered the ship's pumps and winches. Now, it sat crookedly on a bed of coral stones, connected to a serpentine mess of copper piping.

"Will it hold pressure, Mr. Main?" Read asked, his voice rasping.

Main turned, wiping his face with a rag that was black with soot. "The shell is sound, Paymaster. The fire-tubes are choked with salt, but we are clearing them. The problem isn't making steam. It's catching it."

Main gestured to the sand where a bizarre collection of scavenged parts lay spread out. There were lengths of copper piping, brass fittings, and, most strangely, long, coiled sections of gutta-percha and metal tubing.

Read recognized them instantly. "The speaking-tubes," he said.

"Aye," Main nodded grimly. "We cut them out of the pilot house before she broke up. Yesterday they carried the Captain's orders to the engine room. Today, God willing, they will carry water."

They were building a condenser from the corpse of the ship. The donkey boiler would heat the seawater. The steam would rise and be forced into the speaking-tubes, which would act as a cooling coil.

"We need a trough," Main barked, turning back to his crew. "We need to submerge the coils. Bring the cooler-box from the gig. And bring wet sand. Pack it tight."

Read watched as the contraption took shape. It was a plumber's nightmare. The copper pipes were bent by hand, kinked and irregular. They sealed the joints with canvas strips and white lead, their hands fumbling with the marline as the salt-shakes took them. To Read, the contraption looked less like an engine and more like a desperate, iron lung designed to breathe for ninety dying men who had forgotten the taste of anything but sand. The cooling trough was a wooden crate lined with tin, filled with seawater that the men had bucketed up from the lagoon.

The donkey boiler sat at the head of this serpentine assembly, looking like a pagan idol demanding sacrifice.

"Fuel," Main ordered.

A gang of sailors began to feed the furnace. They did not use coal; there was none. They used the *Saginaw* herself. Splintered pieces of the paddle-wheel boxes, fragments of the bulwarks, and dried branches of the naupaka scrub were shoved into the firebox.

"Light it."

A match flared. The dry wood caught instantly. A plume of acrid smoke, smelling of old paint and varnish, rose into the still air.

The camp went silent.

Word had spread. The men began to emerge from their shelters, drawn by the smoke and the promise it represented. They gathered in a wide circle around the machine, keeping a respectful distance but leaning forward with a collective, desperate intensity. Captain Sicard stood at the front, his arms crossed, his face an unreadable mask.

Read felt the tension. It tightened the skin on his scalp. If this failed, if the boiler leaked, if the pipes burst, if the steam simply evaporated into the tropical air, there was no Plan B. The brackish wells were poison. This iron pot was their only hope.

The fire roared. The heat radiating from the boiler was intense, shimmering the air above the sand. Main circled the machine, his eyes fixed on the pressure gauge. The needle, rusted and sticky, began to twitch.

"She's making steam," Main whispered.

A hiss escaped from a loose joint near the top. A jet of white vapor shot out.

"Caulk that!" Main shouted. A fireman lunged forward with a hammer and a piece of lead, pounding the leak shut while the steam scalded his hands. He did not flinch.

The pressure rose. The water inside the boiler, scooped from the ocean, was boiling. The steam, invisible and superheated, was pushing into the speaking-tubes.

Read watched the cooling trough. The copper pipes submerged in the water began to vibrate. The seawater in the trough started to steam as it absorbed the heat from the coils.

"More water in the trough!" Main yelled. "Keep the coils cool!"

Men scrambled to pour buckets of lagoon water over the pipes.

At the end of the line, a single copper tube protruded from the trough, hovering over a tin cup placed in the sand.

Ninety-three pairs of eyes fixed on that tube.

Nothing happened.

The fire crackled. The boiler groaned, the metal expanding under the heat. The sun beat down.

"Come on," Read breathed.

A wisp of steam curled from the end of the pipe. Then, a sputter. A sound like a throat clearing.

Plip.

A single, dark drop fell into the tin cup.

A collective sound, half-gasp, half-sob, went through the crowd.

Plip. Plip. Plip.

The drops came faster now, coalescing into a steady, thin trickle. The liquid was not the crystal-clear water of a mountain spring. It was brown. It was discolored by the rust of the boiler, the verdigris of the copper, and the oil of the fittings. It looked like runoff from a gutter.

Main watched the cup fill an inch. He reached out, his hand trembling slightly, and lifted it. He did not drink. He held it out to Captain Sicard.

"Captain," Main said.

Sicard took the cup. He looked at the dark liquid. He raised it to his nose and sniffed. The smell of hot metal and rubber reached Read even from where he stood.

Sicard took a sip. He held the liquid in his mouth for a long moment, analyzing it, before swallowing.

He lowered the cup. He looked at Main, and then at the men.

"It is fresh," Sicard announced.

A cheer erupted, ragged, hoarse, and wild. It was the sound of men who had just been granted a stay of execution.

Sicard passed the cup to Read. "Paymaster."

Read took the vessel. The metal was warm. He tipped the liquid into his mouth.

It was revolting. It tasted of tallow, scorched iron, and the rubbery tang of the gutta-percha speaking tubes. It was warm and oily, coating the tongue with a chemical film.

But it lacked the one thing that would kill them: salt.

It was sweet, fresh water.

"It is nectar," Read said, handing the cup back to Main.

"Keep the fire fed!" Main roared, his authority expanding with the success. "I want a bucket brigade to the lagoon! Keep that trough cold! We run twenty-four hours a day!"

The paralysis of the thirst broke. The camp transformed instantly. Men who had been too weak to stand were now scrambling to gather driftwood. The machine, this ugly, hissing, leaking collection of junk, was suddenly the holiest object on the island.

Read watched the brown trickle splatter into the cup. It was slow, painfully slow. Main estimated perhaps ten gallons a day if they ran the boiler hard. That was barely a pint per man. It was still a starvation ration. It was still a slow death.

But it was death deferred.

He looked at the speaking-tubes coiling through the trough. A week ago, those tubes had carried the Captain's voice, commanding the ship's speed and direction. Now, they carried life itself. The ship was dead, but her arteries were keeping them alive.

Read wiped the sweat from his eyes. The metallic taste in his mouth was foul, lingering on the back of his throat like a stain.

***

Inside the tent, the mercury in the glass barometer fell with a steady, mechanical precision. Sicard tapped the instrument. The needle remained fixed in its downward trajectory, a leaden weight pulling toward a storm. The light outside had turned a sulfurous, bruised yellow, bleeding the blue out of the Pacific and turning the white coral sand into the color of old bone.

Ninety-three men. Ten gallons. The calculation hummed. The failed wells yielded only a bitter, brackish liquid that parched the throat and triggered the bowels. Fuel remained the only path to survival. Sicard looked toward the main island's wood pile, now a heap of splinters and twigs.

A mile to the west, the spit offered a graveyard of Pacific refuse, bleached timber, ships' ribs, and massive, salt-pitted trunks.

Sicard's boots sank into the hot sand as he stepped toward the waterline. The air was stagnant. The spit was a low, white rib, shimmering in the heat. To stay was to let the fires die. To go was to lead a crew into a falling glass. He signaled to Manning.

"Mr. Manning, prepare the cutter. We make for the western spit."

"The glass is falling hard, sir," Manning said, his eyes scanning the sickly horizon.

"I am aware of the glass, Mr. Manning. But the distiller is thirsty. We cannot wait for the wind to decide our ration."

The words felt like dry gravel in his mouth. Manning didn't answer, only nodded. The men hauled the cedar cutter into the shallows, their feet splashing in the tepid water. Sicard took his place at the stern, his hand closing over the tiller. The wood was warm, grit-stained, and vibrating with the low thrum of the reef.

"Give way."

The oars bit. The lagoon floor shifted below the keel, a mosaic of pale sand and dark, antler-like coral heads. The cedar planks hummed as the boat gained momentum.

Halfway across, the tiller kicked. A low, resonant thrum moved through the wood and up Sicard's arm. The water, previously a flat sheet of turquoise, rippled in tight, nervous patterns. A mile to the north, the breakers on the outer reef roared with a new, aggressive frequency. The turquoise turned to a leaden, metallic sheen.

The wind arrived without a preceding breeze. It slammed into the starboard quarter, heaving the cutter onto its beam-ends.

"Pull!" Manning's shout was a scrap of sound lost in the rising din. "Keep her head to it!"

The oarsmen strained, tendons standing out like cordage in their necks. The yellow sky vanished behind a curtain of gray. Rain, horizontal and hard as birdshot, raked across the boat. Sicard leaned his entire weight against the tiller, forcing the bow to bite into the rising chop.

"We can't make the return, sir!" Manning yelled over the spray.

"We make for the spit!" Sicard shouted back. "Beach her high!"

The boat grounded hard on the coral shelf. The impact jarred Sicard's spine. The men tumbled over the gunwales, boots sliding on slick, algae-covered rock. They hauled the painter taut, the line vibrating in the gale as they lashed it to the iron-hard roots of a stump.

The spit was a wasteland. Bleached logs and massive trunks lay scattered like the bones of a giant, but they offered no lee. The men scrambled toward a cluster of silvered trunks, pressing their backs against the wood. It was useless. The gale did not break against the logs; it curled over the rounded surfaces, a freezing vortex that lashed them with pulverized shell and salt spray. They huddled in pairs, shoulders hunched, but the wind scoured the very hollows they tried to claim. The gale stripped the warmth from Sicard's body. He watched Manning's hands; the lieutenant was fumbling with a knot, his fingers stiff and useless. A violent, involuntary jerking took hold of Manning's shoulders.

"Manning, eyes on me." Sicard's voice was a flat crack. He saw the onset of the 'umbles', the clumsy fumbles of the hands and the violent, rhythmic shivering of a body that had lost the war for its own heat. Manning's lips were the color of a bruised plum. His teeth chattered in a frantic, mechanical clatter that sounded like a telegraph key on a dying ship. The marrow in Sicard's own bones was turning to ice. They would be dead of exposure long before the wood reached the boiler. "The air is the enemy. We go below it."

"Below it, sir?" Manning's voice was thick, his teeth chattering a frantic rhythm.

"Dig! Use your hands! Two feet down the sand holds the sun's heat. That is our stove tonight."

Sicard dropped to his knees. The sand was a mixture of pulverized shell and jagged coral. It sliced into his fingertips, but he felt nothing but the drive to reach the warmth. He threw the grit behind him, carving a trench into the spine of the spit. He signaled the others to do the same, each man spaced five feet apart.

He slid into the burrow, pulling the damp, heavy sand over his legs, his torso, and finally up to his chin.

The weight of the earth pressed against his ribs. It restricted his breath, but the shivering slowed. Below the surface, the trapped heat of the afternoon sun hummed against his skin. Above, the freezing lash of the gale continued its work. The spit became a field of decapitated heads.

"Manning," Sicard called out, his voice low to save strength. "Stay awake. If the tide breaches the ridge, we move for the boat. Until then, hold your heat."

"Aye, sir," came the muffled reply from the next mound of sand.

Night fell. The gray world turned to a total, sightless black. The roar of the ocean was an unbroken wall of sound that vibrated through the sand and into Sicard's skull. Hours passed. He tracked the time by the pulse in his neck. Then, through the roar, a new sound emerged. A heavy clack.

Shapes darker than the storm-tossed sea emerged from the white foam. They moved with a slow, agonizing heave, their heavy carapaces slick with brine.

Manning's head turned in the sand, his eyes wide. "Meat, sir," he hissed, the word wet with sudden saliva. "The turtles. We can take them before they turn back."

"Wait," Sicard commanded. He did not move a muscle. "Let them clear the surf. If we strike now, they'll bolt for the foam and we'll lose them in the dark. We need them on the high sand where they lose their purchase."

Sicard looked at the row of heads protruding from the spit. "Pass the word down. No man moves until I give the mark."

Manning turned his face toward the next mound of sand. "Wait for the Captain's mark," he whispered. "Hold your heat. Pass it on."

The command rippled down the spine of the spit, a series of low, urgent murmurs that were swallowed almost instantly by the roar of the gale. The men stayed entombed, a line of silent observers.

The green sea turtles hauled three hundred pounds of ancient muscle up the incline. Sicard heard their breathing, a wet, labored huffing. The air filled with a visceral scent of ancient brine and cold mud. A beast crawled within a yard of Sicard's head. Its flipper sprayed a fan of grit across his face.

The turtles reached the crest of the spit, their pace slowing as the sand became drier and deeper. They began to settle, their weight pinning them into the grit.

"Now! Together!"

Sicard erupted from the sand. He rose, white-shrouded and gaunt. The men followed, ghost-like figures emerging from their graves.

"Manning, take the flank! Heave on my mark!"

They fell upon the nearest beast. The turtle hissed, its beak snapping at the air with the sound of breaking dry wood. Sicard grabbed the leading edge of the massive shell. It was cold and slime-slick. He braced his boots into the shifting sand and heaved. His muscles screamed.

"Heave!"

The turtle flipped. It hit the sand with a heavy, wet thud. Its pale, yellowish belly lay exposed to the rain, its flippers flailing in the void.

"The next one! Before they turn!"

They worked with a frantic energy born of cold and hunger. By the time the last beast was overturned, ten white bellies gleamed in the gloom. The turtles groaned, a low, resonant sound that vibrated through the ground beneath Sicard's feet.

"Back to the burrows," Sicard ordered. "The wind is still high. We guard the meat from the holes."

He returned to the trench. He lay entombed once more, listening to the gale. The wind began to veer. The shrieking in the cutter's rigging dropped an octave. The horizontal rain transitioned into a fine, vertical mist.

A hard, gray light bled into the eastern sky. The men stood among the driftwood, caked in white salt and sand. Their eyes were bloodshot and rimmed with rime.

"Load the timber first," Sicard ordered, his voice cracking with the salt rime. "Pack it tight between the thwarts. We don't come back to this godforsaken spit twice."

The men worked in the gray, pre-dawn light, their movements stiff. They hauled bleached trunks and the jagged ribs of long-dead ships, jamming them into the bottom of the cutter until the gunwales sat low in the water. Then came the turtles. The combined strength of the crew hoisted each beast over the side, resting their heavy, mossy shells atop the wood. The cutter settled deep, the cedar planks groaning under the weight of fuel and flesh.

The lagoon had settled into a long, oily swell. Sicard took the tiller and pushed off. The oars dipped into the gray water, pulling the heavy load toward the smudge of the main island. The turtles' flippers moved like the blades of a slow-turning engine, slapping uselessly against the dry logs beneath them.

On the beach of Green Island, the camp was a wreckage of shredded canvas and half-buried crates. The gale had scoured the sand from beneath the storehouse, leaving the structure listing toward the lagoon. Near the high-tide mark, the fire beneath the distiller had dwindled to a pathetic, flickering orange. George Read stood near the water's edge, his brass telescope leveled at the western horizon. His eyes were stinging from the salt spray of the night's gale. He had spent the dark hours watching the spit vanish under the white transition of the storm, certain that the Captain and the cutter's crew had been swept into the Pacific.

"The boat," a lookout shouted, his voice thin from thirst. "The cutter is in sight!"

Read adjusted the focus. Through the circular frame of the lens, the boat appeared not as a sleek naval craft, but as a low, dark slug wallowing in the swell. It moved with a funereal slowness.

"They're deep in the water," Read murmured. "Too deep."

As the boat cleared the inner reef and entered the shallows, the men of the camp drifted toward the shoreline. They looked like a tattered army, many bore the marks of the gale, raw, red abrasions from clinging to the tent-poles. No one cheered. They had spent the last of their strength simply holding the camp against the wind.

The cutter's bow hissed into the sand. Sicard was the first to step out. He moved with a rigid, mechanical dignity, though his uniform was a map of salt-stains and his hands were raw, red meat.

"Mr. Read," Sicard said, his voice a dry rasp that barely carried.

"Captain. We feared the spit had been overtopped."

"The spit held," Sicard replied. He turned back to the boat, gesturing with a trembling hand. "We have the fuel. And we have something else."

The men of the camp crowded the gunwales. For a moment, there was a stunned, collective silence. Below the thwarts, resting on a bed of silvered driftwood, the ten turtles lay on their backs. Their pale plastrons, the underside of the shells, gleamed like wet bone in the morning light. One of the beasts let out a long, wheezing sigh, its beak snapping shut with a sharp, hollow clack.

"Meat," a sailor whispered.

"Fresh meat," another echoed, his hand reaching out to touch the cold, leathery skin of a flipper.

"Begin the unloading," Sicard commanded, leaning heavily against the bow of the boat. "Get the wood to the boiler immediately. I want the fires at full head. Then, Mr. Read, you will oversee the slaughter."

***

The men of the "flagstaff gang" were preparing to raise the timber. It was a massive undertaking for a crew subsisting on a pint of water and a few ounces of meat a day. They moved with the slow, brittle motion of the elderly, their joints stiff, their skin hanging loose on their frames.

"All ready with the guys!" shouted Boatswain's Mate O'Connell. His voice, usually a roar that could carry from the foretop to the quarterdeck, was now a cracked rasp.

"Heave away!"

The sheer-legs, constructed from shorter spars lashed together in an A-frame, took the strain. The heavy hawser tightened, groaning as the fibers stretched. The topmast lifted from the sand, the butt end hovering over the deep pit they had excavated near the center of the camp.

Read held his breath. The flagpole was more than a piece of wood; it was a prayer. Without it, they were invisible, a speck of biology lost in the millions of square miles of the North Pacific. With it, flying the reversed ensign of distress, they might catch the eye of a passing whaler.

"Steady... handsomely now!" Captain Sicard commanded, watching the ascent with critical eyes.

The mast rose to forty-five degrees. The men on the guy-lines leaned back, their bare feet digging into the coral sand, sweat streaming through the soot and grime on their faces. The silence in the camp was heavy, save for the creaking of the block and tackle. Even the albatrosses seemed to pause in their clacking.

Then, the sound of a pistol shot shattered the morning.

Snap.

The corroded iron strap of the block, weakened by the salt and the strain, gave way.

"Stand from under!"

The cry came too late for anyone to move, but instinct took over. Men scrambled, throwing themselves flat as the heavy spar plummeted. It twisted in the air, the top hamper crashing into the scrub, while the butt end slammed down violently, not into the hole, but onto the edge of it.

The impact shook the ground. The sand walls of the pit, laboriously dug to a depth of five feet, collapsed inward, burying the bottom in a cascade of white grit.

A groan went up from the crew, a collective exhalation of pure defeat.

Read closed his eyes. It was an omen. It had to be. The island was rejecting them. They had fought the sea and won, fought the reef and won, but the island was a passive, sullen enemy that simply refused to cooperate. The condenser was producing its oily trickle, yes, but it was barely enough to wet the lips. Now, their signal mast lay in the dirt, their labor wasted.

"Is anyone hurt?" Sicard's voice cut through the despair, immediate and practical.

"No, sir. Just shaken."

"Then clear the wreckage," Sicard ordered. "We dig it out and we try again. Providence does not reward the idle."

Providence. Read looked at the Captain. Sicard's faith in the rituals of duty was unshakable, but Read wondered if God was even watching this desolate coordinate.

A young coal-heaver, a lad named Thomas Hennessey, grabbed a shovel and jumped into the ruined pit. He attacked the sand with a fury born of frustration, throwing shovelfuls over his shoulder. He was digging out the collapse, trying to reach the bottom so they could reseat the mast.

Read watched him. The boy was working too hard. He would exhaust himself.

"Easy, lad," O'Connell warned. "Pace yourself."

Hennessey ignored him. He dug deeper, the shovel biting into the damp sand at the bottom of the hole. He paused. He leaned on the handle, staring down at his feet.

He stooped.

Read frowned. What was he doing? The boy was on his knees in the bottom of the pit, scraping at the sand with his hands. The hole was perhaps six feet deep now, the lowest point they had reached on the island.

Halford scooped up a handful of the slurry that was seeping into the depression. He held it to his nose. Then, tentatively, he touched his tongue to his palm.

He froze.

For a second, Read thought the boy had been poisoned. The ciguatera fish, the brackish wells, everything here was toxic.

Then Hennessey looked up. His face was streaked with mud, his eyes wide and white in the sun. He opened his mouth, and a sound came out that Read would remember for the rest of his life, a primal scream of deliverance.

"Boys! Fresh water! By God, fresh water!"

The tableau of the camp shattered.

"What?"

"Water!" Hennessey screamed, scooping another handful and splashing it over his face, laughing and choking at the same time. "It's sweet! It's sweet as the rain!"

The discipline of the Navy dissolved. The men dropped the guy-lines. They dropped the block and tackle. They rushed the hole.

"Stand back!" Sicard roared, but he was moving toward the pit himself. "Make room! Give him air!"

Read found himself running. He reached the edge of the excavation just as Hennessey filled a tin cup that was passed down to him. The water in the cup was muddy, clouded with the white silt of the coral, but it was plentiful. It was seeping rapidly from the sides of the pit, rising around Hennessey's ankles.

The cup was passed up to the Captain.

Sicard held it. The camp went silent again, a repetition of the scene at the condenser, but the tension was different. This was not the tension of mechanics; this was the tension of a miracle.

Sicard drank. He didn't sip. He drank.

He lowered the cup, water dripping from his beard. A genuine smile, rare and brilliant, broke across his face.

"It is fresh," Sicard announced, his voice trembling with emotion. "It is perfectly fresh."

Pandemonium.

Men were crying. They were hugging each other, dancing a jagged, limping jig on the hot sand.

"A bucket!" O'Connell yelled. "Form a line! Don't foul the well!"

Read watched as the first bucket came up. The water was grey and cloudy, but to ninety-three men dying of thirst, it looked like vintage champagne. He took his turn, receiving a pannikin of the precious fluid.

He drank.

It was cool. It had a slight earthy taste, the flavor of the coral and the roots, but it was devoid of salt. It washed the oily, metallic taste of the condenser water from his throat. It went down his gullet like life itself, expanding in his stomach, cooling his blood.

He looked up at the sky. The sun was still a hammer, the horizon was still empty, and they were still trapped. But the island had yielded.

"Providence," Read whispered, wiping his mouth with the back of his hand.

He looked at the fallen mast. It lay in the sand, a failure of engineering that had become an instrument of salvation. They would raise it eventually. They would fly their flag. But for now, the message had been received, not by a ship, but by the earth itself.

"Fill the breakers!" Sicard ordered, his voice strong, the rasp of thirst gone. "Fill every cask! We shall drink our fill tonight, gentlemen! The *Saginaw* is dead, but her crew is alive!"

Chapter 7

The relief of the fresh water well had lasted exactly twenty-four hours. It was a reprieve, certainly, the men were no longer dying of thirst, but in the unforgiving arithmetic of the quarterdeck, solving one variable only exposed the lethality of the next.

Captain Montgomery Sicard sat at his makeshift desk, the salvaged packing crate leveled on the sand. The canvas walls of the tent beat softly in the trade wind, a sound that mimicked the luffing of a sail.

He dipped his pen into the inkwell. The ink was thickening in the heat, dragging across the page of the logbook.

November 4, 1870. Ration of salt beef reduced to one-quarter. Hardtack issued by count, not weight.

He stared at the numbers. Paymaster Read's inventory was meticulous, reflecting the man's professionalism, but the totals were terrifying. They had saved perhaps a quarter of the ship's stores. Ninety-three mouths were a relentless engine of consumption. The albatrosses were plentiful now, stupidly sitting on their nests while the sailors clubbed them, but the birds were migratory. They would leave. The monk seals, already wary, would retreat to the outer reefs.

Sicard closed the book. He did not need to do the math again. He knew the answer. Three months. Perhaps four, if they starved themselves to the edge of functionality.

He stood and walked to the tent flap. Outside, the camp was a bustle of activity that masked the underlying desperation. Men were drying clothes on the scrub, salting seal meat, and reinforcing the shelters. It looked like a colony. It looked permanent.

That was the danger.

Kure Atoll was not a destination; it was a void. The charts in his head were clear. They were twelve hundred miles from Honolulu, in a direction that ships simply did not travel. The trade routes from Japan to California lay far to the north. The routes from Australia to the Sandwich Islands lay far to the south. They were in the dead zone of the North Pacific.

To wait for a passing ship was to gamble ninety-three lives on a lottery ticket that had not paid out in thirty years. The *Gledstanes* men had waited five months. The *Parker* men, eight. Sicard looked at his crew, the firemen, the coal-heavers, the landsmen. They were good men, but they were not whalers accustomed to years of deprivation. Discipline was holding, welded together by the chain of command, but starvation was a solvent that dissolved even the strongest iron.

"Mr. Hershberger," Sicard called to the officer of the watch.

"Sir."

"Present my compliments to Lieutenant Talbot and Paymaster Read. Ask them to attend me here."

"Aye, aye, sir."

Sicard turned back to the interior of the tent. He smoothed the chart of the Pacific he had salvaged from his cabin. It was water-stained and wrinkled, but the distances remained fixed. He took his dividers and spanned the gap between the tiny speck of Ocean Island and the cluster of islands to the southeast.

The dividers stretched wide. Too wide.

Talbot and Read entered a moment later, ducking under the canvas. They looked ragged. Talbot's uniform was bleached white by the sun; Read looked thinner, his face gaunt under a week's growth of beard.

"Gentlemen," Sicard said, motioning to the empty ammunition crates that served as chairs. "Please, sit."

They sat, the silence heavy between them. They knew why they were here. The euphoria of the water discovery had faded, replaced by the grinding reality provisions ledger.

"I have reviewed the Paymaster's inventory," Sicard began, his voice level. "The situation is clear. We have water, for which we must thank Providence. But we cannot eat water."

"The seal meat is spoiling, Captain," Read added quietly. "The salt we recovered is wet and full of sand. We are losing pounds of meat every day to the heat and the flies."

"Precisely," Sicard said. "And the birds will fly soon. When they do, we are left with the salt pork. At one-quarter ration, we have supplies for three months. After that..." He let the sentence hang.

Talbot leaned forward, resting his elbows on his knees. "We are off the track, Captain. No steamer calls here. No China trader comes this far north unless she is blown here by a typhoon."

"Then we are agreed," Sicard said. "We cannot wait."

He turned the chart so they could see it. He placed his finger on the paper.

"We must send a boat."

The words were spoken, and the room seemed to shrink. Sending a boat was not a simple evolution. It was a desperate, last-ditch gambit.

Sicard stepped to the opening of the tent and tied back the canvas flap. The view framed the beach where the salvage parties had hauled the surviving craft.

Sicard stared at the two boats resting on the sand.

On the left, the Second Cutter. Heavy. Intact. A draft horse. On the right, the Gig. A splintered hole in her starboard bow. Her keel scarred. A thoroughbred with a broken leg.

"The Cutter is sound, sir," Talbot said, following his gaze. "She's ready to launch."

"The Cutter is a tub," Sicard muttered. "She sails like a brick. It would take you forty days to reach Honolulu in that. We have food for thirty."

He turned to the broken Gig. "Can Chips patch the hull?"

"He can. But she's too low in the water, Captain. One gale would swamp her."

"Then we raise her," Sicard said. "We build up the gunwales. We deck her over. We turn a harbor boat into a deep-ocean flyer. It's speed or death, Mr. Talbot. We have to bet on speed."

Read spoke up, his voice thoughtful. "It is the only way, Captain. If we stay, we starve. If we send the boat... five men might die, but eighty-eight might live."

Sicard looked at the Paymaster. Read had the accountant's gift for boiling tragedy down to percentages.

"It is a suicide mission," Talbot murmured. "Or near enough."

"It is a duty," Sicard corrected him sharply. "We are the Navy. We do not sit on a sandbar and wait for death. We act."

He stood up, signaling the end of the debate. He paced the small length of the tent, his hands clasped behind his back.

"Mr. Talbot, you will oversee the modifications to the gig. Have the carpenter raise the gunwales eight inches. Deck her over completely, leaving only a small cockpit for the steersman. She must be watertight."

"Aye, sir. And the crew?"

Sicard stopped pacing. This was the hardest part. He was sending men into the throat of the Pacific. He was asking them to sail a boat the size of a large dining table through the most desolate stretch of water on earth, battling the storms of November and December.

"Volunteers," Sicard said softly. "I will not order a man into that boat. Must be volunteers only. And only the best. I want an officer to command, and four men. No more. We cannot provision more."

"I will ask for an officer," Sicard said. "And four men. But understand this: once that boat leaves the lagoon, they are beyond our help. They will have a sextant, a pocket chronometer, and twenty-five days of rations. If they miss the islands... if they are dismasted... if the boat is pooped by a heavy sea..."

He looked at the chart again. The blue space between Kure and Kauai looked infinite.

"They are our only hope," Sicard finished. "Prepare the gig, Mr. Talbot. We sail as soon as she is ready."

"Aye, aye, sir."

The officers filed out, leaving Sicard alone with the ledger and the flies. He sat back down, the wood of the crate biting into his spine. He was effectively signing the death warrants of five men. He hoped, desperate and silent, that he wasn't signing them for all ninety-three.

He stood up and gave the signal. The boatswain's pipe shrilled, a sharp, silver command that shattered the silence. All hands.

Read, having just stepped outside the canvas flaps, stopped and wiped the sweat from his eyes.

***

The heat was a tangible burden, pressing down on the island with a suffocating intensity. Around him, the crew of the *Saginaw* shuffled toward the appointed meeting place, a patch of hard-packed sand near the Captain's tent.

They were a sorry sight. In the weeks since the wreck, the crisp blue uniforms of the United States Navy had dissolved into rags. Trousers were cut off at the knee to save fabric for patches; shirts were stained with the grey grime of the coral dust and the grease of the seal hunts. The men themselves were gaunt, their cheekbones pressing against skin that was bronzed and leathery from exposure.

Captain Sicard stood waiting for them. He was flanked by Lieutenant Talbot and the other officers. Sicard stood rigidly at attention, his posture a silent rebuke to the disintegration of their world. When the shuffling stopped and the ranks were formed, the silence that descended was heavy, filled only by the ceaseless, churning roar of the surf on the outer reef.

"Men," Sicard began. His voice was not loud, but it carried to the back ranks without effort. "I have called you here to speak plainly. We have secured water. We have shelter. We have established a routine of life."

He paused, his grey eyes scanning the lines of faces.

"But we cannot remain here."

A ripple of unease went through the crowd. A cough from a coal-heaver sounded like a gunshot.

"The Paymaster's calculations are exact," Sicard continued, gesturing briefly to Read. "At our current ration, a ration that I know leaves you hungry every hour of the day, we have food for three months. Perhaps four, if the seals return. But no longer."

Read watched the men. He saw the realization hit them. Three months was a death sentence. It was a finite number. It put a date on their end.

"We are twelve hundred miles from the Sandwich Islands," Sicard said. "We are off the shipping lanes. To wait here for a rescue that may never come is to choose a slow death. Therefore, I have decided to act."

He pointed to the beach, where the Captain's gig lay under a canvas tarp. It was a small boat, twenty-two feet of cedar planking, fragile and elegant.

"We will deck over the gig," Sicard announced. "We will rig her for sailing. And we will send her to Honolulu to bring relief."

Read felt a chill that had nothing to do with the wind. To send that nutshell into the winter gales of the North Pacific was madness. It was a voyage that would test a large ship; for an open boat, it was suicide.

"I can spare only five men," Sicard said. "The boat cannot carry provisions for more. She requires a crew of reliability. And she requires a commander."

Sicard straightened his shoulders. The moment had come.

"I am asking for an officer to volunteer."

The silence stretched. It was a heavy, terrified silence. Every officer knew the odds. To step forward was to leave the relative safety of the island, where there was at least water and ground, for the terror of the open ocean. It was to accept the likelihood of drowning, or thirst, or exposure.

"I volunteer, sir."

The voice was immediate, clear, and devoid of hesitation.

Lieutenant John G. Talbot took one step forward from the line of officers.

Read looked at the Executive Officer. Talbot was a young man, barely thirty, with a face that often seemed too gentle for the service. He was not a brawler like Halford or a disciplinarian like Sicard. He was a man of quiet faith, zealous in his duty, with a chivalrous streak that belonged to an earlier century. Standing there in the glaring sun, his uniform bleached and torn, he looked almost beatific.

Sicard looked at his second-in-command. Read saw a flicker of pain in the Captain's eyes, the knowledge that by accepting this offer, he was likely sending his friend to his grave.

"Mr. Talbot," Sicard said softly. "You understand the hazards? The season is late. The distance is great."

"I understand, Captain," Talbot replied. He stood with his hands clasped behind his back, his chin lifted. "I believe I can navigate her, sir. And if relief is to be brought, it is my place to bring it."

There was a nobility in the gesture that silenced the cynics in the crew. Read felt a lump form in his throat. Talbot was the Executive Officer; his place was here, managing the camp. He could have stayed. He could have let a junior officer take the risk. But that was not John Talbot's way. He was offering himself as the sacrifice for the ninety-two men behind him.

"Very well," Sicard said, his voice thick. "I accept your offer, Mr. Talbot. You shall command the gig."

A sound went through the crew, a murmur of respect that bordered on awe. The men knew Talbot. They knew he was kind, that he was fair, and that he was the best navigator among them.

"I shall need four men," Sicard addressed the crew. "Four volunteers to go with Mr. Talbot. I will not pick you. You must choose this yourselves."

Read held his breath. He looked at the fragility of the boat and the violence of the surf, expecting the men to calculate the odds and step back. It was, after all, a suicide pact.

But the hesitation never came.

"I'll go, Captain!"

"Take me, sir! I can pull!"

"I've sailed open boats in the Arctic, sir!"

The line of enlisted men bowed outward as nearly every sailor in the company stepped forward. It was a mass movement, a collective rejection of the passive death of the island in favor of the active death of the voyage. They pushed and shoved, elbowing each other for a position near the front, raising their hands like schoolboys answering a question.

Sicard held up a hand, but the tumult was hard to quell. These men were starving. They were scorched by the sun and bitten by rats. The boat represented action, and to a sailor, action was always preferable to waiting.

"Steady!" Sicard roared. "I cannot take you all. Mr. Talbot will select his crew."

Talbot stepped forward. He did not look at the ledger or the service records. He looked at the men. He knew them. He knew who slept on watch, and he knew who could splice a wire in a gale.

"Halford," Talbot said instantly.

There was no murmuring at that choice. William Halford, the Captain's Coxswain, stepped out of the crowd. He was a man hewn from oak and wrapped in leather. At thirty-three, he was one of the older enlisted men, a career sailor with a face that looked like a topographical map of bad weather. He was broad-shouldered, thick-necked, and possessed of a density that made him seem heavier than his displacement. He was "unvarnished," as the officers said, rough, illiterate, and competent. He walked to Talbot's side, his bare feet planting heavily in the sand, his expression bored. He looked as if he were volunteering to peel potatoes, not cross an ocean.

"Francis," Talbot called next.

Peter Francis, the Quartermaster, nodded solemnly. He was a different breed, quiet, dark, a man of few words but immense endurance. He was a half-caste, born in Manila, with the natural affinity for the sea that seemed bred into the islanders. He stepped out, touching his knuckle to his forehead.

"Andrews," Talbot said.

John Andrews, the captain of the hold, joined the line. He was a solid, dependable man from Boston, the kind of sailor who kept his head when the topsail sheet parted.

That left one spot.

The crowd pressed closer. The desperation spiked. The men who had not been called were frantic now, realizing the door was closing.

"I need a strong hand," Talbot murmured to Sicard, his eyes scanning the remaining faces. "A man who can handle the sheet and bail for hours."

"Muir!" a voice shouted from the back. "James Muir!"

A tall, wire-thin sailor pushed his way to the front. It was Muir, the Captain of the Forecastle. He was a Scot, hard as iron, with a reputation for a short temper and a long memory.

"I'm your man, Mr. Talbot," Muir declared, breathing hard. "I have got the reach, and I have the wind."

"Stand down, Muir!" another voice cracked. "You've got the fever shakes! Look at his hands!"

A stocky, bull-necked coal-heaver named Dougherty shouldered Muir aside. "I'm stronger than him, Captain. I can lift the boat myself. Take me."

Muir turned on the interloper, his eyes narrowing. He wasn't fighting for a seat; he was fighting the image of his own bones bleaching in the Scaevola bushes. The discipline of the quarterdeck, already frayed, dissolved into a primal Scottish fury.

"Get back, you coal-dust sweeper," Muir spat. "This is a seaman's job."

"Make me," Dougherty growled.

It happened in a flash. There was no formal challenge, no squaring off. It was an explosion of frustration and adrenaline. Dougherty lunged, grabbing Muir by the throat. Muir, faster and meaner, ducked the grapple and slammed his shoulder into the bigger man's chest.

They hit the sand in a tangle of limbs.

"Halt!" Sicard shouted, stepping forward, but the men were beyond hearing.

Read watched, horrified and mesmerized. It was a "hard-fought wrestling-match," a brutal, silent struggle in the white dust. There was no technique here, no Marquess of Queensberry rules. They rolled over the hot sand, grunting, kicking, gouging. Sand flew in gritty clouds, coating their sweating backs.

Dougherty had the weight. He pinned Muir, his forearm pressing down on the Scot's windpipe. "I'm going!" he hissed, his face purple with exertion. "I'm going home!"

But Muir was a creature of sinew and leverage. He bucked his hips, twisting violently to the left. As Dougherty shifted his weight to compensate, Muir drove a knee into the coal-heaver's ribs and flipped him.

The reversal was sudden. Muir was on top now. He didn't strike. He simply drove his forearm into Dougherty's chest and leaned his full weight onto it, pressing the man into the coral grit until the fight went out of him.

Muir held him there for a long second, panting, the sweat dripping from his nose onto Dougherty's face. Then he looked up at Talbot.

"I am fit for duty, sir," Muir gasped.

The camp was silent. The violence of the brawl had shocked them all. It was a stark reminder of the animal state that lay just beneath the surface of their naval discipline.

Talbot looked at Sicard. The Captain gave a barely perceptible nod. In a situation like this, you didn't want the polite man. You wanted the man who refused to lose.

"Muir," Talbot said softly. "Fall in."

James Muir stood up. He offered no hand to Dougherty. He brushed the sand from his torn trousers, wiped the blood from a scratch on his cheek, and walked to the line of volunteers. He stood next to Halford. The Coxswain didn't even look at him; he just stared out at the horizon, chewing on a piece of salt rind.

Dougherty lay in the sand for a moment, his chest heaving, his eyes staring up at the sun. Then he rolled over and pounded the ground once with his fist. He looked up at Muir, his face caked in white coral dust and streaked with sudden tears, wearing an expression of such naked, terrified envy that Read had to look away. He knew what that look meant. Dougherty wasn't just mourning the loss of a seat; he was mourning his own life. He had just drawn the short straw for the slow death, and the realization broke something behind his eyes. He had lost his ticket out. He was condemned to the island.

Read looked at the five men standing apart from the rest. Talbot, the idealist officer. Halford, the unvarnished stoic. Francis, the quiet professional. Andrews, the solid yankee. And Muir, the scrapper.

They were a motley collection, stripped of their insignia, barefoot and bearded. Yet as they stood there against the backdrop of the turquoise lagoon and the distant, thundering reef, they looked formidable. They were the best of the *Saginaw*.

"These are the men," Sicard announced formally. "They will be relieved of all camp duties. They are to assist the carpenter in the modification of the gig. Mr. Read, you will issue them double rations starting tonight. We need their strength built up."

"Aye, sir," Read said, noting the flash of envy that rippled through the rest of the crew at the mention of food.

"Dismissed."

The formation broke. The men drifted away, returning to the shade of the scrub, leaving the chosen five standing by the water.

Read walked over to Halford. The big Coxswain was inspecting the hull of the gig, running a callous hand over the cedar planking.

"She's a good boat, Halford," Read said.

Halford spat into the sand. He looked at the Paymaster with eyes that had seen too much of the world to be impressed by heroism.

"She is a bucket, Paymaster," Halford grunted. "But she is a bucket with a keel. We'll deck her over. We'll caulk her tight. If the Lieutenant can find the stars, I can keep the water out of her."

"Do you think you can make it? Fifteen hundred miles?"

Halford looked at the ocean. He narrowed his eyes against the glare.

"It ain't the miles, sir. It's the water. And the wind. And the hunger." He paused, scratching his beard. "But I'd rather drown out there trying to get somewhere than rot here waiting for the rats to finish me. Mr. Talbot is a good man. He's got the Lord with him, he says. That's fine for him."

Halford tapped the handle of the knife at his belt.

"Me, I've got this. Between the Lord and a sharp knife, I reckon we might see San Francisco yet."

He turned back to the boat, dismissing the officer. Read watched him go. He realized then that while Talbot provided the soul of the mission, Halford provided the spine. Talbot would navigate by the stars; Halford would navigate by the waves. One was looking up, the other was looking down.

Read opened his ledger to a fresh page. He wrote down the names.

Lieutenant J.G. Talbot.

William Halford, Coxswain.

Peter Francis, Quartermaster.
John Andrews, Captain of the Hold.
James Muir, Captain of the Forecastle.

He stared at the ink. It looked like a memorial list. He hoped, with a sudden, fierce intensity, that he wasn't writing their epitaphs.

Behind him, the sound of a hammer striking wood rang out. The modification of the gig had begun. Butterfield's mallet struck the planking, *thwack, thwack.*

Chapter 8

The wood was cedar. It was light, straight-grained, and smelled of a clean, resinous memory of a forest that felt a million miles away from this stinking sandbar. Coxswain William Halford ran his hand along the garboard strake of the Captain's gig, feeling for the give that would betray a rot or a crack.

She was twenty-two feet long from stem to stern. On a millpond in San Francisco Bay, she was a fine, fast boat, built to carry officers to shore in dry clothes. Here, sitting on chocks in the blazing sun of Kure Atoll, she looked like a toy.

"She's thin," Halford muttered, pressing his thumb against the planking. The cedar gave slightly, resilient but fragile. "Half an inch of wood between us and the bottom."

"She's sound, Halford," the Carpenter, Mr. Butterfield, said. He was kneeling in the sand, shaping a piece of salvaged ash with a drawknife. "Don't go borrowing trouble. The keel is straight as a rifle barrel."

A fresh cedar patch plugged the gash where the reef had bitten through the garboard. Butterfield had driven the copper nails flush, the metal heads bright against the salt-scoured hull. The breach that once swamped her to the gunwales held tight.

Halford grunted. He didn't trust wood he hadn't cut himself, but Butterfield knew his trade. The boat was their universe now. The *Saginaw* was gone, a skeleton picked clean by the surf. This tiny, double-ended whaleboat was the only thing that mattered.

"The freeboard is the devil," Halford said, standing up and wiping the sweat from his eyes with a forearm that was stained with tar. "As she sits, a steep sea will fill her in a blink. We need more side."

"Eight inches," Butterfield nodded. "The Captain ordered her raised eight inches all around. I've got the strakes cut from the interior paneling of the gig."

Halford watched as the carpenter fitted the new planking. It was a delicate surgery. They were grafting new wood onto the old gunwales, fastening them with copper screws salvaged from the wreck. Every screw had been backed out of the *Saginaw* by hand, straightened on a coral rock, and greased with seal fat before being driven into the gig.

Halford picked up a hammer and tested the new sheer-strake. He struck it, once, hard. The wood rang solid. It held.

"Make the joints tight, Chips," Halford warned. "We won't be able to caulk her once we're out there. If she works in a seaway, she'll spit the oakum and we'll be bailing for twenty days."

"I'm bedding them in white lead," Butterfield replied, not looking up. "She'll be tighter than a bottle."

Halford moved aft. The modification plan was aggressive. They weren't just raising the sides; they were turning an open rowboat into a decked vessel. Mr. Main, the engineer, had designed a decking of light pine boards, covered with canvas and painted with a mixture of linseed oil and tar. It would turn the boat into a sealed capsule.

Halford looked at the hatchways. There were two: a small square hole amidships for the men to go below, and a tiny cockpit aft for the helmsman.

He swung his legs over the side and dropped into the bilge.

It was a coffin. With the deck beams in place, the vertical space was barely eighteen inches. A man would have to lie flat on the ballast, his nose pressing against the underside of the deck. It was dark, hot, and smelled of fresh tar and claustrophobia.

"Five men," Halford whispered to the darkness. "Five men, twenty-five days."

He lay down, testing the length. His shoulders brushed the sides of the hull. If he turned, his hip bone scraped the centerboard trunk. In a storm, with the boat pitching forty degrees and the waves hammering the hull like sledgehammers, this space would be a tumbling machine of bruises and vomit.

He climbed back out, gasping for the hot, salt air.

"She'll do," Halford said, though his stomach tightened at the thought of the confinement. "She has to do."

He walked over to the shade of a large naupaka bush where Quartermaster Peter Francis was sitting cross-legged, a sailmaker's palm strapped to his hand. A pile of heavy canvas, the remains of the *Saginaw's* top-gallants, lay across his lap.

"How does the suit look, Peter?"

Francis pushed the heavy triangular needle through the canvas, using the iron thimble of the palm to drive it. *Punch. Drag. Stitch.*

"Canvas is good," Francis said quietly. "Heavy. Maybe too heavy for light airs, but she'll stand up to a blow."

They were re-rigging her. The standard lug-sail of a whaleboat was too clumsy for long-distance voyaging. They were stepping two masts, a fore and a main, and rigging her as a schooner. It would allow them to balance the helm better and handle the boat if the wind howled.

Halford picked up the leech of the mainsail. The stitching was precise, the twine waxed and doubled. Francis was sewing his soul into the canvas.

"Put a double patch on the clew," Halford advised, fingering the corner of the sail. "That's where the stress comes. If the sheet tears out in the dark, we're done."

"I'm reinforcing all the grommets with leather," Francis said. He looked up, his dark eyes steady. "Mr. Talbot says we sail on the sixteenth."

"If the boat is ready."

"She will be ready. The question is, will we?"

Halford looked at the Quartermaster. Francis was tough, but he was thinning. They all were. The rations were barely enough to keep a man walking, let alone working ten hours a day in the sun. Halford felt the weakness in his own knees when he lifted a heavy timber. His hands, usually steady, had a faint tremor when he held the hammer.

"We're ready enough," Halford spat. "I'd sail her today if the pitch was dry. Every day we wait, we get weaker. And the storms get stronger."

He looked out at the lagoon. The gig sat on her cradle, an ugly, modified hybrid of a boat. She looked top-heavy with the raised sides. She looked small.

Beyond the reef, the Pacific Ocean heaved in a long, rhythmic swell. The waves out there were fifteen feet high, moving with the momentum of a thousand miles of fetch. They would toss this cedar chip around like a cork.

Halford walked back to the boat. He picked up a piece of sandpaper, sand glued to canvas, and began to smooth the new gunwale. He worked with a rhythmic, grinding motion, focusing entirely on the wood.

Distance and hunger were irrelevant. There was only the friction of water against wood. The shear strength of a copper screw. The specific geometry of the knot he would tie in the mainsheet.

A sharp, metallic rasp cut through the dry sound of the sanding.

Ten yards away, Herschel Main ignored the sun blistering the back of his neck. His world had shrunk to a square foot of sand and a collection of scrap metal.

On his knee lay the face of the auxiliary steam gauge. Brass, heavy, and stamped with numbers meant to measure the pressure of a boiler. Now, they had to measure the curve of the earth.

He clamped the zinc sheet, stripped from the *Saginaw's* hull sheathing, between his boots. The file bit into the soft metal. *Rasp. Rasp. Rasp.* Zinc dust coated his knuckles, grey and gritty. He shaped the frame, beveling the edge to accept the gauge face. It had to be rigid. If the frame warped in the heat, the angle would drift. If the angle drifted, the gig would miss the Sandwich Islands by a hundred miles.

He wiped the sweat from his eyes with a greasy forearm.

Next came the optics. A shard of a shaving mirror, jagged at the edges. Main set it into a bed of pine resin, the sticky sap pungent in the heat. He pressed the glass down, checking the alignment with a squinted eye. It had to be perpendicular to the frame. Precision mattered more than aesthetics.

He took the opera glasses, useless luxury items a week ago, and wired one barrel to the zinc frame. He twisted the copper wire tight with pliers, locking the lens in place.

The mechanism came together. A marriage of boiler scrap, hull plating, and vanity glass.

Main stood up. His knees cracked. He held the device up to the horizon. The weight felt good. Balanced. Solid.

"Lieutenant."

Talbot looked up from his charts. He stood and took the instrument. He did not look at it as a piece of junk; he handled it like a weapon.

Talbot raised the frame. He peered through the opera glass. His fingers adjusted the index arm, sliding the vernier scale along the brass curve of the steam gauge.

Main waited. He watched the Lieutenant's hands. Steady.

Talbot lowered the instrument. A nod. A sharp, affirmative motion.

"Zero matches the horizon," Talbot said. "It reads true."

Main took the tool back. He ran a thumb over the filed edge of the zinc. It was ugly. It was covered in resin and sand. But it was no longer scrap. It was the only thing that could find a speck of land in a thousand miles of empty blue.

Halford watched the exchange from the gunwale. He looked at the fragile contraption of wire and glass, then looked back at the solid oak under his hand. Mr. Talbot could have his prayers and his sextant. Those were things of the air and the spirit. Halford dealt in the physical. He would build a boat that refused to leak. He would caulk the seams until they were one with the wood. He would make this coffin watertight. Then, he would climb inside and sail it into the teeth of the North Pacific. "Bring the pitch, Chips!" Halford's voice cut through the sound of the surf. "We seal the deck seams before sundown."

The sharp, chemical reek of hot tar drifted up from the beach, signaling that the work was done. The pitch cooled into a hard, black seal. The gig was as ready as wood and iron could make her.

***

It was Friday, the eighteenth of November.

The heavy canvas flap dropped behind Sicard, cutting the glare. The air inside the command tent was dead, baking the smell of mildewed canvas and dry sand into the atmosphere.

Sicard stood in the center of the small space. He did not move. He waited for the crunch of boots to fade outside, ensuring the perimeter was clear.

He slumped forward, bracing his hands on the crate, head hanging low between his shoulders. He gasped, stripping the air into his lungs as if he had been holding his breath for an hour. He clawed at his neck. The black silk stock was soaked with sweat, a wet noose tight against his throat. He ripped it loose, throwing it onto the cot, and unbuttoned the top of his frock coat.

He ran his hands over his face. His skin felt tight, stretched thin over the bone. His jaw ached with a deep pressure. He realized his teeth were clamped together, ground tight in a subconscious vise he hadn't released since sunrise. He forced his mouth open, massaging the knot of muscle at the hinge, feeling the tension snap and pop.

He caught his reflection in the small shaving mirror tied to the tent pole. The face staring back was not the Commander. It was a stranger. It was a thirty-four-year-old man with hollow eyes and a mouth trembling with exhaustion. He looked young. He looked like a boy wearing his father's coat, playing at war while the water rose around his ankles.

Get up, he told the mirror. Put it back on.

He splashed water from the basin onto his face, washing away the tremor. He slicked his hair back. He re-tied the stock, pulling the knot tight, choking down the panic. He buttoned the coat to the chin, sealing the boy inside the officer. He stood straight, locking his knees, waiting for the facade to harden.

Sicard moved to the packing crate and sat down. He drew the oilskin packet toward him and uncorked the ink. First, the official business. He drafted the report to the Secretary of the Navy with a mechanical ease; the language of disaster, *bilged, stove, total loss,* was a dialect he spoke fluently. He sanded the ink and set the page aside.

But the second sheet of paper, the one addressed to "My Dear Wife," remained a terrifying expanse of white.

He dipped the pen. The ink, thickened by the heat, dragged across the page like tar. *We are sound*, he wrote. The lie sat there, wet and accusatory. He looked at his own hand holding the pen. It was a stranger's claw, the knuckles swollen, the skin stained with indelible grease. He tried to picture her face, to summon the soft geometry of her parlor in New York, but the image was instantly superimposed by the starving, hollow-eyed face of the sentry outside.

A fly landed on the wet ink of *sound*, tracking a black smear across the page. Sicard watched it crawl. A sudden, irrational spike of rage seized him, not at the fly, but at her. At her safety. At the fact that she would read this while sipping tea, while he was drinking water that tasted of hot rubber. He wanted to write: *I am rotting. I am governing a kingdom of rats and dysentery.*

His hand spasmed. The nib caught, then skidded violently across the page, dragging a jagged smear of black ink. He stared at the blot, breathing hard through his nose, fighting the urge to sweep the inkwell off the crate. He crumpled the ruined page, shoving it into his pocket to be burned later. He took a fresh sheet. He composed his face, though there was no one to see him, and wrote with a terrifying, detached precision: *Do not despair. Duty compels us to patience.* It was not a letter from a husband; it was a general order to a subordinate. It was all he had left.

He set the letter aside and picked up the final document: the orders for the gig. The phrasing was standard, the margins precise, yet the reality was grotesque. He was issuing a formal naval directive to a twenty-two-foot rowboat to cross fifteen hundred miles of the most hostile ocean on the planet. He might as well have written an order commanding the tide to stop.

"Mr. Hershberger," Sicard called to the sentry.

"Sir."

"Ask Lieutenant Talbot to step in."

Sicard stood up. He adjusted his frock coat, fastening the top button. The coat was stained with salt and faded by the sun, the gold lace tarnished to a dull brown, but he wore it as if he were receiving an admiral.

Talbot entered a moment later. The Executive Officer had shaved. He wore a clean shirt, perhaps the last clean shirt on the island, and his trousers were brushed free of sand. The hardships of the reef had stripped the flesh from his face, leaving him gaunt, his eyes large and luminous with a strange, calm fervor.

"Reporting as ordered, Captain," Talbot said, snapping a salute that belonged on a parade ground, not a sandbar.

"At ease, Mr. Talbot."

Sicard picked up the oilskin packet. It felt heavy, though it contained only paper.

"These are your despatches," Sicard said formally. "You will find herein my report to the Department, a list of the officers and crew surviving, and a request for immediate relief."

Sicard set the heavy envelope down on the crate, keeping his hand resting upon it as he reached for a second, smaller packet.

"You also have the bill of exchange," Sicard continued, picking up a second, smaller envelope. "It is drawn on the United States Minister in Honolulu for the sum of two hundred pounds sterling. Guard this paper as you would your life, Mr. Talbot. We may rely on Providence for water, but we cannot rely on it for coal. Shipowners are businessmen, not saints. You must have the means to buy our lives on the spot. If you make the islands, you are to charter a schooner immediately. Do not wait for a government vessel. Speed is the only economy that matters now."

"I understand, sir. A fast schooner. Provisions for one hundred days."

Sicard looked at the chart pinned to the tent pole. The distance to Honolulu was a vast, blank expanse of paper.

"The winds are fresh from the Northeast," Sicard observed, his voice dropping a register. "You will have to beat to windward the entire way, John. It will be wet work."

"The gig is tight, Captain. Mr. Main has done wonders with the decking. And Halford... Halford believes she can stand up to a gale."

"Halford is a good seaman," Sicard allowed. "But the ocean does not care about seamanship. It cares only about displacement."

He walked around the crate and stood in front of his friend. The protocol of the service usually kept a respectful distance between captain and executive officer, a buffer zone of rank. Sicard stepped through it.

He placed a hand on Talbot's shoulder. The bone sharp beneath the thin wool.

"You are taking the lives of eighty-eight men with you in that boat," Sicard said quietly. "If you fail, we are ghosts. You know the Paymaster's count. We cannot last past February."

"We will not fail, sir," Talbot said. His voice was gentle, devoid of the fear that gnawed at Sicard's own gut. "I have prayed on it. I feel... I feel a certainty, Captain. We shall bring relief."

Sicard studied him. He envied Talbot that faith. To Sicard, the ocean was a physics equation of wind velocity, current drift, and wave height, an equation that solved for death.

"I have written to my mother," Talbot added, his voice dropping so the sentry outside could not hear. "If the boat... if we do not make the islands, you will see that she gets it?"

Talbot handed the letter to Sicard. The Captain took it, his hand trembling, slipping the envelope into the breast pocket of his coat.

He turned back to the crate. He placed the official reports inside the oilskin packet and sealed them in the watertight tin. He pressed the lid down, the friction of the metal scuffing in the quiet tent, and handed the canister to his executive officer.

"Guard this, John. It is our voice."

Talbot took the box, feeling the weight of the eighty-eight lives inside.

"Check your chronometer daily," Sicard advised, falling back on the technical to mask the emotional. "I have rated it against my own. It is losing two seconds a day. Make the allowance."

"Aye, sir. Two seconds."

"And the water. Put the crew on allowance immediately. Do not trust the rain."

"I will watch it myself."

There was nothing left to say. The orders were given. The navigation was settled. The boat was provisioned with the best food they had, ten days of desiccated potato, five days of beef, and twenty-five days of half-rations.

Sicard held out his hand.

Talbot took it. His grip was firm, his skin dry and hot.

"Godspeed, Mr. Talbot," Sicard said, his voice tightening.

"Goodbye, Captain," Talbot replied. He did not say *au revoir*. He did not say *until we meet again*. He used the finality of the word.

Talbot held the grip for a second longer, his eyes searching Sicard's face, perhaps looking for absolution for the risks he was about to run. Then he stepped back, saluted once more, and turned on his heel.

He ducked under the flap and vanished into the blinding sunlight.

Sicard stood alone in the dim tent. He looked at his hand, the hand that had just sent five men to what he suspected was a watery grave. He felt a sudden, overwhelming urge to call him back, to cancel the order, to say that they would all stay together and wait for the end with dignity.

But the ledger on the desk remained open. *Rations remaining: 80 days.*

That number was the final authority. It silenced the doubt and sealed the orders. Outside, the abstract math of survival was being converted into weight. Paymaster Read stood by the gunwale, watching the transfer.

***

"Easy with the breakers," Coxswain Halford grunted, standing in the cockpit, his bare feet braced against the ribs of the boat. "Stow them low. Keep the weight on the centerline."

The water kegs, the breakers recovered from the wreck and the gig itself, were passed down the line of wading men. They were heavy, sloshing with the precious fluid they had distilled drop by drop and dug from the earth. They were wedged tight under the new decking, packed in with dunnage to prevent them from shifting in a knockdown.

Then came the food. It was the best the island had to offer, yet it looked pathetic. Five tins of cooked beef. Five tins of cooked beans, the iron casings pitted with rust from the bread-room flood. Twenty-five days of half-rations of hardtack, sealed in watertight tins. Two five-pound cans of desiccated potatoes, the Paymaster's hoard. A small bag of coffee. A tin of sugar.

As each item was handed over, the gig settled lower in the water. Read watched the waterline. The freeboard, the distance from the water to the gunwale, was shrinking. Even with the raised sides Mr. Butterfield had added, the boat looked dangerously heavy. She was laden not just with supplies, but with the desperate hopes of eighty-eight men.

"That's the lot," Halford announced, wiping his hands on his trousers. "She's down by the head a fraction. Move that aft keg, Francis."

The Quartermaster shifted the ballast. The boat trimmed level.

The five voyagers stood in the water, taking their final leave. They were a study in contrasts. Lieutenant Talbot, pale and spiritual, shook hands with the officers. His grip was light, his smile serene. He looked less like a sailor embarking on a voyage and more like a priest ascending the scaffold.

Halford was all business. He checked the mainsheet, checked the rudder pintles, checked the knife at his belt. He shook hands with no one. He was already gone, his mind projecting itself into the swells beyond the reef.

Muir and Andrews, the two seamen, looked grim. They hugged their messmates, the rough embraces of men who knew that words were useless.

"Keep her dry, Jimmy," a sailor called out to Muir, his voice cracking.

"I'll bail till my arm falls off," Muir replied, forcing a grin that didn't reach his eyes.

Captain Sicard stood at the water's edge. He looked at his watch. It was four o'clock in the afternoon of November 18th. The tide was turning. The sun was beginning its descent, casting a golden, melancholy light over the scene.

"It is time," Sicard said.

The order rippled through the crowd. The eighty-eight men remaining on the island, officers, sailors, marines, firemen, crowded down to the waterline. They did not form ranks. They stood in a dense, motley mass, a sea of ragged clothes and sunburned faces.

Talbot climbed aboard. He stepped carefully into the small cockpit aft. He sat down, arranging the skirts of his frock coat, and placed the chronometer box between his feet.

"Shove off," Talbot ordered quietly.

Halford and Francis pushed the boat away from the sand. The keel scraped briefly, a harsh, grating sound, and then the gig floated free. They vaulted over the gunwales.

"Out oars."

The long ash sweeps slid into the oarlocks. The men bent to them. The blades dipped, bit the water, and the gig surged forward. She moved sluggishly at first, burdened by her load, but as the momentum built, she gathered way.

The distance between the boat and the shore opened. Ten yards. Twenty yards.

"Three cheers for the gig!" Boatswain's Mate O'Connell bellowed, turning to face the crew. "Hip, hip!"

"Hurrah!"

The shout roared out from eighty-eight throats. It was a sound of defiance, a sonic weapon hurled against the silence of the Pacific. It echoed off the dunes and startled the albatrosses from their nests.

"Hip, hip!"

"Hurrah!"

Read shouted until his lungs burned. He shouted to drown out the fear in his own heart. He shouted to tell Talbot that they were with him, that every heart on that beach was beating in the hull of that tiny boat.

"Hip, hip!"

"Hurrah!"

The third cheer died away, swallowed instantly by the trade wind.

From the boat, a response drifted back. The five men had stopped rowing for a moment. They stood up in the cockpit, waving their hats. A faint, thin cheer came across the water. It sounded incredibly fragile, like the cry of a bird lost in a storm.

Then they sat down. The oars dipped again. *Thump-splash. Thump-splash.*

Read watched them go. The gig moved steadily across the lagoon, heading for the western channel.

The boat grew smaller. It ceased to be a collection of wood and men and became a shape, a silhouette against the blinding glare of the setting sun. Read raised his hand to shield his eyes. The oars were shipped. The masts were stepped. The white canvas of the schooner rig blossomed, filling with the breeze.

The boat heeled. She picked up speed, a white bone of foam appearing at her bow. She looked elegant then, a tiny, brave thing skimming over the turquoise glass.

Then she reached the channel.

Read saw the transition. The calm water of the lagoon gave way to the chaotic energy of the pass. The boat began to pitch. She rose and fell, disappearing into the troughs of the swells. She was leaving the sanctuary.

The men on the beach stood frozen, a tableau of statues, watching their salvation recede. No one spoke. The jokes, the complaints, the petty arguments of the camp, all were suspended. There was only the collective, agonizing focus on that diminishing speck of white.

The gig cleared the reef. She turned north, then east, beginning the long beat to windward.

She grew smaller. She became a dot. Then a smudge.

And then, she was gone.

The horizon was empty. The line between the blue of the sea and the blue of the sky was unbroken. The Pacific Ocean had swallowed them.

Read lowered his hand. He blinked, his eyes stinging from the strain and the salt. He looked around.

The "rousing cheers" were a memory. The only sound was the wind in the scrub and the rhythmic, relentless crashing of the surf on the outer reef.

It was a heavy silence. It was the silence of a house after the guests have left, but magnified a thousand times. The energy had been sucked out of the island. The focus, the purpose, the hope, it had all sailed away in that boat.

Now, there was only the waiting.

"They are well away," Captain Sicard said. His voice was low, devoid of its usual command resonance. He was staring at the empty horizon, his face unreadable.

"Yes, sir," Read replied. "They have a fair wind."

"For now."

The Captain turned. He looked at the men. They were still standing there, staring at nothing. They looked suddenly smaller, more vulnerable. Without the gig to work on, without the immediate goal of the launch, the reality of their situation was settling back in.

"Mr. Hershberger," Sicard said, "Secure the muster. Set the evening watch."

"Aye, sir."

The men began to disperse. They moved slowly, dragging their feet in the sand. There was no skylarking tonight. They walked back to their tents in twos and threes, their heads down.

Read remained by the water. The sun was touching the water now, painting the lagoon in shades of blood and violet. As long as the gig was on the beach, they had an escape plan. Now, the plan was gone. They were truly marooned.

He looked at the water lapping at his feet. It was the same water that was slapping against the hull of the gig, miles away now. It connected them, yet it separated them.

He thought of Talbot, checking his chronometer in the dark. He thought of Halford, gripping the tiller, his eyes scanning the waves for the rogue sea that could end it all.

"God be with you," Read whispered to the emptiness.

He turned and walked back up the beach toward the camp. The shadows of the naupaka bushes were long and twisted, reaching out like grasping fingers. The rats would be coming out soon. The night was coming. And for the first time in three weeks, George Read felt truly, terrifiedly alone.

Chapter 9

The stench of the colony hit Read before he reached the scrub, a thick, ammonia-heavy musk of guano and rotting fish that coated the back of his throat. Thousands of Laysan Albatross sat in a dense, shifting mosaic of white and gray, their black eyes tracking the intruders with an indifference that felt like a challenge.

Beside him, Miller gripped a heavy wooden club, his knuckles white against the grain. Two young Marines, Jensen and O'Malley, followed in his shadow, their faces pale despite the blistering sun.

"Listen to the clack," Miller said, his voice a low rasp. He gestured with the club toward a large bull nesting near a clump of scaevola. "That beak sounds like dry oak for a reason. But it's the wing you watch for. The bone at the shoulder is thick as a man's wrist."

Read stepped closer, but Miller's arm shot out, barring his path. "Stay back, Mr. Read. This isn't a stroll on the quarterdeck."

Miller turned his focus back to the Marines. "The wing is double-jointed. It's built for the gale, not the sand. They need a runway to lift. If we get to the windward of 'em, they're pinned to the earth. Jensen, take the left. O'Malley, stay behind me. Don't let him turn his breast into the breeze."

The Gooney stood its ground, arching its neck and spreading its wings, a terrifying six-foot span of muscle and quill. Jensen moved too quickly, his boot slipping on a patch of loose coral. He stumbled into the bird's reach.

The strike was a blur. The bird pivoted with a sudden, prehistoric agility. The leading edge of the wing caught Jensen across the thigh with a sound like a wet towel snapped against stone. Jensen let out a choked cry, collapsing into the sand as the blow split his trousers and left a dark, blooming welt across the skin.

"Get up!" Miller barked, already lunging. "Keep your feet!"

Miller swung the club. A sickening, flat *thud* echoed across the dunes. The great wings flailed once, a frantic, rhythmic beating that sent a cloud of white feathers and sand into Read's face. Miller dropped to his knees, pinning the bird's neck with his forearm. His knife flashed, a quick silver arc in the sun, and the struggling stopped.

Miller hoisted the carcass by its feet, the magnificent wings dragging uselessly in the sand. He nodded toward the injured Marine. "Rub some salt water on that, Jensen. You're lucky he didn't catch you on the shin."

Miller slung the dead bird over his shoulder and began the trek back. Read followed, his stomach tightening as the rhythmic *clack-clack-clack* of ten thousand beaks filled the air like a clock ticking down the hours of their exile.

Read approached the cooking fire, forcing himself to navigate the abattoir that served as their galley. To his left lay the carcass of a monk seal, dragged up from the tide line. The butchers had peeled the blubber back in thick, white sheets, exposing the dark red meat of the muscle to the sun. The sand surrounding the animal had turned into a black paste of coagulated blood, buzzing with a carpet of flies that rose in a sudden, angry cloud as his boot sank into the slurry.

He stepped wide to avoid the offal, only to brush against a mound of plucked albatross feathers shifting in the trade wind. They were matted with gray lice and glued together by the dried, yellow oil that had leaked from the birds' crop. The stench, a suffocating wall of rendering fat, wet plumage, and the tang of opened bowels.

Read reached the circle of drift-logs and sat down heavily, deliberately turning his back to the flayed carcass. It was the hour of the evening mess, the focal point of their existence, yet it was a ritual that inspired more dread than anticipation. He looked down at the grey, fibrous lump on his plate, the same bird Miller had silenced in the scrub only an hour ago.

"Eat up, Mr. Read," Dr. Frank said, sitting beside him. The surgeon was chewing slowly, his jaw working with a mechanical, grim determination. "It is protein. The body requires it."

"It requires mastication, at the very least," Read muttered. He cut a piece of the meat. It resisted the knife, rubbery and dense. He put it in his mouth. The taste was instant and overpowering. It did not taste like poultry. It tasted of the ocean floor. The flesh was saturated with the fish oil that constituted the bird's diet. It was rank, fishy, and possessed of a peculiar, musk-like bitterness that coated the roof of the mouth and refused to be washed away.

He swallowed. The gorge rose in his throat, a rejection, but he suppressed it.

"The seal is worse today," Lieutenant Commander Sicard observed from across the circle. The Captain was eating with the same rigid discipline he applied to everything, but his face was pale.

Read looked at the second component of their feast. A slab of monk seal meat, fried in its own blubber. It lay on the plate like a piece of coal, dark red, almost black. The seal was a deceptive meat. It looked like beef, a rich, dark steak that should have been succulent. But the taste was a betrayal. It was coarse, stringy, and permeated with the flavor of "train oil," the heavy, cloying taste of rendered blubber. It smelled of the slaughterhouse and the swamp.

Read pressed a hand to his stomach. It felt wrong. His belt was tight, digging into his flesh, yet his arms were spindly, the wrists loose in his cuffs. His belly was hard as a drum, distended with water and gas. He pushed a finger into the flesh just above his waistband. The skin dimpled, leaving a white pit that did not spring back.

"It is the dropsy," Dr. Frank murmured, watching Read's finger. "Just as Liebig described. The blood has turned watery for want of vegetables and bread. It is not fat, Paymaster. It is leakage. We are drowning from the inside out."

The diagnosis hung in the humid air, heavier than the smoke. The men around the fire stopped chewing. They looked at their own bodies, at the swollen ankles and the protruding ribs. The stillness pressed down on them, filled only by the crackle of the burning driftwood. They needed an escape. They needed to be anywhere but here.

"I dreamt of bread last night," a young landsman whispered from the darkness beyond the officers' circle. "Soft bread. With butter. And a potato. A hot potato with the skin on."

"Stow that," a boatswain's mate growled. "Don't talk of it."

But the dam had broken. The terror of the Doctor's words fueled a desperate retreat into fantasy.

"No, not boiled," a fireman snapped, leaning into the firelight, his voice trembling with a terrifying, serious rage. "You ruin the flour if you make a paste. It must be a duff. A plum duff, steamed in the bag for four hours until it's heavy as lead." He clenched a fist, the knuckles white and sharp against the translucent skin. "And the sauce... it must be hard sauce. Butter and sugar whipped white. So sweet it makes your teeth ache."

"Peaches," another whispered from the shadows, eyes fixed on the dancing flames. "A tin of preserved peaches. Swimming in heavy syrup. Yellow and soft." He swallowed, a dry, clicking sound in the quiet. "I would drink the syrup first. I would drink it straight from the can."

"And beer," the fireman added, his voice thick with phlegm. "Steam beer. In a heavy glass that sweats on the table."

The argument flared, a feverish debate not over politics or survival, but over the viscosity of gravy and the specific crunch of a pickle. For ten minutes, the stagnant air of the camp was filled with the phantom scents of a banquet that existed only in their starving synapses, a collective delirium of starch and sugar.

Read closed his eyes. The description of the heavy, sweet syrup made his salivary glands ache with a sharp, stinging pain. It was a torture. It was worse than the hunger itself. To hear them conjure these ghosts while the taste of rancid seal oil coated his tongue was unbearable.

Then the wind shifted. The smoke from the try-pot rolled over them, carrying the cloying stench of rendering blubber, the smell of burning hair and rancid fat. The fantasy collapsed instantly, replaced by the suffocating reality of their larder.

Read stood up, his knees cracking. The sand of the camp felt softer, or perhaps his legs were just weaker. He walked toward the edge of the firelight, away from the smell of the cooking grease and the voices of the dreamers. He could not listen to it anymore.

The night was closing in. The albatrosses were settling onto their nests, making their low, moaning sounds. Read leaned against a naupaka bush, doubling over as a sharp cramp twisted his gut. A rat scurried across his boot, bold as brass. He didn't even kick at it. He was too tired.

He looked at his own hand in the moonlight. It was a claw, the skin loose and translucent. He wondered if Sicard's math was optimistic. At this rate of decay, the gig wouldn't need to return in three months. There would be no one left to rescue.

He turned back to the tent. Sleep. Sleep was the only time he wasn't hungry. In his dreams, the seal meat didn't taste like train oil, and the flour barrel was bottomless. He crawled into the canvas tunnel, pulling his coat over his head to block out the smell of the rendering fat, and prayed for the mercy of unconsciousness.

***

Heat shivered off the white coral dunes, distorting the air until the horizon danced. The trade wind hissed through the naupaka scrub, a dry, rattling sound that scoured the nerves. For four days, the lagoon had remained empty. The white sail of the gig had vanished over the western rim, taking the camp's adrenaline with it.

Captain Montgomery Sicard walked the perimeter. The sand burned through the thin soles of his boots. He clasped his hands behind his back, locking his fingers to keep them from trembling. A group of firemen sat in the shade of a bush. They did not mend clothes. They did not talk. They stared at their feet, their hands limp in their laps.

Inertia. It presented a danger greater than the reef. If they sat, they would rot. The discipline of the command would unravel in the silence, leaving only the rats and the dysentery. He needed a task. He needed a monster to fight.

He turned toward the beach. A mile out, the wreck of the *Saginaw* broke up. The winter swells hammered the hull, stripping the copper and shattering the oak. Every high tide vomited a new piece of timber into the lagoon. Ribs. Planks. Spars. A shipyard in pieces.

"Mr. Butterfield."

The Carpenter sat on a drift-log, sharpening his adze. The stone rasped against the steel. *Scritch. Scritch.* He stood, brushing the coral dust from his trousers.

"Sir."

"The foremast," Sicard said, pointing to the massive pine spar washing in the shallows. "Is it sound?"

Butterfield looked at the log. The sun had bleached it white. The coral had scarred it deep.

"The sapwood is shaken, Captain, but the heart holds true."

"And the wreck timber? The keel pieces?"

"Seasoned oak, sir. Hard as iron."

Sicard looked at the men dozing in the scrub. Their ribs pressed against their skin.

"We have muscle," Sicard said. "We have time."

He turned to the Carpenter.

"Lay a keel, Mr. Butterfield. Tomorrow morning."

Butterfield blinked. He wiped the sweat from his forehead with a dirty forearm. "A keel, sir? For a cutter? To replace the lost boat?"

"No. A schooner. Forty feet on the deck. Beam enough to carry eighty-eight men."

The Carpenter stared at him. To build an ocean-going vessel on a sand-bar without a forge or seasoned lumber defied engineering logic.

"Captain," Butterfield said, his voice low. "We lack the planks. We must rip them by hand. From the wreck timbers."

"Then we rip them. We saw every plank. We straighten every nail. We spin every thread of oakum."

"The men are weak, sir. They subsist on quarter rations. Sawing oak by hand will break them."

"Idleness kills faster."

Sicard looked out at the empty horizon. Mr. Talbot was gone. They prayed for his success, yet they could not bank on it. A second line of retreat required construction. If the gig failed, they must save themselves.

He kicked the drift-log.

"Draw up the lines, Mr. Butterfield. We start at dawn. Keep every man employed."

Butterfield looked at the massive pine log, then at the wasted limbs of the crew. He nodded.

"Aye, sir. We'll lay the keel."

***

"Heave... and... down."

The chant was a whisper compared to the shouts that had moved the boiler weeks ago. In the pit, a coal-heaver named Lynch stood covered in a snow of sawdust, his eyes protected by a rag tied around his forehead. Above him, balancing on the baulk of timber, a fireman pulled the handle of the long rip-saw.

Rasp. Shriek. Pause.

They were "ripping" the planks. It was a task that would have broken strong men on full rations. The *Saginaw* had not carried spare lumber for a forty-foot boat. The material had to be harvested from the wreck. Heavy oak beams, scarred by the reef and hardened by decades of salt water, were dragged from the surf, dried, and then sawed lengthwise by hand to create the thin sheathing for the hull.

It was a contest of friction against malnutrition.

Read watched the muscles in Lynch's back bunch and release. There was no fat left on the man. The skin was draped over the scapula like a wet sheet over a chair back. With every downstroke of the saw, the vertebrae stood out in sharp relief. The man was burning fuel he did not have.

"Rest," Read suggested, though he had no authority over the work gang. "You've been at that beam for an hour."

Lynch looked up. His face was a mask of beige dust, his eyes rimmed with red irritation. He didn't stop. "If we stop, Paymaster, we don't start again. The joints lock up."

"Keep the rhythm, Lynch," the fireman above grunted. "Don't let the blade bind."

The saw moved again. *Rasp. Shriek. Pause.*

Captain Sicard moved through the shipyard with the critical eye of a naval architect. He held a crude ruler fashioned from a barrel stave, measuring the scarf joint on the keel. The keel was a patchwork monster, three separate timbers bolted together because no single piece from the wreck was long enough.

"Mr. Butterfield," Sicard called to the carpenter.

"Sir."

"This knee is checked. It will not hold the strain of the mast step."

"It's the best we have, Captain," Butterfield replied, wiping his adze with an oily rag. "The heartwood is solid. The check is only surface deep."

"Fish it," Sicard ordered. "Bolt a sister-piece alongside. We cannot risk a structural failure in a seaway. This boat must carry ninety men."

Read listened to the exchange. It was surreal. They were discussing structural integrity and load limits while standing barefoot in rags, their bellies distended from the "*Saginaw* bloat." They were building a ship out of garbage, using tools that were dulling by the hour, fueled by seal grease and determination.

He walked over to the pile of finished planks. They were rough, the grain tearing where the saw had wandered, but they were planks. A month ago, they had been part of a gunboat's deck. Now they were the skin of a desperate hope.

A young sailor whose name Read struggled to recall through the fog of his own fatigue, was planing a board. He pushed the tool forward, stumbled, and dropped to one knee. He stayed there, swaying, his head hanging low.

Read stepped forward. "Steady, lad."

The boy waved him off. "Just... just a head spin, sir. Stood up too fast."

Read knew the signs. The blood pressure was dropping. The heart was laboring to pump thin, watery blood to the brain. The *"Saginaw Junior"* was consuming the crew. Every plank that was ripped cost them calories they could not replace. Every nail that was straightened and driven was a withdrawal from a biological bank account that was already overdrawn.

Sicard approached, the ruler clasped behind his back. He looked at the kneeling sailor, then at the half-finished hull rising from the sand.

"They are working well, Mr. Read," Sicard said quietly.

"They are working themselves to death, Captain," Read replied, keeping his voice low. "Look at them. They are spending a pound of flesh for every pound of timber."

Sicard's expression did not change. "I know the cost, Paymaster. I see the ribs. But consider the alternative."

He gestured toward the tents where the sick lay in the shade.

"If they do not build this boat, they will sit. If they sit, they will think. And if they think about the distance to Hawaii, and the silence of the horizon, and the taste of that seal meat... they will go mad. Or they will lay down and die of despair. The work kills the body, Mr. Read, but it saves the mind."

Read looked back at the saw-pit. The saw was still moving. *Rasp. Shriek.* It was a brutal rhythm, but Sicard was right. It was a rhythm of purpose.

"Besides," Sicard added, touching the rough wood of a frame. "We may need her. Mr. Talbot is in God's hands, but God helps those who help themselves. If the gig does not return by February, we sail this scow."

"February," Read repeated. It seemed a century away.

"February," Sicard confirmed. "Make sure your flour lasts, Paymaster."

The Captain moved on to inspect the stern-post, leaving Read with the noise of the labor.

The air smelled of fresh-cut oak and rotting kelp. The sound of the adzes chipping away at the wood, *thwack, thwack, thwack,* was the heartbeat of the camp. It was a sound of defiance.

Read watched Lynch in the pit. The man paused to cough, a dry, hacking sound that rattled his chest, then gripped the handle again. He wasn't building a boat because he wanted to sail; he was building it because the

Captain said so, and because the act of ripping the plank was the only thing that separated him from the albatrosses.

Read opened his ledger, making a mental note to issue an extra ounce of meat to the sawyers tonight, regardless of the inventory. They were buying hope with their sweat, and the price was rising every day.

He closed the book and walked back to the tents as the sun began to fail. The light bled out of the sky, turning the blinding white sand to a bruised purple, and then to black. As the noise of the shipyard faded, the silence was filled by a dry, rustling sound rising from the scrub.

***

Read lay on his back in the officers' tent, his eyes wide open, staring at the canvas ceiling that was faintly illuminated by the moonlight filtering through the clouds. The siege had no beginning, it was simply a permanent state of being. He had not slept, truly slept, since arriving. The exhaustion was no longer a heaviness; it had become a high-pitched, electrical buzzing in his skull, a vibration that made his teeth ache and his vision swim even in the dark.

He held a piece of driftwood, shaped into a heavy club, across his chest. To close his eyes was to invite violation.

The sound was everywhere. It was a continuous, low-frequency thrum of movement, like the sound of dry leaves blowing across pavement, but heavier. *Thump-drag. Thump-drag.* It was the sound of heavy bodies dropping from the scrub and pulling themselves through the sand.

A shadow ran across the ridgepole of the tent. Then another. They were gathering.

"Damn you," Master's Mate Hershberger whispered from the next cot. "Get off."

Hershberger kicked out his leg. There was a dull thud and a high-pitched squeal as a rat was launched against the canvas wall. It hit the ground running, undeterred.

The rats of Ocean Island were changing. When the crew had first landed, the vermin had been small, cunning but skittish creatures, content to scavenge the crumbs of hardtack dropped in the sand. But four weeks of cohabitation with the United States Navy had emboldened them. They had feasted on the offal of the seal slaughter, grown fat on the stolen flour, and sleek on the discarded fish guts.

They had evolved from scavengers into predators. They had grown larger, their bodies thick with muscle, their coats greasy and dark. And they had lost all remaining fear of man.

A weight settled on his shin. It was light, tentative at first, then heavier as the animal shifted its bulk. The individual pressure of the claws pricked through his trousers.

He lay perfectly still, his knuckles whitening on the driftwood club. He waited.

He didn't feel a bite. Not at first. He felt a wet, rhythmic rasping on the sole of his right foot. It was gentle, almost tender, a tongue, rough and warm, licking the salt from the callus on his heel.

Read held his breath, his heart hammering against his ribs like a trapped bird. The licking stopped. Then came a sharp, testing pressure. Teeth. They weren't biting to kill; they were grazing. The rat was nibbling the dead skin at the edge of his heel, tasting him as one might taste a piece of cheese rind. It was an inquisitive, leisurely consumption.

A second weight settled near his head. A nose, cold and wet, pressed against his earlobe. He heard the sniff, a wet *snuffle-snuffle* right against his auditory canal. Then the whiskers tickled his cheek as the animal moved to his mouth, drawn by the scent of the seal grease he had eaten hours ago.

Read squeezed his eyes shut. It was everywhere. *Scritch-crunch. Scritch-crunch.* It came from the leather of the tent straps. It came from the canvas walls. It came from the wooden handle of his club. Thousands of teeth were working in the dark, a ceaseless, industrial grinding. They weren't just invading the camp; they were eating it. They were dissolving the world one bite at a time.

The cold nose touched his lip.

He swung the club with a violent, backhanded motion. Wood connected with bone and soft tissue. The rat shrieked, a high, tearing sound like wet metal. It did not die. It dragged its broken hindquarters across the ground, leaving a smear of dark fluid.

Read went still. A cold, breathless clarity descended upon him. He watched the animal crawl, fascinated by the mechanics of its suffering. He raised the driftwood with the calculated precision of a man canceling a debt.

Thump.

He shattered the spine. The rat twitched and went still. It was over. But Read was not finished. The shape of the thing, the existence of the thing. He struck it again. And again. Holding his breath, his lips pressed into a thin, white line. He pounded the carcass until the geometry of the skull collapsed, until the distinction between the animal and the earth was erased. He was trying to edit the rat out of existence.

He stopped only when his club hit the sand with a dull, wet thud, the resistance gone.

His hands. They were shaking, but not from the exertion. He was looking at his right thumb. A smudge of blue ink was trapped in the whorl of his print, a stubborn crescent of bureaucracy that refused to wash off. It annoyed him more than the blood. The blood was natural; the ink was an error. He rubbed his thumb against the rough wool of his trousers, scraping frantically at the skin until it burned.

He looked up. Hershberger was sitting up in the next cot. The young Master's Mate wasn't stepping in to stop him; he was staring at the Paymaster with a look of naked, unguarded revulsion.

"Got him," Read breathed, his heart hammering against his ribs.

But the victory was meaningless. For the one he had killed, ten more were scratching at the tent flaps. The infestation had become a siege.

"We cannot live like this," Dr. Frank groaned from the corner. The surgeon sounded on the verge of tears. "I treated three men this morning for bites. Deep punctures. The risk of infection is... it is inevitable. They are eating us alive, Paymaster."

The air in the tent smelled of musk and ammonia, the signature scent of the rodent army.

"The storehouse, if they get into the remaining flour, we are dead men regardless of the infection."

He grabbed his lantern and ducked out of the tent. The camp was a scene from a fever dream. The moon painted the dunes in silver and black, and the ground was moving. It twitched with the synchronized movement of a battalion. They swarmed over the cooking pits, gnawed on the leather of the shoes left outside the tents, and fought over scraps of seal bone.

Read made his way to the provision depot. This was the new front line of the war. After the first disastrous night, Captain Sicard had ordered a fortification built to protect their dwindling food supply. It was a structure born of desperate ingenuity.

The storehouse stood on four stout posts, raised six feet above the sand. It looked like a crude altar to the god of starvation. But the genius lay in the supports.

Read held his lantern high. Halfway up each post, the engineers had installed a defense mechanism: a tin pan, inverted and nailed to the wood. It acted as a conical shield.

As Read watched, a large rat began the ascent. It climbed the wooden post with ease, its claws finding purchase in the rough grain. It reached the tin pan. It stretched out a paw, searching for a way around the metal lip. It found nothing but smooth, slippery tin. It scrabbled, slipped, and fell back to the sand with a soft *plop*.

"Gravity," Read murmured. "The one law they cannot break."

But the rats were persistent. A dozen of them were gathered at the base of the posts, jumping, scratching, trying to find a weakness in the citadel.

A group of sailors was standing guard, armed with seal-clubs and shovel handles. They looked like mediaeval warriors defending a grain silo.

"Lively tonight, Mr. Read," said Boatswain's Mate O'Connell. He swung his club casually, crushing the skull of a rat that ventured too close to his boot. "I reckon there's ten thousand of them. Maybe more."

"Do the pans hold?" Read asked, looking up at the precious crates of hardtack and flour stored on the platform.

"They hold, sir. But the little devils are smart. They climb the guy-lines if we don't grease 'em. We have to tar the ropes every evening."

Suddenly, a shout went up from the enlisted men's quarters.

"Turn out! Turn out! They're in the bedding!"

It was the nightly hunt. The men, unable to sleep, were venting their rage. Read watched as sailors poured out of their shelters, weapons in hand. It was a massacre born of frustration.

The thud of wood on flesh echoed across the camp. *Thwack. Thwack.* Men cursed, stomped, and kicked. One of the contractor's men chased a particularly large rat across the open sand, cornering it against a naupaka bush. The rat turned, reared on its hind legs, and hissed, a feral, defiant sound.

The blade of the shovel came down with a dull, wet chop that bisected the animal, but the motion didn't arrest. He struck again, and again, driving the steel into the coral sand with a rhythmic, grunting fury. It ceased to be an act of pest control and became a spasm of pure, kinetic rage, a release for sixty nights of teeth scratching against canvas and the phantom weight of claws on sleeping faces.

With every downward thrust, he seemed to be trying to kill the island itself. Sand flew, mixing with the dark smear of the carcass. He was hyperventilating, a high, thin wheeze escaping his throat, his knuckles white on the ash-wood handle as he pulverized the limestone beneath the body.

He kept pounding the wet red spot long after the creature was obliterated, his eyes wide and fixed on the mess. O'Connell clamped a heavy hand over the shovel shaft, arresting the blow in mid-air.

"Easy, lad," the Boatswain said, his voice low but cutting through the red haze.

"It's dead. You can't kill it twice."

"Filth," the man spat, kicking the carcass into the brush. "Dirty filth."

Read turned away. They were officers and gentlemen of the United States Navy, reduced to fighting vermin for the right to sleep. The rats stole more than food; they stole dignity. They made the men feel unclean. No matter how much they washed in the lagoon, the sensation of those small, cold feet running over their bodies in the dark lingered like a phantom touch.

He walked back toward his tent, carefully stepping over the bodies of the fallen enemy. The ground was littered with them. In the morning, the burial detail would have to dispose of hundreds of carcasses before the sun bloated them and the smell became unbearable.

He reached his tent and checked the perimeter. He had tried to seal the edges with heavy stones, but the rats always found a way. They tunneled. They chewed. They were relentless.

Read crawled back onto his cot. He kept the lantern burning low, a waste of oil, but a necessary comfort. He gripped his driftwood club.

Outside, the scratching continued. The inverted pans on the storehouse might save the flour, but nothing could save their sleep. The island was theirs by day, but at night, the *Saginaw* crew were merely guests in a kingdom of teeth and claws.

He closed his eyes, listening to the *plop, plop* of rats falling from the storehouse posts, a rhythmic drumbeat of the stalemate. It was going to be a long night.

Chapter 10

The tiller was a living thing in William Halford's hand. It was a piece of shaped ash, connected to the rudder head by iron pintles, and through it, he could feel the entire conversation between the ocean and the boat. The wood vibrated when the leech of the mainsail luffed; a sudden heaviness warned him of a following sea trying to slew the stern.

He sat in the small cockpit aft, his legs braced against the coaming. The gig was running close-hauled, her bow punching into the short, steep chop of the trade winds. They were heading North-by-East, fighting for latitude.

The most terrifying thing was the silence. For sixty days, the roar of the reef had been a ceaseless, grinding thunder that defined their world. Now, suddenly, it was gone. The deep water absorbed the sound, leaving only the hiss of the cedar hull cutting the swells and the lonely creak of the spars. It felt less like an escape and more like they had gone deaf.

"She's stiff," Halford said, half to himself and half to Quartermaster Francis, who was coiled in the corner of the cockpit, splicing a chafed line. "Stiffer than I reckoned. That extra planking Mr. Butterfield put on gives her a good shoulder."

"She's wet, though," Francis grunted, shielding his eyes from a burst of spray that flew over the weather rail.

"She's a boat, Peter. Boats are wet. As long as the water stays on the outside of the deck, I don't care if she drowns us in spray."

Halford looked forward. The gig was a hybrid creature now, a Frankenstein of a vessel. The schooner rig they had jury-rigged was drawing well, the canvas taut. The new decking, painted with tar and linseed oil, shone black in the sun, shedding the water that washed over it with every plunge.

Under that deck, in the dark, suffocating crawlspace of the hold, lay Lieutenant Talbot, Andrews, and Muir. They were off-watch. Halford tried not to think about them down there. It was eighteen inches of vertical space, hot as an oven, smelling of bilge water, unwashed bodies, and the sweet, sick scent of the desiccated potatoes. A man couldn't turn over without elbowing his shipmate in the face.

But up here, in the wind, it was different. Up here, it was just physics.

The boat rose on a swell, hung for a second at the crest, and then slid down the backside with a rushing hiss. The motion was violent, a corkscrew twisting that tested the stomach.

He focused on the motion. It was rhythmic. Halford knew this rhythm. He had spent his life on the foredecks of frigates and sloops.

He knew that a boat wasn't a solid object; it was a collection of tensions. The shrouds pulled against the mast, the mast pushed against the keel, the water pushed against the hull. As long as the tensions balanced, you lived. If one failed, if a stay snapped or a plank sprung, the ocean would reclaim the materials.

"Ready about!" Halford called.

The wind had headed them, shifting a point to the east. They needed to tack to keep their northing.

"Ready," Francis said, uncleating the jib sheet.

"Helm's a-lee."

Halford pushed the tiller hard over. The gig spun on her keel, lively as a witch. The sails luffed, a thunderous flapping of canvas that shook the rig, before filling on the new tack. The boom swung over, snapping the sheet taut. The boat heeled sharply to starboard, digging her shoulder in and accelerating.

"She points high," Halford noted with satisfaction. "We'll make thirty-two degrees north inside a week if this holds."

Thirty-two degrees. That was the magic number. Captain Sicard's orders were precise: run north until they hit the thirty-second parallel. There, the trade winds, the easterlies that were currently hitting them in the face, would die out, replaced by the prevailing westerlies. Those winds would catch them and blow them straight down the line of latitude to the Sandwich Islands.

It was a simple plan on paper. On the water, it meant sailing six hundred miles into the empty North Pacific, away from any land, just to turn left.

Talbot's head popped up through the main hatch. His face was flushed, his hair plastered to his forehead with sweat. He gasped for the fresh air like a drowning man surfacing.

"How does she lie, Coxswain?" Talbot asked, pulling himself halfway out of the hole.

Andrews didn't look up from the bilge pump. He stopped the handle for a second, watching the grey water swirl back around his ankles, erasing his work instantly.

"She lies heavy," Andrews whispered. It wasn't a report to the officer; it was a private admission to the floorboards. "The water is coming in faster than we can push it out. We're just borrowing time, Bill."

"Full and by, sir," Halford said, his voice loud, drowning out the doubt. "Making five knots, I'd wager."

Talbot smiled. It was that beatific, calm smile that unnerved Halford. The Lieutenant looked at the horizon, then at the set of the sails. He held his sextant in a protective wooden box against his chest.

"I'll take a sight at noon," Talbot said. "Though the motion is lively. It will be hard to bring the sun down to the horizon."

"You get the numbers, sir," Halford said. "I'll keep the water out."

Talbot nodded and ducked back below. Halford watched him go. He respected the Lieutenant. The man had guts. But navigation was just geometry. Survival was mechanics.

Halford checked the mainsheet. It was humming with tension. He eased it an inch, letting the sail breathe. The boat responded instantly, picking up a fraction of speed.

He looked at the provisions lashed in the cockpit. The tin of hardtack. The breaker of water. They were eating well enough, half rations were a feast compared to the starvation of the island. But Halford noticed the water level in the breaker. They were drinking their allowance, but the heat was sucking the moisture out of them faster than they could replace it. His lips were already cracking. The salt spray dried on his skin, forming a white crust that itched maddeningly.

"Take the helm, Peter," Halford said. "I'm going forward to check the stem."

He traded places with Francis, moving carefully along the narrow side-deck. The boat pitched, throwing him off balance, but he grabbed the shroud, his fingers locking onto the wire. He crawled to the bow.

He looked down at the stem, where the cedar planks met the cutwater. The ocean was hammering this point relentlessly. *Smash. Smash.* White water exploded upward with every impact.

Halford ran his hand over the hood-ends. The caulking was holding. Mr. Butterfield's white lead was doing its job. The wood was wet, soaking up the sea, but it wasn't weeping.

He sat there for a moment, riding the bow like a horse. The horizon was a flat, hard line of blue. There was nothing out here. No birds. No ships. Just the long, rolling swells of the Pacific, marching endlessly from west to east.

He felt a strange surge of optimism. They were doing it. The boat was small, yes, but she was strong. The crew was weak, but they were seamen. They weren't rotting on the sand anymore, waiting for the rats to bite them. They were moving.

He looked back at the cockpit. Francis was steering with a steady hand. The sails were white triangles against the deep blue sky. It was almost beautiful, in a stark, terrifying way.

Halford patted the deck. "Good girl," he whispered. "You hold together, and I'll get you there."

He crawled back aft, the salt spray stinging his face. He didn't know about God, and he didn't know about the westerlies. But he knew this boat. And right now, she felt lucky.

"She's dry forward," Halford reported, dropping back into the cockpit. "Tight as a drum."

"Good," Francis said. "Because the glass is falling."

Halford looked at the barometer mounted under the coaming. The needle had nudged downward. The sky to the north was thickening, the blue fading to a bruised purple.

"Let it fall," Halford said, taking the tiller back. "We need the wind. Let it blow."

He got his wish. The wind backed to the northwest and began to build, driving a cold, confused sea ahead of it.

***

By the third day, Halford sat at the helm, water streaming from his beard. The sky had descended into a permanent, bruising shade of grey that merged seamlessly with the heaving slate of the sea. The gale had stripped the whitecaps off the waves, filling the air with a horizontal sleet of salt spray.

The gig was leaking.

It wasn't a catastrophic failure, Mr. Butterfield's white lead held the seams mostly tight, but the violence of the motion was working the fasteners. Every time the boat slammed into a head sea, the timber groaned, and a little more of the Pacific wept into the bilge.

"Pump," Halford ordered, his voice roughened by the salt air.

Down in the cockpit well, John Andrews worked the handle of the small bilge pump. *Clack-hiss. Clack-hiss.* The stream of grey water spurted out of the discharge hose and over the lee rail.

"She's making water faster, Bill," Andrews shouted over the wind. "The deck seams are working."

"Just keep her clear," Halford replied, his eyes locked on the luff of the mainsail. "As long as it's below the floorboards, we're floating."

The dampness was the real enemy. It was pervasive. It had soaked through the canvas decking, through their oilskins, and into the marrow of their bones. There was no dry place in the boat. The "cabin" below decks, that suffocating eighteen-inch crawlspace, was a humid tomb where condensed breath dripped from the overhead beams onto the sleeping men.

It was a geometry of intimacy that bordered on violence. When Andrews shifted a cramped leg in the bilge, his boot heel dug into Muir's kidney. When Francis coughed, the spray hit Halford's face. There was no retreat from the smell of vomit or the intrusion of another man's shivering limbs. It reminded Halford of the monitor turrets in '64, iron cans sweating in the humid heat of the James River while the rebs took potshots from the banks, only this time the enemy was the whole damn Pacific Ocean and there was no armor plating to hide behind.

Halford shivered. The cold was a dull ache in his joints. He shifted his grip on the tiller, his hands white and puckered, the callouses softened into a sodden mush. He was hungry.

It was a hunger that went beyond the hollowness of the stomach. It was a cellular demand. They had finished the "fresh" rations. Now, they were down to the hard stuff. The iron rations.

Lieutenant Talbot's head appeared in the hatchway. The seasickness had taken him early and refused to let go. He gripped the coaming with white-knuckled fingers, the scent of bile clinging to his beard. A yellowed, waxy pallor masked his features.

"It is noon, Halford," Talbot rasped, clutching the coaming for support as the boat lurched violently. "Issue the dinner ration."

"Aye, sir. Andrews, break out the tins."

Andrews stopped pumping and crawled forward into the dark hold. He returned a moment later, dragging a heavy, square tin of navy biscuit. It was soldered shut, a watertight sarcophagus meant to keep the hardtack crisp for years.

"And the beans," Halford added. "We need the bulk."

Andrews retrieved a second tin. Cooked beans, also sealed.

The five men gathered in the small cockpit, huddled against the spray. This was the high point of the day. The opening of the tins. The promise of dry, solid food. Even Muir, who was curled in the corner trying to sleep, sat up, his eyes bright with anticipation.

"Open her up," Halford said, handing Andrews his knife.

Andrews worked the blade under the soldered lip of the biscuit tin. He leaned his weight on it. The metal sheared with a sharp *pop*.

A smell hit them instantly.

A thick, cloying stench of fermentation, sour and yeasty, underscored by the heavy reek of mold.

Andrews froze. He peeled the lid back.

Halford looked into the tin. There was no biscuit. There was only a green, pulpy mass of corruption. The hardtack had been reduced to a chaotic sludge of mold and slime.

"God in heaven," Francis whispered.

Halford reached in. He pulled out a handful of the stuff. It squelched in his fingers, slimy and cold. It was unrecognizable.

"The wreck," Halford said flatly. "When the *Saginaw* broke up. These tins were in the bread room. They must have been underwater before they were salvaged. The rust ate the seal".

"They've been cooking in the sun on the island for a month," Muir added, his voice hollow. "Rotting in the can."

"Check the beans," Talbot ordered, his voice trembling.

Andrews slashed the second tin open.

A hiss of escaping gas signaled the verdict before the lid was even off. The smell that followed was worse, a sulfurous, sewage-like odor of decayed protein. The beans were a black, bubbling soup.

The men stared at the provisions. This was their fuel. This was the math that was supposed to get them to Honolulu.

"Throw it over," Francis said, turning his head away and spitting into the sea. "It's poison."

"No," Halford said.

The word hung in the cockpit, heavy as lead.

Halford looked at the green mush in his hand. He wiped it off on his trousers, leaving a smear of mold. He looked at Talbot. The Lieutenant was staring at the food with a look of pure despair, his hand covering his mouth.

"We have twenty days of sailing, Mr. Talbot," Halford said, his voice hard. "Maybe thirty, if the wind heads us. We have no other food."

"It is rotten, Halford," Talbot said weakly. "It will kill us."

"Starving will kill us faster," Halford countered. "It's spoiled, aye. But it's mass. It's something for the belly to work on."

He reached into the biscuit tin again. He dug out a lump of the green paste. It smelled of vinegar and dead wet wood. He looked at the other four men. They were waiting. They needed someone to tell them it was possible. They needed to see it done.

Halford put the lump in his mouth.

The taste was a shock to the system, violently sour, with a gritty texture that coated the tongue. It tasted of salt water and mildew. His throat constricted, a natural reflex to reject the foulness, but Halford forced his jaw to work. He chewed the slime. He swallowed.

He felt the bolus slide down his gullet, a cold, heavy weight landing in his empty stomach. He waited a moment, half-expecting to vomit immediately. It stayed down.

"It's wet," Halford grunted. "Don't have to chew it much."

He took another handful and held it out to Andrews.

"Eat it," Halford commanded. "Hold your nose if you have to. But get it down."

Andrews looked at the coxswain, then at the tin. He took the portion. He ate it. He gagged, coughing violently, but he forced himself to swallow.

One by one, the men of the gig partook of the meal. It was a communion of filth. They ate the green biscuit mush. They ate the black, fermented beans. They ate with their eyes closed, trying to separate the sensation of texture from the reality of taste.

Talbot was the last. The officer took his share with a shaking hand. He bowed his head for a moment, perhaps saying grace, perhaps asking for immunity, and then ate.

When the meal was done, they sat in silence, listening to the wind howl in the rigging. The taste lingered in their mouths, a rancid film that the salt spray couldn't wash away.

"The salt," Halford said, wiping his mouth with the back of his hand. "The salt in the mash... it'll make us thirsty."

"We are on one pint a day," Francis reminded him.

"Then we suffer," Halford said. He looked at the empty horizon. The boat plunged into a trough, a sheet of spray breaking over the cockpit, drenching them all in fresh misery.

He checked the compass. North-by-East.

"The rice," Muir asked quietly from the corner. "Is the rice ruined too?"

"We'll find out tomorrow," Halford said. "Stow the tins, Andrews. Cover them with canvas. Keep the spray out."

Andrews pushed the half-eaten tins of rot back under the thwart.

Halford gripped the tiller. His stomach was beginning to churn, a slow, roiling protest against the garbage he had just fed it. He clamped his jaw shut. He would not bring it up. He would digest it. He would turn that green slime into muscle and heat, because that was the job.

The gig crested a wave, hanging in the grey air for a heartbeat before crashing down. The timbers shuddered. The water in the bilge sloshed around their ankles.

"Full and by," Halford whispered to the boat. "You keep the water out, darling. We'll handle the poison."

He looked at Talbot. The Lieutenant was leaning over the lee rail, dry heaving. There was nothing coming up but bile.

That retching sound was the bell tolling for the watch. Within hours, the poison they had swallowed began to digest them.

***

Coxswain William Halford sat at the tiller, a scarf of wet wool wrapped around his nose and mouth. It did little good. The odor was in his clothes, in his beard, in the pores of the wood.

"Bail," Halford croaked.

At his feet, John Andrews slumped against the centerboard trunk. The man was a ruin. His eyes were rolled back in his head, showing the whites, and his hands, clutching the galvanized bucket, shook with a palsy that had nothing to do with the cold.

"I can't, Bill." Andrews did not open his eyes. "The cramps. They're tearing me in two."

"Bail," Halford repeated, his voice flat. "The water don't care about your cramps. Bail or swim."

The gig lurched violently, sliding down the face of a graybeard swell. A sheet of spray, cold as ice, broke over the weather rail, drenching them both. The water in the bilge sloshed aft, brown and foul, washing over Andrews's legs.

The "rotten mass" of the provisions had done its work. The green mold on the biscuit, the fermenting slime of the beans, it was poison. Halford knew it when he ate it, and he knew it now. But the alternative was the slow fading of starvation. So they had eaten the poison, and now they were paying the price in fluids.

It had struck the crew three days ago. It began with a "gripe" in the belly, a sharp, twisting pain that felt like a marlinspike being turned in the gut. Then came the fever. Then the evacuation. It was relentless. There was no dignity in a twenty-two-foot boat. There was no privacy. When the spasm hit, a man simply turned away, hung his backside over the gunwale if he had the strength, or fouled himself if he didn't.

The boat was slick with it. The bilge water was a toxic soup of seawater, vomit, and bloody flux.

Halford felt his own stomach clench. A wave of nausea rolled over him, hot and dizzying. He clamped his jaw shut, grinding his teeth until the ache in his jaw distracted him from the ache in his gut. He adjusted his position on the bench, wincing. The salt-water boils on his buttocks had merged into a single, raw abrasion that made sitting a torture. He shifted his weight to his left hip, then his right, trying to find a patch of skin that wasn't on fire. There wasn't one. He closed his eyes for a second, just to escape the boat, and saw a freshwater creek sliding over green moss. It was silent and sweet. He opened his eyes. The grey ocean was still there. He would not let go. He was the Coxswain. He was the helm. If he let go, the boat would broach, and the Pacific would roll them under.

"Give me the bucket," Halford snarled.

He locked the tiller under his armpit, steering with the pressure of his body. He reached down and snatched the bucket from Andrews's limp hands.

He scooped. *Scrape-splash.* He hurled the water over the lee rail. *Scrape-splash.*

The exertion was agony. Every time he bent forward, his abdominal muscles contracted, triggering the cramps. It felt as if his intestines were being pulled through a hawsepipe. But he kept the rhythm. The boat was heavy; she was laboring in the seas. The extra weight of the water made her sluggish, slow to rise to the waves.

"Mr. Talbot," Halford called out, not breaking his cadence. "How does she lie forward?"

There was no answer from the hatch.

"Mr. Talbot!"

A pale hand appeared on the hatch coaming, followed by the Lieutenant's face. Talbot looked like a corpse that had been dragged from the sea. His skin was translucent, the veins showing blue at his temples. His eyes were glazed with fever.

"She... she is taking water through the stem," Talbot rasped. "The pou nding... it has loosened the hood-ends."

"Is Muir pumping?"

Talbot shook his head weakly. "Muir is... incapacitated. He cannot rise."

Halford cursed. James Muir, the man who had wrestled Dougherty into the sand for a spot on this boat, was currently curled in a fetal ball on the ballast, weeping softly as the cramps ravaged him. The fighter was gone, replaced by a shivering husk.

"Take the helm, Mr. Talbot," Halford ordered. It was a breach of protocol to order an officer, but the ocean had stripped the rank from their sleeves. "Just hold her steady. Keep the wind on the cheek. I have to go forward."

Talbot crawled into the cockpit. He took the tiller, his grip frail. Halford watched him for a second to ensure he had the feel of the boat, then moved.

Walking on the deck was impossible. The boat was pitching forty degrees, slamming into the head seas with bone-jarring force. Halford crawled. He dragged himself along the narrow side-deck, the non-skid of the canvas tearing at his knees.

The cold was marrow-deep. They were constantly wet. Their oilskins, cracked and peeling, were useless against the driving rain and the constant boarding seas. Underneath, their wool uniforms were sodden, heavy sponges that sucked the heat from their bodies. The skin on Halford's hands was white and wrinkled, peeling away in long, raw strips. Salt water sores, "sea boils", festered on his wrists and neck, stinging with every splash of spray.

He reached the forward hatch. He didn't want to go down there.

He lowered himself into the hole. The heat hit him first, a wet, suffocating warmth generated by three feverish bodies decomposing in the dark. It didn't smell of tar anymore. That chemical scent was a memory, replaced by the organic reek of confinement: the sour acidity of bile and the cloying, sweet-rot stench of excrement.

He crawled over the ballast. The bilge water wasn't just under the floorboards; it was washing over them, a tepid gray soup swirling with bodily filth. Every time the gig plunged into a trough, the water rushed forward, soaking his knees and sloshing against the ribs of the hull.

There was no way to rest. To lie down was to lie on a bed of jagged coral rocks used for ballast, their sharp edges digging into the kidneys through the thin mats. There was no personal space. As the boat lurched, Andrews's dead-weight leg slid across the darkness and kicked Halford in the jaw. A foot pressed against his neck. An elbow dug into his ribs. They were a tangle of misery, rolling around in a wet wooden box that amplified the screaming of the ocean outside into a deafening, hollow boom.

Halford wiped the sweat from his eyes and looked around. On the starboard side, Muir lay tangled in a wet blanket.

The man was vibrating. It wasn't the rhythmic shivering of the cold; it was the violent, tectonic shuddering of the "Coast Fever" resurfacing to claim its due. Halford stripped the glove from his hand and pressed his palm against Muir's neck. The skin was dry and burning with a terrifying, radiant heat that seemed to defy the icy slurry sloshing around his hips.

The fever had been waiting in his marrow, biding its time. Halford pulled his hand back, wiping the fever-sweat on his trousers.

On the port side, Francis was slumped against a rib, his eyes closed, his breathing shallow and rapid.

"Francis," Halford said, shaking the Quartermaster's shoulder.

Francis opened one eye. It was red-rimmed and dull. "Bill," he whispered.

"We're heavy forward, Peter. You have to pump."

"I... I have no strength, Bill. The flux... it's taken the legs from me."

Halford looked at the pump handle. It was a simple brass rod. It took perhaps ten pounds of force to move it. A child could do it. But Francis, the man who could sew a sail in a gale, couldn't lift his arm.

Halford grabbed the handle himself. He pumped. *Clack-whoosh. Clack-whoosh.*

He counted the strokes. Ten. Twenty. Fifty.

His arm burned. The lack of food was telling now. His muscles had no glycogen reserve. They were consuming themselves. He felt a trembling in his triceps, a weakness that spread down to his fingers. But the sound of the water gurgling out of the discharge pipe was the only music that mattered.

"The food," Muir groaned from the darkness, the sound of the water seemingly waking his misery. "Don't make us eat the food, Bill. Please."

"You'll eat what I give you," Halford grunted, switching arms. "Or you'll die."

"It's the beans," Muir wept. "They're alive inside me."

Halford ignored him. He knew the feeling. He felt the beans inside him too, fermenting, twisting. But he also knew the alternative. If they stopped eating, the cold would kill them in a night.

He finished pumping. The bilge was relatively clear. He crawled back to the hatch, gasping for the clean, cold air of the deck.

He emerged into the grey light and looked aft. Talbot was slumped over the tiller, his head resting on his chest. The boat had fallen off the wind, the sails luffing dangerously.

"Mr. Talbot!" Halford roared, scrambling aft.

Talbot jerked awake. "I... I rested my eyes. For a moment."

Halford grabbed the tiller, bringing the gig back onto course. The canvas snapped full, and the boat heeled, burying her rail.

"Go below, sir," Halford said, his voice softer now. "Lie down. I have the watch."

"I must... I must navigate," Talbot murmured, fumbling for the sextant box.

"There's no sun, sir. Just clouds. Go below."

Talbot didn't argue. He looked at Halford with a mixture of gratitude and shame. He was the commander. He was supposed to be the strength. But the dysentery respected no commission. He crawled into the hatch, vanishing into the reeking dark.

Halford was alone.

He sat on the wet bench, the tiller in hand. He looked at his own legs. The trousers were stained and stiff. He could feel the sores on his thighs rubbing against the wet wool.

He was tired. God, he was tired. He wanted to close his eyes. He wanted to curl up in the bottom of the boat and let the cramps take him. He wanted to stop fighting the ocean, stop fighting the leaks, stop fighting the smell.

He looked at the compass. North-by-East.

He reached into his pocket and pulled out a piece of the spoiled hardtack he had saved from the noon ration. It was a green, slimy lump. He looked at it.

"Fuel," he whispered.

He put it in his mouth. He chewed. The taste was vile, sour and moldy. He forced his throat to open. He swallowed.

He waited for the cramp. It came, a sharp spasm that doubled him over for a second. He rode it out, gripping the gunwale, breathing through his nose.

The pain passed, leaving a dull ache.

Halford straightened up. He wiped the rain from his eyes. He looked at the empty horizon, gray and indifferent.

"Is that all you got?" he asked the ocean.

He checked the sheet. He checked the luff. He checked the bailer.

"My watch," Halford said.

He settled in. He would bail for Andrews. He would pump for Francis. He would steer for Talbot. He was the hull. He was the iron. The rest of them could rot, but he would not let this boat sink. He would drag this floating coffin to Hawaii if he had to row it with his own bones.

Chapter 11

The wind had become a solid, screaming wall. It tore the tops off the waves and hurled them horizontally, a sheet of stinging shot that flayed the skin and blinded the eyes.

Coxswain William Halford crouched in the cockpit of the gig, his knees locked against the thwarts, his hands frozen into claws around the tiller. The world had reduced itself to a terrifying geometry of grey and white. The horizon was gone. The sky was gone. There was only the immediate, towering reality of the sea.

They were in the trough. It was a dark valley between two moving mountains. The water around the boat was black and streaked with foam, hissing like a nest of vipers. Then, the next wave arrived.

It rose astern, a vertical cliff of water that blocked out the faint light of the moon. It lifted the stern of the gig, higher and higher, until they were looking down into the abyss of the next trough. The boat surged forward, surfing with a terrifying speed that threatened to bury the bow in the sea ahead.

"She won't hold!" Halford roared, though the wind snatched the words away before they reached the hatch. "It's too much!"

The gig was surfing. For a racing yacht, this was sport. For a twenty-two-foot open boat, heavy and weakened by rot, it was a death sentence. If the bow dug in, they would pitch-pole, flip end over end. If the stern slew around, they would broach, roll sideways and be crushed.

Lieutenant Talbot crawled out of the hatch. He was soaked, his face a mask of exhausted terror. He dragged himself to the cockpit coaming.

"The wind has backed!" Talbot screamed, pointing to the tell-tales on the shrouds. "It's a gale, Halford! A full gale!"

"We have to heave to!" Halford yelled back, wrestling the tiller as the boat tried to yaw. "We can't run before it! The seas will poop us!"

To "poop" the boat, to have a breaking wave crash over the stern and fill the cockpit, was the end. The gig had eight inches of freeboard. One solid sea would fill her, and she would sink like a stone.

"The drag!" Talbot ordered. "Get the drag over!"

The sea anchor. It was their only brake. A conical canvas bag, reinforced with an iron hoop, designed to grip the water and hold the boat's bow into the wind.

"Francis! Andrews!" Halford bellowed. "On deck! Bear a hand with the drag!"

The two men emerged from the hold, moving with the sluggish, jerky motions of the sick. The dysentery had drained them, but the terror of the storm injected a dose of adrenaline. They crawled forward, clinging to the lifeline that ran along the center of the deck.

The boat plunged into another trough, slamming the hull with a force that jarred Halford's spine. A sheet of water swept the deck, burying Francis for a second. He held on, coughing, and kept crawling.

"Bend the hawser!" Halford shouted. "Make it fast to the bitts! Double turn!"

Francis reached the bow. He fumbled with the heavy coil of hemp line. His hands were shaking, numbed by the cold and the wet. He shackled the line to the canvas drogue.

"Ready!" Francis waved his arm.

"Stream it!"

They threw the canvas cone over the side.

For a moment, nothing happened. The line paid out, snaking into the dark water. Then, the slack was eaten up.

Twang.

The hawser went taut, vibrating like a bass string. The drag bit into the water fifty yards ahead. The effect was immediate. The gig's bow was pulled around, swinging into the wind. The terrifying surfing motion stopped. The boat settled, rising and falling with the seas instead of racing them.

Halford let out a breath he didn't know he was holding. He wiped the salt from his eyes. The gig was now "hove to," riding the gale like a duck, tethered to the friction of the ocean itself.

"She rides easier," Talbot gasped, slumping against the washboard.

"Aye," Halford said, flexing his cramped fingers. "But watch the line. It's chafing in the chock."

For an hour, they existed in a state of suspended catastrophe. The gale howled, the waves crashed, but the thin hemp line held them safe. The boat pitched violently, up, down, up, down, a sickening elevator ride that churned the contents of their ruined stomachs. But they were afloat.

Halford watched the hawser. It was their lifeline. As long as it held, the bow stayed into the wind. As long as the bow stayed into the wind, the waves broke around them, not over them.

The strain on the rope. Every time a massive comber struck the boat, the line stretched, shedding water droplets in a fine mist. It was old rope, salvaged from the *Saginaw*. It had been baked in the sun and rotted by the damp.

"Freshen the nip," Halford called out to Francis, who was huddled near the mast. "Let out a foot of line! Don't let it rub in one spot!"

Francis moved to obey. He reached for the bitt.

Then, the ocean decided to end the truce.

A rogue wave, taller and steeper than the rest, rose out of the darkness. It had no back; it was a wall of black water topped with a curling crest of white foam. It hit the gig with the force of a train collision.

The boat was thrown backward. The drag held fast in the water. The opposing forces, the immovable canvas bag and the unstoppable mass of the wave, met in the fibers of the hemp rope.

Crack.

It sounded like a pistol shot.

The line whiplashed back toward the boat, the frayed end flying in the wind.

"Lost!" Francis screamed. "The drag is gone!"

The reaction of the boat was instantaneous and terrifying. Freed from its tether, the bow fell off. The wind caught the high sides of the gig and shoved her sideways.

"She's broaching!" Halford roared.

The gig swung broadside to the sea. She was now lying in the trough, paralyzed, exposing her vulnerable flank to the next mountain of water.

Halford threw himself at the tiller. He jammed it hard over, trying to force the rudder to bite, trying to turn the stern into the wind. But the boat had no way on. The rudder was useless dead wood.

"Oars!" Halford screamed. "Get the oars out! Row, you bastards! Row for your lives!"

He didn't wait for them. He let go of the tiller and scrambled for the starboard sweep. He jammed the heavy ash oar into the lock.

"Pull!"

Talbot and Andrews grabbed the other oars. They were weak, sick men, but they saw the wave coming. It was towering above them, a suspended avalanche of water. If it broke now, it would fill the boat and roll her over.

Halford put his back into the stroke. He pulled until the muscles in his shoulders tore. He wasn't rowing to move the boat forward; he was rowing to spin her. He needed to get the stern around. He needed to present the narrow profile of the boat to the wave.

"Heave!"

The boat began to turn. Slowly. Agonizingly slowly.

The wave crested. The white water at the top began to curl. It hung there, twenty feet above their heads, hissing.

"Hold on!"

The wave broke.

It missed the full broadside by degrees. It struck the quarter, smashing into the boat with a shuddering impact. A deluge of green water poured over the rail, filling the cockpit, washing over Halford's legs, filling the bilge.

The boat reeled, heeling over until the lee rail was buried. Halford was thrown across the cockpit, his ribs slamming into the centerboard trunk. He gasped, swallowing salt water.

For a second, the gig hung on the edge of capsizing. She was heavy, sluggish, full of water.

Then, slowly, heavily, she righted herself.

"Bail!" Halford choked, scrambling back to his knees. "Bail!"

He grabbed a bucket. Andrews grabbed a pot. They threw the water out frantically, blind with panic. The boat was sitting low, wallowing like a log. The next wave was already forming.

"We have to run!" Halford yelled at Talbot. "We can't hold her head up! We have to run before it!"

To run before a gale in a small boat was a desperate gamble. It meant surfing the waves again, risking the pitch-pole every time. But they had no drag. They couldn't hold position.

"The sail!" Halford ordered. "Show a corner of the mainsail! Just enough to give her steerage!"

Francis hauled on the halyard. A scrap of canvas rose. The wind filled it instantly with a crack.

The boat surged forward. Halford grabbed the tiller again. The kick of the rudder returned as they gathered speed.

"Hang on!"

They were racing again. The gig lifted on the next swell, accelerating down the face. The speed was terrifying. The vibration hummed through the hull planks. Halford fought the tiller, his arms burning, keeping the stern square to the wave.

He looked back. The wave they had just survived was rolling away into the darkness, a white-capped monster that had failed to kill them.

But the drag was gone. Their safety brake was at the bottom of the Pacific.

"We run," Halford whispered, the salt water dripping from his beard onto his hands. "We run until we drop."

He looked at the men. They were slumped in the bottom of the boat, exhausted, shivering violently.

Halford tightened his grip on the wood. He could feel the ocean searching for a weakness, testing the rudder, testing his grip.

Then the wave took them. The stern lifted, the bow dropped, and the gig began to slide. The vibration returned instantly, traveling up the rudder post and shaking the bones of Halford's shoulders as the boat exceeded her hull speed. The hum of the water rushing past the planks rose to a shriek.

***

"She steers wild!" Quartermaster Francis shouted from the cockpit floor, where he was baling. "She wants to gripe to windward!"

"I have her!" Halford roared back, though his forearms were burning with the lactic fire of the effort. He fought the tiller, correcting the yaw with sharp, brutal movements. If she turned broadside now, at this speed, the keel would trip on the water and they would cartwheel into oblivion.

The darkness was thinning. A gray, sickly dawn was bleeding into the sky, revealing the true scale of the gale. The waves were not mountains, that was a poet's word, they were moving landscapes. Gray valleys of water, streaked with white scars of foam, stretching quarter of a mile from crest to crest. The wind whipped the tops off them, filling the air with a horizontal sleet of salt spray that stung the eyes like sand.

The gig crested a massive sea. For a moment, they hung suspended in the gale, the wind shrieking in the shrouds. Then the bow dropped. The stern lifted. Gravity took hold.

They began the slide.

The boat accelerated. The hum in the tiller pitched up to a scream. Halford narrowed his eyes against the spray, staring into the trough ahead. The water down there was a churning confusion of foam and black depth.

There. Hard. Black. Stationary in the moving water.

It lay directly across their path, wallowing in the trough. A log. A massive trunk of drift-timber, perhaps forty feet long and four feet thick, stripped of its bark and bleached by years in the gyre. It was a battering ram of solid redwood, floating low and heavy, rolling lazily in the wash.

They were doing ten knots. They were sliding downhill on a fifty-ton wave. There were no brakes.

"Timber!" Halford screamed. "Dead ahead!"

Talbot scrambled up from the hatch, his face white. He saw the log. The distance closing. Fifty yards. Thirty.

"Hard over!" Talbot yelled. "Sheer off!"

"I can't!" Halford snarled, gripping the tiller with both hands. "If I turn, we broach! We hit it broadside!"

The rudder had no bite at this speed. To turn the boat now, while surfing the face of the wave, would present the full length of the hull to the breaking crest behind them. They would be rolled over and crushed instantly.

The only way out was through.

Halford squared his shoulders. He lined the bow up directly on the center of the log. He didn't try to miss it. He aimed for it.

"Hold fast!" he bellowed. "For God's sake, hold fast!"

The gig rushed down the face of the wave. The log loomed, massive and unforgiving. It looked like a breakwater. Halford braced his feet against the thwart, tensing his body for the impact that would shatter the cedar planking and send them all into the gray water.

Ten yards. Five.

The bow of the gig reached the bottom of the trough just as the wave behind them arrived.

The ocean did not crush them. It lifted them.

The immense volume of water displaced by the breaking crest surged underneath the hull. The buoyancy of the gig, combined with her terrifying forward momentum, launched her upward. The bow rose, lifting clear of the water, pointing at the gray sky.

They didn't hit the log. They flew.

For a breathless, suspended second, the twenty-two-foot boat was airborne. Halford felt the tiller go slack in his hand as the rudder left the water. He saw the dark, wet wood of the log passing underneath them, close enough to touch. The barnacles encrusting its surface. A crab clinging to a knot.

Then, the sound.

Thump-scrape.

The keel grazed the timber. It was a heavy, shuddering vibration that ran the length of the spine, a tactile report of inches. The false keel, the sacrificial strip of ironwood on the bottom, kissed the driftwood as they vaulted over it.

The gig slammed back into the water on the far side of the log.

Spray exploded outward in a white geyser. The boat shuddered violently, groaning in every timber, but she kept moving. The rudder bit the water again. The tiller kicked in Halford's hand, alive and resisting.

"Check the bilge!" Halford shouted, his voice cracking. "Did we start a plank?"

Francis scrambled to the pump. He worked the handle frantically. *Clack-whoosh. Clack-whoosh.* The water that came out was gray, but it wasn't gushing.

"She's tight!" Francis yelled, looking back with eyes wide as saucers. "God almighty, Bill. We jumped it. We jumped it like a horse!"

Halford didn't answer. He couldn't. The adrenaline was draining out of him, leaving him shaking. He looked astern. The log was already vanishing into the spray and distance, a silent killer left behind in the wake.

He looked at his hands. They were locked onto the tiller in a death grip. He had to pry his fingers loose one by one to get the blood flowing again.

"That was close," Andrews whispered from the bottom of the cockpit. The man was curled in a ball, vomiting bile into the bilge. "Too close."

Halford spat the salt taste from his mouth. He looked at the next wave rising ahead of them. It was just water. Soft, yielding water. Compared to the timber, it looked friendly.

"We missed," Halford said, his voice flat and hard. "That's all that matters. Now bail the boat, damn you. The ocean ain't done with us yet."

Francis didn't move. He remained on his knees, his hand slipping off the iron handle to hang limp at his side. He stared down at the water swirling around his shins, grey, cold, and infinite.

"It's the salt," he whispered. The sound was thin, cutting through the roar of the wind like a wire.

Halford frowned, sparing a sharp glance from the following sea. "What?"

"That's the part they don't tell you," Francis said, looking up. His eyes were dark holes in a face scrubbed raw by the spray. "It burns. When the water goes into the lung, it isn't peaceful. It's like inhaling fire. It scrubs the air out of you with steel wool."

He looked back at the black water, terrified not of the depth, but of the taste. "I won't breathe it in again, Bill. I'll hold my breath until the heart stops. I won't let the salt in."

Halford looked away, unnerved by the specific anatomy of the man's fear. He gripped the tiller until his knuckles popped, forcing his eyes back to the compass to drown out the image.

His hands began to shake uncontrollably, the adrenaline draining out of his system and leaving him hollow. His vision grayed at the edges, a tunnel of exhaustion closing in. He slumped forward, his forehead resting against the wet wood of the tiller, gasping for air that felt too thin to fill his lungs.

He pulled the tiller toward him, correcting the course, and drove the gig back into the fight.

The fight continued long after the adrenaline of the near-miss had faded to a cold, shaking exhaustion. The grey light of the day bled away, swallowed by the storm clouds, until the horizon was extinguished completely. Sight became a memory, replaced by a terrifying, rhythmic blindness.

***

The gig fell down the mine-shafts of the troughs and climbed the invisible cliffs of the crests, over and over, a pendulum swinging in the dark.

Coxswain William Halford sat at the tiller, his eyes squeezed shut against the stinging spray. Sight was useless here. He steered by the feel of the wind on his left cheek and the vibration of the rudder in his palm. He knew the boat's speed by the hum of the hull, a low, resonant note that rose in pitch as they surfed and dropped to a shuddering bass as they buried the bow in the foam.

They were making seven knots, blind.

"Relieve the helm," Halford said.

His voice was a croak, swallowed instantly by the gale. He didn't know if anyone heard him. He kicked the boot of the man slumped in the bottom of the cockpit.

"Francis," Halford barked. "Wake up. My hands are froze."

Peter Francis stirred. The Quartermaster was a dark shape in the gloom, huddled under a sodden blanket that smelled of mildew and dysentery. He groaned, a sound of pure exhaustion, and pulled himself up to his knees.

"Aye, Bill," Francis rasped. "I have her."

The transfer of the helm was a dangerous dance. In a twenty-two-foot boat pitching forty degrees, standing up was an invitation to gravity. Francis moved slowly, gripping the gunwale with one hand and reaching for the tiller with the other.

Halford waited until he felt Francis's weight settle on the bench before he let go of the wood. His fingers were locked in a claw shape, stiff as iron. He began to massage the blood back into them, hissing through his teeth as the circulation returned with a burning prickle.

"Watch the leech," Halford warned, leaning close to Francis's ear. "She's luffing in the gusts. Keep her full, or she'll roll the sticks out of her."

"I see it," Francis said. He sounded weak. The sickness had taken the meat off him. He was steering by instinct now, his body swaying with the boat, but his reactions were slow.

Halford moved forward. He needed to check the mainsheet cleat. The rope had been complaining under the strain, and he worried about chafe. He crawled on his hands and knees along the narrow floorboards, sliding over the sleeping forms of Andrews and Muir.

The boat rose. It felt like an elevator cable had snapped. Up, up into the screaming dark, hanging for a breathless second at the apex.

Then the lurch.

A cross-sea, a rogue wave running counter to the wind, slammed into the starboard quarter. The gig was kicked sideways with a violence that jarred Halford's teeth. The boom gibed across, the heavy spar sweeping the cockpit like a scythe before the sheet snapped it back.

"Jesus!" Halford shouted, grabbing a thwart to keep from being thrown into the bilge.

He looked aft.

The cockpit was empty.

The tiller was swinging wild, banging against the stops. The bench where Peter Francis had been sitting was bare wet wood, glistening in the faint phosphorescence of the wake.

"Man overboard!"

The scream tore out of Halford's throat, raw and terrified.

He scrambled aft, throwing himself at the tiller just as the boat began to broach. He jammed the rudder hard over, fighting the ocean's attempt to roll them. The gig shuddered, hesitated, and then swung back downwind, picking up speed again.

"Talbot! Andrews! On deck!"

Halford stared into the wake. It was a churning trail of white foam vanishing into the blackness. There was nothing there. No head bobbing. No arm waving. Just the ocean, moving away at seven knots.

"Peter!" Halford yelled at the dark.

A sound came back. Faint. Impossible. A scream, thin and high, drifting over the roar of the wind.

Help!

He was alive. He was in the water, alone in the middle of the North Pacific, in a gale, at night.

"We have to turn!" Talbot gasped, crawling out of the hatch, his face a ghost in the gloom.

"We can't!" Halford snarled, the tears of frustration hot in his eyes. "We have no drag! If I bring her about now, the sea will catch us broadside!"

It was the cruelest mathematics of the sea. To save one man, he would have to kill four. The boat could not handle a turn in these seas. They were surfing. They were committed to the run. Every second that passed put another thirty feet between them and the Quartermaster.

"Throw a line!" Andrews shouted, grabbing a coil of rope.

"He's gone!" Halford shouted back, the despair crushing his chest. "He's too far astern! He's gone!"

The scream came again, fainter this time. A cry from the grave.

Halford gripped the tiller, his knuckles white. He had lost men before. He had seen them washed off the yards, seen them crushed by cannon. But this, to leave a shipmate behind in the dark, conscious, watching the boat sail away, it was a horror that froze the blood.

Then, the boat shuddered.

A jerk. A heavy, rhythmic tugging on the stern.

Halford looked down.

Trailing from the stern cleat was a thin line. A fishing line. They had streamed it hours ago, a desperate, passive attempt to catch a bonitol or a dolphin fish to supplement the rotten rations. It trailed two hundred feet behind the boat, invisible in the wake.

The line was taut. It was singing. It cut through the water, vibrating with a tension that threatened to snap it.

"The line!" Halford roared. "The fishing line!"

Talbot lunged for the cleat. He grabbed the thin cord.

"I have him!" Talbot screamed. "I feel weight! There is weight on the line!"

It wasn't a fish. No fish pulled with the dead, heavy drag of a soaked wool uniform.

"Heave!" Halford bellowed. "For the love of God, heave gently! It's rotten cord!"

Talbot and Andrews grabbed the line. It was thin stuff, barely strong enough to land a twenty-pound fish. Now it was holding the weight of a grown man being dragged through the water at seven knots.

"Easy," Halford warned, his heart in his throat. "Don't jerk it. If it part s..."

He didn't finish the sentence.

They hauled. Hand over hand. The line cut into their palms, slick with water and slime. They pulled with a desperate, fluid motion, trying to keep a steady tension as the boat surged and slowed in the waves.

Every time the gig accelerated down a wave, the line hummed, stretching to its breaking point. Halford watched it, waiting for the snap.

"He's still there," Andrews gasped, bracing his foot against the transom. "He's fighting."

Ten feet. Twenty feet. Fifty feet.

A dark shape emerged from the foam of the wake. A head. A hand, wrapped in a death grip around the cord.

"Peter!" Talbot cried out.

Francis was being towed like a lure. His face was underwater for seconds at a time as the wake washed over him. He was drowning on the end of a string.

"Get him to the rail!" Halford shouted. "Wait for the pitch!"

The stern dropped into a trough. The water level rose to the gunwale.

"Now!"

Talbot and Andrews reached over the side. They grabbed the sodden mass of Francis's coat. They grabbed his hair. They grabbed his belt.

"Heave!"

They pulled. Francis was dead weight, heavy with water and exhaustion. They dragged him over the rail, scraping his ribs against the wood. He tumbled into the cockpit, landing in a wet heap on the floorboards.

He lay there, retching. Sea water poured from his mouth and nose, shivering violently. He wasn't looking at Halford; he was staring at his own right hand.

The fingers were frozen in a claw, locked tight in the shape of the fishing line. He struck his fist against the floorboards, once, twice, sobbing with a mixture of rage and grief.

"It wouldn't open," Francis choked out, his voice a wet, broken rasp. "I tried to let go, Bill. I wanted to sink. But the hand... it wouldn't open."

Halford didn't speak. He looked at the fishing line. It was frayed, worn almost through where it had rubbed against the stern. One more strand, one more minute, and Francis would have been lost to the darkness forever.

Francis rolled onto his back. His eyes were wide, staring up at the empty sky. He was shivering so violently his teeth clattered like castanets.

"I saw the boat," Francis whispered. "I saw the sail going away. I thought... I thought I was dead."

"You were dead," Halford said. "You were dead and buried."

He looked at Talbot. The Lieutenant was weeping silently, his hand resting on Francis's shoulder. It was too much. The hunger, the dysentery, the rot, and now this. The ocean was playing with them. It was catching them and throwing them back, just to see how much terror they could absorb before they broke.

"Get him below," Halford ordered roughly. "Strip him. Put him in the blanket. Get some body heat into him."

Talbot and Andrews wrestled the Quartermaster toward the hatch. They shoved him into the black hole of the cabin, crawling in after him to chafe his limbs.

Halford was alone at the tiller again.

He looked at the fishing line, still trailing in the water. He pulled his knife from his belt. He reached back and cut the line.

He watched the end drift away into the wake.

"No more fishing," Halford whispered. "No more."

He didn't want to catch anything else. He didn't want to be connected to the black water by even a single thread. He gripped the tiller, feeling the hum of the boat, and steered north, driving the gig away from the grave that had just opened and closed behind them. The night was still black, the wind was still screaming, but the boat felt heavier now. It carried the weight of a ghost that had been dragged back to the land of the living.

Chapter 12

The disintegration of the command was no longer measured in days, but in the failure of materials. The canvas of the tent, once white and taut, had succumbed to the unrelenting violence of the sun. It was now a brittle, grey skin that flaked like dead flesh when the trade wind gusted, dusting the interior with a fine powder of rotten cotton.

Outside, the iron hoops of the water casks were shedding layers of red scale, bleeding oxide stains into the white sand. Even the brass buttons on Sicard's uniform had surrendered, turning a dull, verdigris green that refused to shine no matter how aggressively he rubbed them. The island was digesting them. It was breaking down the chemistry of their civilization, the fiber, the iron, the leather, and returning it to the mineral state of the reef.

Sicard looked down at the logbook, the white page glaring under the vertical sun. The date at the head of the entry sat heavy and immovable on the page, an administrative impossibility that his mind struggled to reconcile with the heat. According to the regulations and the calendar, he should have been bracing against a northerly gale or seeking the warmth of a wardroom stove.

There was no biting frost to redden the cheeks, no smell of pine needles or roasting goose. There was only the blinding, white-hot glare of the coral sand and the suffocating blanket of the trade wind, which carried the stench of guano and rotting kelp.

Inside the command tent, Sicard gripped the pen. The date was December 25th, 1870. Christmas. The column for "Remarks" waited, a blank white indictment. He looked through the open flap. Fifty yards away, a landsman was sitting in the dirt, gnawing on the raw, purple carapace of a shore crab, weeping silently as he cracked the shell with his teeth.

Sicard looked back at the page. The truth, we are dissolving, was inadmissible. To record despair was to make it official; it was a failure of command that would exist forever in the archives of the Department. He dipped his pen. The nib scratched loud in the humid silence, the ink flowing black and permanent.

The crew are well, his script tight, angular, and unyielding. *Morale is high. We celebrate the day with a grateful spirit.*

He blotted the line, watching the ink dry.

The logbook demanded optimism, but the silence of the camp offered none. Fifty yards away, in the stifling gloom of the officers' tent, the reality was far less orderly.

Paymaster George Read sat on the edge of his cot, his feet resting in the sand that perpetually carpeted the floor of the officers' tent. He held his head in his hands, trying to summon the fortitude to face the day.

In Philadelphia, the gas lamps would be glowing against the early winter dusk. Carriages would be rattling over cobblestones, the horses' breath steaming in the cold air. Families would be gathering in parlors festooned with holly, the air thick with the scent of cinnamon, cloves, and the rich, savory smoke of a roasting bird.

Here, the only smoke came from the cook-fire where the seal blubber was rendering, sending a plume of greasy, black soot into the pristine sky.

Read stood up, his joints cracking. The *"Saginaw* bloat" had settled into his abdomen. He buttoned the heavy wool across his chest. It was a ridiculous garment for a castaway, stained with mildew and salt, but today, of all days, the propriety of the uniform felt like a necessary armor.

He moved to the packing crate that served as his desk and opened the ledger. The smell rose up to meet him, not the clean scent of stationery, but the damp, mushroom-like odor of a cellar. The humidity was dissolving the book from the spine outward. The pages, once crisp and white, were now soft, swollen, and spotted with brown blooms of foxing like dead leaves rotting in a gutter.

He dipped his pen. He intended to rule a double line beneath the week's expenditure of salt beef, a standard closure to the accounts.

He placed the straightedge against the paper. He applied the nib. But his hand, betrayed by the palsy of starvation, would not hold the line. The pen skittered. It jerked sideways, dragging a jagged, ugly scar of black ink across the pristine column of figures.

Read stopped. He stared at the smudge. It was a violation. It was a disorderly mark that rendered the entire page unofficial. A cold, irrational logic seized him: *If the ledger is messy, the inventory is suspect. If the inventory is suspect, the ration is invalid. If the ration is invalid, we are already dead.*

He grabbed his penknife to scrape the error away. He scratched frantically at the heavy paper, the blade *scritch-scritching* like a rat's claw, until the fiber tore and a hole opened up, revealing the rough wood of the crate beneath. He froze. He stared at the abyss he had just created in the government's records. He pressed his thumb over the tear, pushing down hard as if to staunch a wound, his lungs seizing in a dry, silent spasm. He sat there, pinning the hole shut, terrified to lift his thumb. The silence of the tent roared in his ears. He stared at the nail of his own thumb, pressing white against the paper, anchoring the reality of the ledger against the chaos outside. *Breathe,* he told himself. *It is just paper. It is just a mark.* But the air wouldn't come. His chest hitched, fighting the lock in his diaphragm. He focused on the blue grid lines, counting them, one, two, three, forcing his mind to trace the geometry until his lungs finally obeyed.

He sucked in a breath, a sharp, ragged gasp that broke the paralysis. He lifted his thumb. The hole remained, jagged and raw, but the world held.

He stepped out of the tent.

The camp was silent. Captain Sicard had ordered a suspension of all labor. The *"Saginaw Junior,"* the schooner they were hacking out of the wreck timber, lay dormant in the saw-pit, a half-finished ribcage of oak rising from the sand. The hammers were still. The saws were silent.

The idleness, meant as a mercy, felt like a curse. Without the anesthesia of exhausting labor, the men were left alone with their thoughts. They sat in small clusters under the shade of the naupaka bushes, staring out at the lagoon. They looked like specters. Their eyes were sunken dark pits in faces stretched tight over the bone. They picked at the scabs on their arms, salt-water sores that refused to heal on the starvation rations.

"Merry Christmas, Paymaster," Dr. Frank said. The surgeon was sitting on a drift-log, whittling a piece of coral with a penknife. He did not look up.

"And to you, Doctor," Read replied. The words tasted like ash. "How is the sick list?"

"Growing," Frank said, blowing the white dust from his carving. "The dysentery is constant. The scurvy is making introductions. I have three men with loose teeth this morning. And the melancholy... well, that is general."

Read looked toward the fire. The "feast" was in preparation. It was a tragic pantomime of a holiday dinner. There would be no turkey. The island offered only two sources of flesh: the monk seal and the albatross.

Read approached the cooking area. The smell hit him at twenty paces, a thick, cloying odor of musk and fish oil.

"What is the menu, Cook?" Read asked.

The ship's cook, Graves, stood over a copper cauldron salvaged from the galley. He looked thinner than the rest, his once-rotund belly now hanging in loose folds beneath his apron. He stirred the pot with a piece of driftwood.

"Albatross stew, sir," Graves said, tapping the spoon against the rim. "With a side of fried seal liver." He pointed to a second pot, where small, grey lumps bobbed in boiling grease. "And the Captain's special order. Doughboys. Graves kicked a small barrel lying on its side in the sand. The wood rang hollow.

"That's the end of it, Paymaster. I scraped the staves with a knife to get the dust. There isn't enough left in there to powder a wig."

Read looked at the bubbling fat. The "doughboys" were dense dumplings, a tablespoon of flour mixed with salt water and boiled in the rancid oil. They were heavy, grey, and represented the last ounce of civilized starch on the island. After this, there was only meat.

"It looks... substantial," Read lied.

"It's hot, sir. And it's the last of the bread locker."

Graves wiped his hands on his apron. "My mother called 'em 'sinkers", an Ordinary Seaman muttered, eyeing the boiling grease. "If they float, they're dumplings. If they kill a rat when you drop 'em, they're sinkers. These here are lethal weapons." A ripple of dry, hacking laughter went through the line. It wasn't funny, but it was a distraction.

The boatswain's whistle chirped. *Tweet-tweeeeeee.*

"Pipe to dinner!"

The men shuffled toward the fire. There was no rushing, no jostling. They moved with the brittle fragility of the elderly. They held out their tin pannikins and plates, their eyes fixed on the ladle with a predatory intensity that was disturbing to witness.

Captain Sicard stood at the head of the line. He was clean-shaven, his jaw set in a line of granite. He looked at each man as they passed, nodding a silent greeting. He was trying to hold the center, to maintain the fiction that they were a naval company and not a tribe of dying castaways.

"Mr. Read," Sicard said as the Paymaster approached. "Join us."

The officers sat in a circle on the sand, separate from the enlisted men but close enough to share the mood. Read looked down at his plate.

The albatross meat was gray and stringy, swimming in a broth that had separated into a layer of clear water and a slick of yellow oil. Beside it lay the seal liver, black as coal, and the single "doughboy," a heavy, glistening lump.

"Gentlemen," Sicard said, raising his tin cup of water. "To our shipmates in the gig. Wherever they may be."

A silence fell over the circle. It had been thirty-seven days since the gig sailed. Thirty-seven days. If they had made a good passage, they should have reached Honolulu in twenty-five. Relief should be on the way.

Or, the boat was gone. Swamped in a gale. Smashed on a reef. Drifting with five corpses desiccating in the sun.

"To the gig," Read murmured. He drank the warm, brackish water.

He cut a piece of the albatross. The knife sawed through the muscle fibers. He put it in his mouth.

The taste was vile. It was the flavor of the bird's life, a distillation of raw squid and surface fish, concentrated into a musk that coated the tongue and throat. It was tough, requiring endless chewing, which only released more of the rank oil.

Read swallowed, fighting the urge to gag. He looked at the doughboy. He bit into it. The exterior was crisp, fried hard in the seal fat, but the interior was a gummy, uncooked paste of flour and salt water. It tasted of the "train-oil" stench of the seal.

Yet, it was food. His stomach clamped around it, grateful for the mass.

"I recall," Lieutenant Hershberger said softly, staring at his fork, "the Christmas of '68. We were in Nice. The wardroom had a roast suckling pig. And champagne. Cold champagne."

"Don't," Master's Mate Blye, hissed. "Don't do it, Hershberger."

"The skin was crisp," Hershberger continued, his eyes glazed. "And the stuffing... chestnuts and sage."

"Silence," Sicard ordered. His voice was not loud, but it cut the air like a lash. "We do not dwell on what is absent. We are grateful for what is present. We have life. We have water."

Hershberger ducked his head. "Aye, sir. Apologies."

But the damage was done. The image of the suckling pig hung in the air, shimmering like a mirage over the plate of gray bird meat. Read felt a cramp of hunger so sharp it nearly doubled him over. It was a biological scream for nutrition. His body wanted a potato. It wanted a lemon. It wanted roast pork and fresh vegetables.

He looked over at the enlisted men. They were eating in silence. There was no laughter, no skylarking. Usually, a sailor's Christmas was a time of riotous behavior, of extra grog and songs. Here, it was a funeral wake for their former lives.

A young coal-heaver, a boy named Donnelly, was sitting alone near the edge of the scrub. He was holding his doughboy in both hands, looking at it. He wasn't eating it. He was crying. Silent, shaking sobs that racked his thin shoulders.

Read watched him. He wanted to go over, to offer a word of comfort, but he stayed seated. He had no comfort to give. To offer false hope was a cruelty. To say "Next Christmas will be better" was a gamble he couldn't back.

He finished his meal. The grease lay heavy in his gut.

The silence in the camp was unbearable; the sight of the men weeping over their doughboys was a suffocation. Read could not sit there and watch the afternoon drag on into a hopeless twilight. He needed distance. He needed altitude. He stood up, leaving his tin plate in the sand, and turned his back on the feast.

***

He walked away from the camp, passing the rugged, plank-sheathed hull of the schooner and headed toward the eastern dune. Here, the men had erected a lookout post, a crude tripod of spars lashed together, surmounted by a crow's nest salvaged from the wreck. It stood like a gallows against the bright sky, the highest point on *Hōlanikū*, offering a view that promised salvation but delivered only emptiness.

The climb was a penance. In his prime, Read could have ascended the ratlines of the *Saginaw* with the ease of a midshipman. Now, every rung of the makeshift ladder was a negotiation with gravity. His arms, wasted by the diet of seal grease and flour-paste, trembled as he hauled his weight upward. His heart hammered a frantic, uneven rhythm against his ribs, protesting the exertion. *Thump-thump-pause. Thump-thump-pause.* The scurvy was in his blood, thinning it, robbing him of the oxygen needed to drive his muscles.

He reached the platform, a small square of planking swaying gently in the trade wind, and collapsed against the railing. He gasped for air, the salt dust of the island coating his throat. He closed his eyes, waiting for the black spots to clear from his vision, waiting for the dizziness of the ascent to subside.

When he opened them, the world had expanded.

From the ground, the horizon was a close, confining circle, broken by the scrub brush and the dunes. From here, sixty feet up, it was an infinite, terrifying circumference. The Pacific Ocean stretched away in every direction, a vast, heaving pavement of blue slate. It was beautiful, in the way that a glacier or a desert is beautiful, flawless, immense, and utterly unconcerned with human biology.

Read adjusted his cap against the glare and began his watch. It was a ritual performed by every officer and man on the island, a daily liturgy of hope. Squinting against the sun, he scanned the northern quadrant first, then turned slowly to the east, toward the inhabited world and home, before sweeping south and west, finding the horizon unbroken in every direction. It was a hard, sharp line where the water met the sky, unblemished by a sail, a funnel, or a wisp of smoke.

Read picked a splinter from the railing. He spent ten minutes working it loose, examining the grain, and then flicking it into the void. Then he found another. It was an occupation. It required no calories and provided a measurable result, unlike the staring.

He leaned his elbows on the weathered wood of the rail. He let his chin rest in his hands. It had been thirty-seven days since the gig sailed.

He did the arithmetic in his head, though he had done it a thousand times before in the silence of his tent. Departure: November 18th. Destination: Honolulu. Distance: Twelve hundred miles, perhaps fifteen hundred with the tacking.

If the gig had averaged four knots, a conservative estimate for a twenty-two-foot boat with a fair wind, they would have covered a hundred miles a day. They should have reached the islands in two weeks. Three weeks at the outside, allowing for calms.

That would put their arrival around the tenth of December.

If they had found the U.S. Minister immediately... if a fast schooner had been chartered the same day... if the winds were favorable for the return trip...

Read looked at the empty sea. A rescue ship could have been here five days ago.

The delay was a fact. The interpretation of the fact was the torture.

Perhaps the winds had been contrary. Perhaps the government bureaucracy in Honolulu was slow. Perhaps they were currently beating up against a headwind, just below the horizon, hull-down and invisible.

Or perhaps the gig was gone.

The thought was a cold stone in his stomach, heavier than the dough-boys he had eaten for dinner. A rogue wave in the night. A broach in a gale. A plank sprung by the constant pounding. Five men in the water, watching their boat sink, treading water in the dark until the cold took them.

Read shivered, despite the heat of the sun. He looked out toward the northeast, the direction the gig had taken.

There.

His heart stopped.

On the edge of the world, just where the blue faded into the white haze of the atmosphere, a shape broke the line.

It was white. Triangular. Distinct.

"A sail," Read whispered. The sound was barely a breath.

He rubbed his eyes furiously, pressing the heels of his hands into the sockets until stars exploded in his vision. He looked again.

It was still there. A top-sail schooner, running free, her canvas bright against the dark water. She was hull-down, but the upper yards were un-mistakable. She was heading straight for the atoll.

A surge of adrenaline, hot and electric, flooded his wasted body. It washed away the lethargy, the hunger, the despair.

"Sail ho!"

The white triangle sharpened into focus, resolving with a sudden, hyper-real clarity. The dark sheer of the hull rising on a swell, the wet gleam of the copper sheathing. The davits swing out. Cutting through the wind, the sharp clang-clang of a ship's bell striking the watch and the squeal of the falls as the relief boat was lowered.

He was already composing the first sentence he would shout to the deck officer, a formal, absurd greeting from a scarecrow in rags to a man in clean linen. We are the *Saginaw*. We are all here.

He leaned far over the rail, his breath hitching in a dry sob, his hand raised to wave at the men who were finally coming for them.

The cry was rising in his throat, ready to be shouted down to the camp. He imagined the scene: the men pouring out of the tents, the cheers, the frantic lighting of the signal fire. He could see the boat lowering from the schooner's davits. He could taste the fresh bread, the cold water, the beef.

He leaned far over the rail, his eyes watering. He needed to be sure. He needed to see the hull.

He watched the white shape. It seemed to hover, suspended above the water. It shimmered.

It was perfect. Too perfect. The canvas shone with a brilliant, impossible purity, untarnished by weather or coal dust, glowing like a pearl against the hard blue wall of the sky. It didn't roll with the swell; it floated, detached from the violence of the ocean, a fever-dream of salvation painted in cloud-vapor.

Then, slowly, silently, the topsail dissolved.

The sharp triangle softened, losing its edge. The canvas detached itself from the mast that wasn't there. Read blinked, his eyelids grating over eyeballs that lacked the moisture to rotate smoothly. The optic nerve, starved of blood and sugar, finally fired and collapsed the image. The form drifted upward, pulled apart by the upper atmosphere winds, and elongated into a wisp of cirrus cloud.

The ship vanished.

Read stared at the empty spot on the horizon where his salvation had been. He stared until his eyes burned and his vision blurred.

It was a phantom. A trick of the light and the desperate mind.

He slumped back against the mast of the lookout, sliding down until he hit the deck planks. He pulled his knees to his chest and buried his face in his arms. A sob wrenched itself from his chest, a dry, hacking sound that hurt his throat.

To be given the vision of life, only to have it evaporate into vapor.

He sat there for a long time, the sun beating down on his neck. The adrenaline faded, leaving him more exhausted than before. The "melancholy" that Dr. Frank spoke of settled over him. It was not a sharp pain anymore; it was a dull, heavy acceptance.

The gig was lost.

Talbot was dead. Halford, with his knife and his grit, was dead. Muir, Francis, Andrews, all dead. They were gone, swallowed by the same indifferent force that was slowly killing the ninety-three men on the island.

Read lifted his head and looked down at the camp. From this height, the tents were dirty canvas smudges on the white sand. The men were tiny, dark figures moving with the slow, aimless torpor of insects in winter.

He saw the *"Saginaw Junior"* in the pit. From up here, it didn't look like a boat. It looked like a scarred beast.

They were building a coffin. That was the truth of it. The Captain could call it a schooner, he could talk of sailing to the islands, but it was a delusion. A forty-foot boat built of rotten wood, fastened with rusted iron, sailed by skeletons? It would never survive the voyage. It would break up in the first gale.

They were trapped. And now they were simply waiting for the end.

Read watched a figure, likely Sicard, walking the perimeter of the camp, head down, hands clasped behind his back. The Captain was still fighting. He was still calculating rations, measuring water, inspecting seams.

But Read knew the ledger was closed. The credits were exhausted. The debits were overwhelming.

He looked back at the horizon one last time. It was clean, empty, and horrifyingly vast. The sun glared off the water, mocking their silence.

"No one is coming," Read said aloud. The wind took the words and scattered them over the lagoon.

He stood up, his legs trembling. He had to go back down. He had to descend the ladder and walk back into the camp. He had to look the men in the eye and say nothing of the phantom sail. He had to eat his ration of seal meat and pretend that February was a deadline, not a death date.

He placed his hand on the rough wood of the spar. It felt warm, solid. Real. Unlike the ship in the clouds.

He turned his back on the world and began the long, shaky climb down to the earth, carrying the weight of the empty horizon on his shoulders. The descent was a controlled fall. His boots scrabbled for purchase on the rungs, his knees locking with a scurvy-induced stiffness that turned every step into a jarring impact. When his feet finally struck the soft coral sand, he did not walk away immediately. He leaned his forehead against the rough upright of the shear-legs, closing his eyes against the swimming vertigo. He had to compose his face. He had to put the mask of the Paymaster back on before the men saw the terror that was currently eating his composure. He took a breath, holding it until his lungs burned, then exhaled the phantom ship. He wiped his eyes with a rough, salt-stained cuff, scouring away the evidence of his hope.

***

The deep gloom of the afternoon seemed to rise from the sand to meet him, wrapping the island in a shroud that the bright sun could not penetrate. The prospect of the canvas walls and the silent, staring faces of his messmates was intolerable. He turned away from the tents and moved toward the surf, needing the violence of the breakers to drown out the silence ringing in his ears. He walked with his head down, staring at his boots to avoid looking at the horizon he knew was empty.

"Mr. Read."

He turned, startled. Boatswain's Mate O'Connell stood a few paces back. The man looked rough, his beard matted, his shirt open to reveal ribs that pressed against his skin like the hull framing of the *Saginaw*.

"A quiet day, O'Connell," Read said, his voice sounding thin to his own ears.

"Aye, sir. Dreary enough."

O'Connell kicked at a piece of coral, grinding it into the wet sand. He didn't look at the officer; he looked at the dark shape of the unfinished schooner rising from the dunes behind them.

"The men are talking, sir. About the launch."

"We must finish her first," Read said, reciting the standard deflection. "Mr. Butterfield needs another week."

"It isn't the work," O'Connell said softly. "It's the loading."

The sailor turned to face the water.

"Eighty-eight men, Paymaster. We've paced it out. We'll be packed in that hold like salted fish in a barrel. Shoulder to shoulder in the dark."

Read felt the chill of the image. He had calculated the cubic footage for supplies, but he hadn't let himself visualize the humanity.

"It is the only way home, O'Connell."

"It's a mass grave, sir," O'Connell whispered. "Chips says there's no way to reach the deck from the center of the hold once the hatches are battened down. If she rolls, we're just loose ballast. We won't be sailors fighting a storm, sir; we'll be rats in a drowning cage, clawing at each other in the dark."

He looked at Read, his eyes wide and unblinking in the twilight.

"The gig took the best of us. This boat... she takes the rest. And she'll take us all at once."

Read looked at the sailor. There was no point in offering platitudes about buoyancy or pumps. O'Connell knew the sea. He knew that eighty-eight men trapped in a sealed hull during a capsize had no chance.

"We sail together, O'Connell," Read said, his voice flat. "Or we rot here one by one. I prefer the boat."

O'Connell nodded slowly. He spat into the surf. "Aye. I suppose the drowning is quicker."

"Merry Christmas, O'Connell."

"Merry Christmas, sir."

The sailor walked away, heading back toward the tents where the rats were already beginning to stir in the gathering dusk.

Read remained on the beach until the sun touched the water. The sunset was spectacular, a violent bruising of purple and gold that stained the lagoon. He hated it. He hated the beauty of the tropics. He wanted grey slate roofs. He wanted mud. He wanted the ugly, industrial noise of a city.

As the light failed, the first rat emerged from the scrub. It scurried across the sand, sniffing at a piece of kelp. Then another. Then a dozen.

The night shift was starting. Read turned his back on the ocean. The "feast" was over. The holiday was done. They had survived Christmas. Now they had to survive the night, and the day after that, and the day after that.

He walked back toward his tent, his boots crunching on the coral. He felt a profound, crushing loneliness. He looked back at the beach one last time. There was no fire, no signal, only the white noise of the surf and the empty dark.

Chapter 13

The hunger was no longer a sharp pain; it was a hollow silence in the center of the body. It felt as though the stomach had digested itself and was now working on the spine. Coxswain William Halford sat in the bottom of the cockpit, his legs splayed out before him. The tiller was lashed. The wind was light, a gray, damp breath from the northwest that barely filled the sails.

The gig rolled sluggishly. She felt different now, corky and light, riding high in the water. The ballast of the provisions was gone.

The tins of beef were gone. The green, moldy hardtack and the fermented beans, the poison that had ravaged their bowels for a week, were finished three days ago. Since then, the locker had been empty.

For seventy-two hours, they had eaten nothing but wind and spray. The violent cramps of the dysentery had faded, replaced by a cold, vibrating weakness that made Halford's hands shake on the tiller. His stomach had stopped demanding food and begun to digest his own muscle.

There was nothing left in the lockers but the tin canister of desiccated potatoes.

Halford picked it up. It rattled. The sound was dry and brittle, like gravel shaking in a skull.

"Dinner," Halford croaked. His voice was a stranger's voice, thin, reedy, lacking the bass resonance of the quarterdeck.

He looked at his crew. They were not sailors anymore. They were bundles of wet rags and bones. Lieutenant Talbot lay under the thwart, his knees drawn up to his chest. His face was a skull with skin stretched over it, the eyes sunken so deep they were merely shadows. Quartermaster Francis was slumped against the centerboard trunk, staring at his own hands as if they belonged to someone else. Andrews and Muir were in the dark hold, silent. They hadn't moved in two days.

Halford took his knife and pried the lid off the tin.

Inside lay the miracle of naval preservation: dried, granulated tubers, processed to remove every ounce of moisture and flavor, reduced to a coarse yellow gravel. On the *Saginaw*, the cooks would boil these in the galley coppers for hours, whipping them with butter and salt until they resembled food.

Here, there was no fire. The matches were damp. The wood was soaked. Even if they had dry tinder, risking a flame in the cockpit with the canvas decking so close was madness.

Halford reached for the water breaker. He poured a careful ration of water into the empty beef tin he used as a mixing bowl. The water was precious, but without it, the potato gravel was inedible.

He poured a cup of the yellow grit into the water.

He waited.

He stirred it with the blade of his knife. The granules absorbed the fluid slowly, grudgingly. They didn't swell into fluffy mounds; they slumped into a dense, cold paste. It looked like wet sawdust. It smelled of nothing, no earth, no starch, just a vague, chemical neutrality.

"Mr. Talbot," Halford said, crawling forward on his knees. The movement cost him. His joints ground together, he felt lightheaded, the world swimming at the edges of his vision.

Talbot opened his eyes. It took him a moment to focus.

"Halford," the Lieutenant whispered.

"Rations, sir."

Halford scooped a lump of the mush onto the blade of his knife and held it out.

Talbot stared at it. He tried to lift his head, but the neck muscles failed him. He slumped back. Halford shifted his position, sliding an arm behind the officer's shoulders to prop him up. He felt the vertebrae of Talbot's spine through the damp wool of his coat. They felt sharp, like knuckles.

"Eat it, sir."

Talbot opened his mouth. Halford slid the paste in.

The Lieutenant chewed slowly. The mush was gritty. The cold water hadn't fully penetrated the center of the granules, leaving hard, sandy kernels in the midst of the slime. It coated the tongue and teeth, a cloying, gluey substance that required saliva to swallow, saliva that none of them had.

Talbot gagged, a weak convulsion of the throat, then swallowed.

"It is... cold," Talbot murmured.

"It's fuel," Halford said, dipping the knife again. "Take another."

He fed the officer three portions. It was like feeding an infant.

Halford watched the yellow paste disappear between Talbot's cracked lips. A dark, ugly thought uncoiled in his belly, distinct from the hunger. *If I stopped,* the voice whispered. *If I just stopped putting the spoon in his mouth.* He looked at the Lieutenant's throat working to swallow. For a second, he imagined tipping the tin into the sea, or shoving it all into his own mouth, letting the officer starve. The urge was so violent, so rational, that his hand jerked back, spilling a drop of mush on the officer's coat. He stared at the spot, horrified and mesmerized by the monster living in his own gut. He wanted to hit him. He wanted to shake him for being weak. The dignity of command was gone, Talbot was no longer the leader; he was a mouth to be filled, a metabolism to be sustained.

Halford moved to Francis. The Quartermaster took the tin himself, his hands shaking so violently that the spoon rattled against his teeth. He ate with a desperate, animal focus, scraping the sides of the tin to get the smear of starch.

"Andrews! Muir!" Halford shouted into the hatch. "Grub!"

A groan answered him.

"We can't come out," Andrews's voice drifted up, hollow and echoing. "Legs won't work."

Halford sighed. He scraped the remainder of the mush onto the tin plate and crawled to the hatch. He slid down into the bilge.

The smell down here was the scent of the grave. It was the smell of men who were slowly decomposing while still alive. Muir lay on the ballast stones, his face pressed against a rib of the hull. He didn't look up.

"Eat," Halford commanded, holding the plate under Muir's nose.

Muir turned his head. His lips were cracked and bleeding, his gums swollen with scurvy.

"Leave me be, Bill," Muir whispered. "I'm tired."

"You eat, or I'll force it down you," Halford snarled. He didn't have the strength to force anything, but the habit of authority was the only thing keeping him upright.

Muir ate. He took small, bird-like bites of the cold paste.

When the others were fed, Halford returned to the cockpit. He scraped the mixing tin. There was a tablespoon of the yellow sludge left, sticking to the corners.

He put his finger in the tin, wiping it clean, and put the finger in his mouth.

The taste was wretched. It was the taste of raw starch and metal. It was grainy, leaving a residue of grit between his teeth. It sat in his stomach like a stone, cold and heavy. It provided no warmth. It gave no pleasure. It was merely mass.

He looked at his hands. The skin was translucent, stretched tight over the tendons. He flexed his fingers. They moved slowly, like the limbs of a crushed insect.

He looked at the horizon. It was empty. The grey sky met the grey water in a seamless line of indifference.

They were five skeletons in a cedar box, floating on a desert of water. The excitement of the gale, the terror of the broach, the adrenaline of the near-miss, all of that was gone. This was the reality of the voyage. It was a slow, quiet erasure.

Halford licked the last of the potato starch from his thumb. He felt the cold wind cut through his sodden coat. He wrapped his arms around himself and leaned back against the tiller, staring at the tell-tales on the shroud.

"North by East," he whispered to the empty air.

He checked the compass. The needle swung lazily. He nudged the tiller with his foot. The boat responded, sluggish and heavy.

But the boat wasn't the only thing failing to answer the helm. The men were shutting down. As the sun dipped below the horizon, dragging the temperature down with it, the potato starch in their bellies turned into a cold, inert lump. It provided mass, but it offered no fire. The shivering started again, a violent, bone-rattling that threatened to shake the boat apart. Halford knew the signs. They were freezing to death from the inside out. They needed fuel. Not starch, but heat.

He looked at the locker under the stern sheets. There was one tin left. It wasn't food. It was light.

***

Halford jammed his knee against the tiller to hold the course, freeing his hands. He leaned forward, his joints popping with the dry, brittle sound of twigs snapping, and clawed at the locker latch. The iron was rusted shut, fused by weeks of salt spray. He took his knife, inserted the blade into the gap, and twisted. The hasp gave way with a screech of tormented metal that cut through the wind's moan like a shriek.

He dragged the tin out. It was a heavy, square canister, battered and streaked with corrosion, sloshing heavily as the boat rolled.

"What is it?" Francis whispered from the darkness of the bilge. His voice was barely a husk, a dry rustling of air. "More potatoes?"

"Better," Halford grunted.

He unscrewed the brass cap. The threads ground against the salt crust, resisting, then breaking free.

The smell wafted out, instantly filling the small, wet cockpit. It was not the smell of food. It was a thick, heavy scent, distinct from the sharp, fishy reek of the albatross or the rancid, fermented stink of the seal meat. This was the smell of pure, concentrated animal fat, rich and cloying, with an undertone of musk and the deep, pressure-crushed depths of the ocean. To a well-fed man in a San Francisco parlor, the odor of sperm oil was the smell of a lamp burning in the hallway. To a starving man in an open boat, it smelled of pure, sustenance.

"Oil," Halford announced, his voice rough. "Sperm oil. Five gallons of it. It's fat. It's heat."

He looked down into the black opening of the tin. The liquid inside was viscous, thickened by the cold into a sluggish syrup. He knew what it was. It was the rendered case matter of a sperm whale's head, the finest fuel on earth. It burned hot and bright in a lantern. It had to burn hot in a belly.

"Pass me a cup," Halford ordered.

Talbot stirred under the thwart. The Lieutenant pulled himself up to a sitting position, his movements jerky and uncoordinated, like a marionette with tangled strings. His eyes were dark hollows in a face that had lost all human softness.

"Oil, Coxswain?" Talbot asked, the words slurring. "We cannot drink lamp oil. It will scour us."

"We can if we want to see morning, sir," Halford replied. He didn't wait for permission. He tipped the heavy can. The oil flowed slowly, glugging out like molasses, coating the bottom of the tin cup with a golden, greasy sheen.

He held it out to the officer. "Drink it, sir. It'll coat the stomach. It'll stop the shivering."

Talbot looked at the cup. His hands, emerging from the sodden sleeves of his frock coat, were trembling so violently that the oil sloshed over the rim, coating his fingers in a slick, water-repellent film. He brought the cup to his lips. He hesitated. The smell flared his nostrils, a sudden intrusion of life and grease in a world of salt and sterility.

"Drink," Halford urged.

Talbot tipped his head back. He swallowed.

Halford watched the officer's throat work. The Adam's apple bobbed. Once. Twice. The oil was thick; it didn't splash down like water. It had to be swallowed with intention. It coated the tongue, the teeth, the esophagus.

Talbot lowered the cup. He gasped, a wet, rattling inhalation. He looked at Halford, his eyes wide with a sudden, desperate hope.

"It is... warm," Talbot whispered. "It feels warm going down."

"It's the life of the whale, sir," Halford said. "Pass it to Francis."

Talbot handed the cup to the Quartermaster. Francis didn't hesitate. He was past the point of squeamishness. He drank his measure with a desperate, animal focus, licking the rim of the cup to catch the last drops.

"Andrews. Muir." Halford called into the forward hatch.

There was no movement from the gloom.

"Drag them out, Peter," Halford said. "They take their ration or they die tonight."

Francis, fortified by the oil or perhaps just the command, crawled forward. He dragged Andrews by the collar. The man was a dead weight, moaning softly as his hips scraped the floorboards. Muir followed, crawling on his elbows, his legs dragging uselessly behind him.

They huddled in the cockpit, a pile of wet wool and shivering limbs. Halford poured the oil. He forced the cup between Muir's cracked lips.

"Swallow," Halford commanded.

Muir choked, coughed, and then swallowed.

For a long moment, there was silence in the boat. The wind whistled through the shrouds, the waves slapped against the hull, but inside the cockpit, there was a strange, suspended peace. The oil seemed to settle the boat. The heavy, musk-scented fat masked the smell of dysentery and decay that had plagued them for weeks.

Halford corked the tin. He felt a flicker of optimism. It was fuel. It was the highest grade of energy available to man. If they could metabolize this, they could last another week. They could make the islands.

Then, the sound of retching shattered the peace.

It started with Talbot. The Lieutenant doubled over, clutching his mid-section as if he had been stabbed. He let out a low groan that escalated into a violent, spasmodic heave.

"No," Halford whispered.

Talbot retched again. His body jackknifed. The oil, rejected by a stomach that had forgotten how to process fat, came up in a torrent. It was mixed with bile and the undigested grit of the desiccated potatoes. It splashed onto the floorboards, slick and glistening in the moonlight.

Halford stared at the golden smear sliding with the roll of the boat. It wasn't just a mess; it was theft. That oil was his blood, his heat, and the

Lieutenant had just spilt it like bilge water. A spike of pure, white-hot hatred pierced Halford's exhaustion. It was the food aggression of a starving dog watching a runt vomit up the kill. *Dead weight,* the voice hissed in his skull. *Just a dying mouth. A waste.* He looked at Talbot's heaving shoulders and felt a violent, electric impulse to kick him, to stomp the life out of him right there and save the rest of the fuel for the only man who could still burn it. He gripped the tiller until the wood groaned in his fist, strangling the scream that wanted to tear out of his throat.

"I... I cannot," Talbot gasped, wiping his mouth with a shaking hand. Spittle hung from his chin. "It will not stay."

The reaction was contagious. The smell of the regurgitated oil, sharper and more acidic than before, triggered Francis. The Quartermaster lunged for the gunwale, hanging his head over the side. He heaved, his back arching, his ribs threatening to punch through his skin.

"It's too rich," Francis choked out, spitting into the sea. "The stomach... it's too weak. It shuts down."

Halford watched them with a growing horror. Andrews was next, vomiting weakly onto his own legs, too exhausted to move. Muir simply let the fluid dribble from his mouth, his head lolling on his chest.

The floor of the cockpit was slick with it. It lay on the wood, separating from the water, shining with a mocking, golden luster.

The dysentery had stripped the lining of their guts; the starvation had atrophied the digestive muscles. They were like lamps with no wicks. Their bodies, whether refined like the Lieutenant's or simply ravaged by the fever like the others, went into shock at the sudden, violent introduction of rich fat. It was a cruel irony: the cure was too potent for the patient. But Halford was built of coarser stuff. His constitution was a cast-iron boiler, scarred by years of salt pork and bad whiskey, capable of burning any fuel thrown into the firebox, no matter how dirty.

"Try again," Halford urged, though his voice lacked the iron it had carried a moment ago. "Small sips, sir. You have to keep it down."

Talbot curled back into a ball on the wet wood, pulling his coat over his head. "No," he whispered from beneath the wool. "No more. Let me be."

Halford looked at the tin. He looked at the mess on the deck. The boat rolled, and the spilled oil sloshed, coating the bare feet of the dying men.

He looked at the horizon. It was black. There was no line between sea and sky, only a wall of cold neutrality. They were going to die here. Not from lack of supplies, but from the inability to use them. They were going to starve to death with five gallons of food sitting in the locker.

He uncorked the tin again. The smell hit him, heavy and cloying. His own stomach clenched, a warning spasm.

***

He lifted the heavy square tin to his lips. The brass rim was cold against his teeth, tasting of verdigris and salt. He tilted his head back.

The oil hit his tongue. It was not a liquid; it was a sludge. It coated the roof of his mouth, clinging to his gums with a tenacious, suffocating film. It tasted of deep pressure and ancient fat, a flavor so concentrated it bordered on metallic.

He forced his throat to open. He swallowed.

It was like swallowing warm candle wax. The grease clotted at the back of his throat, triggering a violent gag reflex that he had to fight down with a convulsive swallow. It coated his teeth, a thick, suffocating film. The bolus of fat slid down his esophagus, a slow, heavy weight moving through his chest. It struck the pit of his stomach like a dropped lead weight.

Halford lowered the can. He waited.

His body rebelled instantly. The nausea rose, a hot, acidic wave rushing up from his gut, demanding expulsion. His diaphragm spasmed. He clamped his jaw shut, grinding his teeth together until the jaw muscles popped. He breathed through his nose, short, sharp inhalations, forcing the bile back down.

Hold, he told himself. *You hold this.*

He gripped the gunwale with his free hand, his fingernails digging into the soft cedar. The boat pitched, sending his stomach rolling, but he locked his core. He treated his own digestion like a unruly sail that had to be sheeted home.

The spasm passed. The oil stayed down.

He took a breath. Then he lifted the can again.

He drank. Swallow after swallow. The grease lubricated his parched throat. It filled the hollow ache in his belly, replacing the vacuum with a dense, heavy solidity. He drank until the nausea was replaced by a feeling of immense, greasy satiety.

He wiped his mouth with the back of his hand, smearing the oil into his beard. He capped the tin and wedged it back into the locker, lashing it tight.

He sat still in the dark, listening to the wind hiss through the shrouds.

The reaction was almost chemical. Within twenty minutes, the violent shivering that had racked his frame for three days began to subside. The heat didn't come from the outside; it bloomed in his center.

He looked at his hands. The trembling had stopped. He flexed his fingers. The skin was still translucent, the tendons standing out like wire, but the grip was there. The weakness that had made his knees buckle was receding, replaced by a hard, mechanical endurance.

He looked down at the cockpit floor.

Talbot lay in a heap, his head resting on a coil of wet rope. The Lieutenant was fading. His breathing was shallow, a desperate, rattling gasp that barely seemed to fill his lungs. His face was a skull in the moonlight, the eyes sunk deep into the sockets, open but seeing nothing.

Francis was curled against the centerboard trunk, groaning softly with every roll of the boat. Andrews and Muir were silent in the hold.

They were dying. Their bodies were consuming themselves, burning the last of their muscle tissue to keep the heart beating. They had rejected the fuel, and now the fire was going out.

Halford felt a strange, cold distance from them. He was no longer one of them. They were men, fragile and failing. He was becoming something else. He was an boiler, fueled by the rendered fat of a leviathan, built to outlast the ocean.

He reached for the tiller. The wood felt solid in his hand. The boat yawed as a wave caught the quarter, but Halford corrected it instantly, his arm moving with a new, fluid strength.

"North by East," he said.

The wind picked up, singing in the rigging. Halford narrowed his eyes against the spray. He was alone now. The others were just cargo. He would sail this boat until the wood rotted or the land appeared, and he would do it on a belly full of grease.

Chapter 14

T he sound of the saw was a rhythmic scream that tore through the heavy afternoon heat. *Rasp-shriek. Rasp-shriek.* It was the only sound on the island that competed with the surf, a mechanical cry of agony that mirrored the physical torture of the men pulling the blade.

Captain Montgomery Sicard stood at the edge of the pit, his hands clasped behind his back, watching the sawdust settle on the shoulders of the man below.

It was January 3rd.

He did not need to consult the calendar in his tent to know the significance of the date. He carried the tally in his head, a number that grew heavier with each sunrise. Forty-six days.

It had been forty-six days since the gig had vanished through the western channel.

Sicard adjusted his stance, feeling the sand shift under his boots. He kept his face impassive, a mask of command that he wore like armor, but behind his eyes, the calculations were running cold and final.

Honolulu was fifteen hundred miles away. A boat like the gig, even sailing conservatively, should have made the crossing in twenty-five days. Allow five days for calms. Allow five days for the government bureaucracy to charter a rescue vessel. Allow five days for the return passage.

Forty days was the outside limit of optimism. Forty-six days was a verdict.

Sicard snapped the book shut. The period of waiting was over. The *Saginaw Junior* ceased to be a therapeutic exercise designed to stave off mutiny; she was now their only reality. The gig was a ghost, and if they did not finish the schooner before the provisions ran out, they would be ghosts alongside her.

They are gone, Sicard thought. The realization did not come with a surge of grief; he had no energy left for grief. It came with the dull, heavy thud of a hatch closing.

Talbot was dead. Halford, Francis, Andrews, Muir. They were all dead. Swamped in a gale, perhaps. Or starved in the doldrums, drifting until the thirst took them. He had sent them out, and the ocean had swallowed them without a belch.

He looked up at the horizon. It was a hard, blue line, unblemished by smoke or sail.

"Rest," Sicard ordered.

The sawing stopped instantly.

In the pit, the coal-heaver Lynch let go of the lower handle. He didn't climb out; he simply leaned his forehead against the massive oak timber, his chest heaving. He was naked to the waist, his ribs standing out like the hoops of a barrel, his skin burned to the color of mahogany and peeling in ragged strips.

Above him, the fireman handling the top of the saw straightened up, wiping sweat from his eyes with a forearm that looked like a knotted stick.

"Drink," Sicard said. "Mr. Hershberger, issue the water."

The men drank their ration, warm, metallic water from the condenser, with a reverence that was painful to watch. They swirled it in their mouths, wetting their cracked lips, before swallowing.

Sicard looked at the timber they were cutting. It was a piece of the *Saginaw's* keelson, a massive baulk of seasoned live oak that had survived the wreck. It was hard as iron, cured by salt water and decades of stress.

To build a boat on a beach with proper lumber is a difficult task. To build a forty-foot ocean-going schooner out of a shipwreck, using tools that were dulling by the hour, was a form of madness.

They were not just sawing wood; they were "ripping" it. Because the *Saginaw* had carried no spare planks, every board for the new boat's hull had to be sliced by hand from the heavy structural timbers of the wreck.

Sicard watched Lynch in the pit. The man was covered in a fine, beige powder. The dust mixed with his sweat to form a paste that coated his skin, clogging his pores.

"It is hard going, Captain," the Carpenter, Mr. Butterfield, said, stepping up beside Sicard. "The grain is twisted. And the fasteners... we hit a copper drift-bolt every three feet. It ruins the teeth."

Sicard looked at the men. The rest had been too short to heal, but long enough for the lethargy of the island to take hold. If they sat any longer, the heat would weld them to the sand.

"Back to the handle," Sicard commanded.

Lynch adjusted his grip on the lower bar, his calloused palms sliding against the sweat-slicked wood. Above him, the fireman took his stance. The saw groaned as they dragged the steel back into the narrow cut, the rhythmic screech of the ripping blade beginning anew.

A high-pitched spang pistol-whipped the air.

The saw blade buckled in the kerf, binding hard against the live oak, then sprang free with a shudder that vibrated through the handles.

The fireman on the top timber froze. He pulled the blade up, exposing the steel. A jagged gap marred the row of teeth where the metal had sheared against the hidden copper.

"She is stripped," Butterfield muttered, running his thumb over the ruin. "Three inches of teeth gone. That's the end of it."

"The end?" Sicard asked.

"We have no spare blades, Captain. The others are snapped or rusted through. We cannot rip planking with a smooth bar of iron."

The rhythm of the shipyard died. The hammers stopped ringing on the anvil. The adzes stopped chipping. The silence pressed down, heavy and suffocating, broken only by the rasp of the surf. The men stared at the broken tool as if it were a dead body.

"File it down," Sicard ordered. His voice was level, devoid of the panic that constricted his throat.

"Sir?"

"File the gap smooth. Cut new teeth into the metal. Make a jagged edge if you must, but make it cut."

"It will bind, sir. It will tear the wood to shreds. The friction will be double."

"Then pull harder," Sicard said. "We do not stop."

Lynch let go of the bottom handle. He didn't climb out. He simply folded, sliding down the side of the pit until he hit the sawdust. He sat there, his head hanging between his knees, his ribcage heaving with dry, sobbing breaths that had no tears left to lubricate them. He looked like a pile of discarded rags.

Butterfield looked at the broken tooth, then at the wreck, then at the Captain. The look said: We are done. Metal cannot cut iron.

"Sharpen the saw," Sicard replied, his voice level. "And keep cutting."

"The men are failing, sir. Lynch has the shakes. He can barely hold the handle."

Sicard turned to look at the Carpenter. Butterfield was gaunt, his eyes sunk deep in his skull, but he was still thinking like a craftsman. He was worried about the tool. Sicard was worried about the timeline.

"I cannot manufacture strength, Mr. Butterfield," Sicard said. "But I can manufacture purpose. If we stop, we die. Is that clear?"

"Aye, sir. Clear."

"Then sharpen the saw."

Sicard walked away, moving down the length of the keel that lay bedded in the sand. He paused at the garboard strake. The plank was sound, hewn from the *Saginaw's* own heart, but the face was ragged where the dull saw had wandered. Splinters bristled along the grain. It was strong enough to turn the sea, but it offended him. It looked wild. It looked like the work of desperate men.

"Mr. Butterfield," Sicard said, his voice cutting through the rasp of the files. "Have this timber planed."

The Carpenter straightened up, swaying slightly on his feet. He looked at the wood, then at the Captain. "Planed, sir? It will be underwater. The barnacles will not mind the grain."

"I mind the grain, sir," Sicard snapped. The objection sparked a flash of disproportionate anger. "We are building a schooner of the United States Navy, Mr. Butterfield, not a Polynesian canoe. Smooth it down".

Butterfield looked at the plank. To plane that hard, seasoned oak would cost a thousand strokes. It would cost a day of life for the man who pushed the tool. He looked at O'Neil, who was currently sitting in the sand, unable to lift a hammer.

"Aye, sir," Butterfield whispered, defeat heavy in his voice. "Smooth it down."

Sicard turned from the carpenter to survey the hull. The skeleton had vanished. In its place, a rough, wooden beast crouched in the sand. The planking gangs had driven themselves harder than the sawyers, closing in the hull with a desperation that ignored craftsmanship.

She was fully planked, but she was ugly. The strakes were uneven, marked by the dull teeth of the saw. Gaps between the boards yawned wide, waiting for oakum the men didn't have the strength to spin. Her stem rose proudly from the sand, a curved piece of oak that Sicard himself had helped to shape.

She was forty feet long. She was ugly, rough-hewn, and fastened with rusted iron. But she was substantial. She was large enough to carry the remaining eighty-eight men, if they packed themselves in like cargo.

Sicard ran his hand over a frame.

He felt a fierce, possessive pride in this ugly boat. She was his answer to the silence of the horizon. She was his refusal to accept the verdict of the forty-six days.

If the government would not come for them, if the gig had failed, then he would sail this scow to Hawaii himself. He would load his starving crew into her belly and command her across the ocean, or he would sink with her. There would be no dying in the sand.

Sicard turned back to the work, his resolve hardened.

***

A hundred yards away, Paymaster Read was making his slow ascent from the hospital tent, his boots sinking into the hot coral. He passed Dr. Frank, who sat on a nail keg, his Medical Journal splayed open on his knees. Read glanced at the wet ink. It was a terrifying counter-narrative to the Captain's log. Where Sicard recorded "duty" and "progress," Frank recorded rot.

Case 14: Vitality depressed. Scorbutic fungosity of the gums. Ancient cicatrices breaking down. Case 22: Profound prostration. Blood impoverished and watery.

Frank noticed the shadow across his page. He didn't look up; he just stared at the row of glass phials lined up on a crate: Opium, Quinine, Blue Mass. He picked up a bottle of laudanum, his hand trembling so violently the amber liquid foamed inside the glass.

"I have the entire Pharmacopoeia," Frank whispered, clutching the bottle. "But I have no remedy for starvation."

He dropped the bottle. It landed in the soft sand with a dull thud, unbroken. He pointed his quill toward the dark interior of the tent. The canvas trapped the heat, baking the air into a heavy, sour stew.

"Come and look, Paymaster."

Frank walked into the gloom. He knelt beside a sleeping marine and pulled back the dirty sheet covering the man's feet.

"Look at the heel."

Read leaned closer. The callus was gone. The raw pink flesh underneath had been gnawed away in a jagged circle, weeping clear fluid.

"The rats?" Read asked, his stomach turning.

"He didn't even wake up," Frank dropped the sheet and moved to the head of the cot. With a thumb stained yellow from iodine, he peeled back the marine's upper lip. The gums were a swollen, dark purple ridge, burying the teeth in dead flesh.

"It is the scurvy, Paymaster. It doesn't just dissolve the blood; it dissolves the will. The coast fever in Mexico hollowed them out months ago. It drank their reserves. Now this..."

Frank let the lip snap back into place. He wiped his hands on his trousers, as if trying to wipe off the contagion.

"Old wounds are opening. We are unspooling."

Read turned away, the taste of bile rising in his throat. He pushed through the canvas flap and stumbled out into the blinding white glare of the coral sand.

He took a breath of the trade wind, trying to clear the scent of decay from his nose. He fixed his eyes on the unfinished hull of the schooner, the only structure on the island that wasn't rotting, and forced his legs to move. He walked ten yards, putting the doctor's voice behind him, before the compulsion overtook him.

He ran his tongue over his gums. They felt soft, like wet velvet. He pushed against a molar. The tooth gave way without a sound, sliding out of the socket as easily as a seed from a ripe fruit. He spat it into his palm. It was white, with a long, yellow root that looked startlingly clean. There was no blood, only a thin, pink serum.

He stared at the object. It was a part of him. A piece of his skull. Yet there it lay in his hand, separate and inert, lighter than a piece of coral. A cold, quiet dread settled in his chest. It wasn't the pain that frightened him, there was no pain, it was the ease of it. The glue that held him together was dissolving, and he was simply falling apart.

He closed his fingers over the tooth, making a tight fist, hiding it from the glare of the sun. He couldn't drop it in the sand. He couldn't let the island have it. He shoved the fist into his pocket, keeping the bone close against his hip, and clamped his jaw shut, terrified that if he opened his mouth to speak, more of him would spill out.

He trudged toward the hull.

"Captain."

Sicard looked up. The Paymaster stood before him, ghostly, his uniform hanging on him like a shroud. He held the ration book, clutching it to his chest as if it were a bible

"Mr. Read," Sicard acknowledged.

"The inventory, sir," Read said, his voice a raspy whisper. "I have completed the weekly tally."

"And?"

"The albatross are leaving, sir. The colony is thinning out. We took only three birds yesterday."

Sicard nodded. He had noticed the silence in the scrub. The birds were migratory; they were following a calendar that did not care about the *Saginaw*.

"And the seals?"

"None seen on the north beach for two days. The hunting parties are ranging further, out to the sand spits on the reef, but the animals are wary. They dive as soon as they see us."

Sicard looked at the hull of the schooner. The math was tightening. The birds were leaving. The seals were wise. The salt pork was gone. The flour was a memory.

They were subsisting on "*Saginaw* belly", a distended, gas-filled mockery of fullness caused by the indigestible seal blubber and the sheer volume of water the men drank to quell the pangs.

"How long, Paymaster?" Sicard asked. "On the present ration of dried potato and what we can catch?"

Read hesitated. He looked at the ground, then at the Captain.

He choked back the report on the Surgeon. He could not bring himself to tell Sicard what he had witnessed in the stifling heat of the hospital tent. Read hesitated. He looked at the ground, then at the Captain. The memory of the purple, liquefying gums churned in his gut, sending a hot wash of nausea up his throat.

"February, sir. Perhaps mid-February. But the men... the men will be too weak to work long before the food runs out. The scurvy is loosening their teeth. The dysentery is taking the rest."

Sicard looked at Lynch, who was climbing back into the saw-pit. The man stumbled, caught himself on the timber, and slid down into the hole. He picked up the saw handle. He didn't complain. He just waited for the downstroke.

"February," Sicard repeated.

It was six weeks away.

"We must launch by the first of February," Sicard said. "Regardless of the state of the fitting out. If she floats, we sail."

"Sir, the sails are not even cut," Read said gently. "We have no canvas left. The sailmakers have exhausted every scrap of duck we salvaged from the wreck. As it stands, the schooner will be a monument, not a vessel."

"Then we sail under rags," Sicard snapped, a flash of the old quarterdeck steel cutting through his fatigue. "Find a way, Mr. Read. Use the men's spare frocks if you must. We are not fitting out a yacht, Mr. Read. We are building a life raft with a keel. We need a hull that keeps the water out and a rag to catch the wind. The rest is luxury."

He turned back to the shipyard. The activity was a slow-motion pantomime of industry. A gang of men was straightening nails on a coral anvil. *Clink. Clink. Clink.*

They worked with agonizing slowness. A man would lift the hammer, pause to breathe, strike, and pause again. They were operating on the very edge of metabolic failure.

Sicard stopped at the saw-pit. A fireman, a veteran of the Mobile Bay blockade, was leaning against the timber, clutching his left thigh. His trousers were dark with a wet, spreading stain that wasn't sweat.

"Report," Sicard ordered, pointing at the leg.

The man looked up, his eyes dull. He peeled back the sodden wool. There was no fresh cut, no splinter. There was only a long, jagged line of purple flesh, a shrapnel scar from '64, healed for six years. Now, it was unzipping. The grey, necrotic tissue was dissolving, the skin parting like wet paper to reveal the raw meat beneath. The body was cannibalizing its own history, melting down the binding agents of old scars to keep the heart beating.

The smell was distinct, sweet, copper-tinged, and rotten.

"Bind it," Sicard said, his voice tight. "And keep sawing."

Sicard watched a marine named O'Neil carrying a plank. He walked ten paces, stopped, swayed, and sat down in the sand. He didn't drop the wood; he just lowered himself and the burden together, as if his legs had simply ceased to receive instructions from his brain.

Sicard walked over to him.

"O'Neil."

The marine looked up. His eyes were glazed, the pupils pinpricks in the sun. "Sorry, Captain. Just... a moment."

"Take your time, O'Neil," Sicard said softly. "But don't lie down. If you lie down, you won't get up."

"Aye, sir. I'm just... the board is heavy today."

It was a one-inch pine plank. A child could have carried it.

Sicard reached down and took one end of the board. "Up," he said.

O'Neil struggled to his feet, shamed by the Captain's assistance. Together, they carried the plank to the hull.

Sicard let go and dusted his hands. He felt the weakness in his own arms, a trembling tremor in the triceps. He was starving too. He ate the same seal gut and drank the same warm water as the coal-heavers.

But he could not show it. He was the mainspring of the watch. If he wound down, the whole mechanism stopped.

He walked back to the saw-pit. The rhythm had resumed. *Rasp-shriek. Rasp-shriek.*

He looked at the pile of finished planks. It was growing, but agonizingly slowly. They needed hundreds of feet of sheathing.

A mile away on the reef, the wreck of the *Saginaw* was breaking up under the hammer-blows of the winter swells; the boiler had washed away and the paddle-shafts had collapsed, warning him that soon there would be no more timber to harvest.

He felt a sudden, crushing sense of isolation. He was the only one who truly understood the race they were running. The men thought they were building a boat to leave. Sicard knew they were building a boat to beat the grave.

Every shaving of wood that curled from the carpenter's plane was a minute bought from death.

He thought of Talbot. He pictured the gig sailing into Honolulu harbor, the flags flying, the cheers. He held onto that image for a second, letting it warm him.

Then he let it go. It was a fantasy. A dangerous one.

Talbot was gone. The empty horizon proved it. The silence of the last forty-six days proved it.

Sicard was alone. He was the commander of a sandbar and a skeleton crew.

He looked at the "*Saginaw Junior.*" She was ugly. She was rough. Her lines were distorted by the warped timber.

But she was real. She was here.

"Mr. Butterfield," Sicard called out.

"Sir."

"Double the gangs on the planking. I want the garboard strake fitted by retreat."

"We do not have the clamps, sir."

"Use wedges. Use levers. I don't care how you force the wood, just get it on the frames."

"Aye, sir."

"One more thing, Mr. Butterfield," Sicard added, his voice dropping so the men in the pit would not hear the tremor in it. "We must know. Before we commit to the tide, we must prove the physics."

He signaled the Boatswain. "All hands to the hull! Man the gunwales!"

The mobilization was not the snap to quarters of a drilled crew; it was a slow, painful resurrection. Men who had been dozing in the shade of the scrub struggled to rise, using their neighbors for leverage. Knees locked by scurvy cracked audibly. It took five minutes for the men to shuffle through the sand and surround the vessel. They looked like a press-gang of ghosts, starvelings in rags, their collarbones protruding against their skin like yokes.

They wedged their shoulders against the rough-hewn oak of the *Saginaw Junior*. They crowded the length of the hull, boots digging into the soft coral grit, trying to find purchase. They didn't need to launch her today; they just needed to break the static friction, to roll the keel even an inch along the ways to prove that their collective muscle mass still exceeded the drag of the sand.

"Heave!" Sicard commanded.

The men drove their legs into the ground. They groaned, a collective, ragged exhalation of effort. Knuckles whitened on the rail. Veins bulged in thin necks. They gave everything they had, burning the last caloric reserves of the seal meat in a single, desperate spasm of force.

The boat did not move. It did not shudder. It did not creak.

It sat on the rollers, an inert mass of tons, mocking the simple mathematics of their starvation. The men fell back, gasping, coughing up pink spittle. They stared at the hull. In that moment of stillness, the illusion broke. They weren't building a vessel; they were building a monument. They would never have the strength to push this thing into the water.

Sicard saw the terror rising in their eyes. He had to kill it.

"Very well," Sicard lied, his voice loud and steady. "She is heavy, but she will slide on the ways when they are greased. Carry on, Mr. Butterfield."

Sicard turned his back on the sea. He would not look at the horizon again today.

He walked toward his tent, his boots crunching on the coral. He would write in his log. He would record the day's progress. He would note the lack of birds.

***

In the public square of the camp, where the men gathered to scrape the last of the seal grease from their mess tins. Paymaster Read sat in the shadows of the provision tent, listening to the murmur of the voices. For weeks, the conversation had been a single, repetitive loop of speculation about the horizon. Tonight, the tense had changed.

The shift was subtle, a change in the wind that only a sailor would notice, but to George Read, it was as loud as a cannon shot.

"She'll need deeper bilges if we're to stow the water casks low," a fireman named O'Shea mumbled, picking at a callous on his palm. "If we stack 'em high, she'll be tender."

"Captain says we ballasting with coral rock," another voice replied from the darkness near the fire. "Tons of it. She'll stand up to a breeze."

"Aye. But where do we sleep? If the hold is full of rock and water, where do ninety men lay their heads?"

"On the deck, likely. Or we don't sleep. Watch and watch."

"And that's if she'll even take the ways," a voice muttered from the shadows. "We put the levers to her this afternoon and she didn't budge a hair. Five tons of seasoned oak bedded in the silt." "She'll slide," O'Connell said, his eyes fixed on the embers. "With enough seal oil rendered down to grease the timbers, she'll slip in like a shore-bird."

Read stopped his pen, the ink drying on the tip. He looked up.

For forty days, the talk had been exclusively external. *When the steamer comes. When Mr. Talbot returns. When the Navy sends a ship.* They had spoken of rescue as a passive event, a miracle that would arrive from the east to pluck them from the sand.

Now, the pronouns had shifted.

We. Us. The boat.

The *Saginaw Junior* was no longer a distraction or a busy-work project ordered by the officers to prevent mutiny. It had become the vessel of their reality.

The gig was dead.

No one said it aloud. To speak the words *Talbot is lost* would be a court-martial offense against hope, a crime against the fragile morale that held the camp together. They had stopped scanning the horizon with that desperate, frantic energy of the first month. Now, they looked at the saw-pit.

They had accepted their abandonment.

Read closed his ledger. The emotional weight of this acceptance was heavy, yet it brought a strange, grim clarity. The waiting was over. The acting had begun.

He crawled out of the tent and walked toward the fire. The night was cool, the trade wind cutting through his thin, patched coat.

A group of men sat around the embers of the cooking fire, not for warmth, but for the primitive comfort of the light. The flames served as the only wall against the grey tide of rats that swarmed the dunes, their dry, skittering footfalls audible just beyond the reach of the glow.

"She's under-canvassed," Boatswain's Mate O'Connell argued, drawing a line in the sand with a stick. "That mainmast is too short. She will be a slug in light airs. And we have not the cloth for a foresail, let alone a jib."

"Better a slug than a coffin," a coal-heaver retorted. "We ain't racing. We just need to get there."

"We need canvas," O'Connell insisted, his voice rising with a frantic edge. "We've got the spars, but the mother ship didn't leave us enough duck to clothe the men, let alone dress a schooner. Unless we want to row forty feet of oak to Kauai, we're at a standstill."

Read stepped into the circle of light. He had been listening to this same circular argument for three nights.

The conversation halted instantly. The men, trained by years of discipline, instinctively tried to scramble to their feet, though their starved limbs made the movement slow and painful.

"As you were," Read said quietly, raising a hand to stop them.

They settled back down, but the easy intimacy of the gripe session was gone. They watched him warily, their eyes hollow in the firelight. An officer was present; the mask of duty was back in place.

"You are concerned about the sail area, O'Connell?" Read asked.

"Aye, sir," O'Connell said, touching his forehead. "Mr. Butterfield has the spars, but the sail-locker is empty. We've used every scrap of duck for the tents and the men's trousers."

Read looked at the fire. He didn't offer false hope. He didn't tell them the gig might still return. He treated the problem with the seriousness of a supply requisition.

"The hammocks," Read said.

O'Connell frowned. "Sir?"

"We have ninety canvas hammocks," Read explained, his voice steady. "It is light cotton, yes, not proper sailcloth. But if you unpick the seams and double-stitch them flat... double thickness..."

O'Connell's eyes widened slightly. He looked at the fire, calculating. "It would take a lot of twine, sir."

"We make twine," a seaman ventured, emboldened by the officer's engagement. "From the signal halyards. We can pick 'em apart."

"Precisely," Read nodded. "It will be tedious work. But it will give us a suit of sails."

The change in their faces. It wasn't joy, there was no joy in the prospect of unstitching ninety hammocks with clumsy, starving fingers, but it was a solution. It was a task.

"I shall speak to the Captain," Read said formally. "If he approves, you may begin the work tomorrow."

"Thank you, sir," O'Connell said.

Read turned to leave. He paused for a moment, looking at the frame of the schooner rising from the sand in the moonlight. It looked primitive, almost prehistoric.

He wanted to ask them if they thought it would float. He wanted to ask them if they were afraid. But he was an officer. He could not share his fear.

"Carry on, men," Read said.

"Goodnight, sir."

He walked back toward his tent, his boots crunching on the coral. The rats were rustling in the scrub, a constant, chattering reminder of the island's hostility.

He felt a profound sense of isolation. He was with them, starving with them, rotting with them, yet separated by the invisible wall of his commission. But as he listened to the murmur of voices resuming behind him, focused now on the mechanics of stitching hammocks, he felt a grim satisfaction.

They weren't looking at the horizon anymore. They were looking at the work.

He crawled into his tent and lay down, pulling his coat over his shoulders. For the first time in forty days, he didn't dream of a steamer's smoke. He dreamed of the sound of a needle piercing canvas, over and over again.

Chapter 15

The silence of the doldrums was a deception. To Coxswain William Halford, the Pacific was a deafening cacophony of fresh water.

The ocean lapped against the cedar strakes of the gig, *slosh, plip, slosh,* but the sound did not register in his brain as the sea. In the broken architecture of his mind, it was the rhythmic squeak of an iron handle working a village pump. It was the heavy, glugging sound of dark ale pouring from a cask into a pewter mug. It was the rush of a river breaking over cold stones in a valley he had not seen in twenty years.

He opened his mouth to breathe. The air hit the back of his throat like a rasp file.

Thirst had become a structural failure of the anatomy. His tongue had ceased to be a muscle. It was a foreign object, a swollen wedge of dry felt that filled his oral cavity, pressing against the hard palate, blocking the airway. It felt too large for his skull.

He tried to swallow. The reflex fired, a spasmodic jerk of the throat muscles, but there was nothing to move. His saliva had transformed into a thick, white glue. It coated his teeth in a film that had to be hooked out with a finger to prevent suffocation.

The horizon jumped. The blue line of the water vibrated, bending into shapes that looked like trees, then waterfalls, then nothing.

"Unacceptable," a voice hissed. It was distinct, sharp, and terrifyingly lucid.

Halford turned his head. Lieutenant Talbot was sitting bolt upright, his spine stiffened by a phantom corset of duty. He was not looking at the sea; he was staring at his own wrist, where a salt-water boil had ulcerated into a black, gangrenous crater about the size of a coin.

"Your brightwork, Coxswain," Talbot murmured, his cracked lips shaping the words with a disappointed formality. "It is tarnished."

He reached out with his other hand, a skeletal claw, and began to scrub at the open sore. He wasn't scratching an itch; he was polishing a brass stanchion. The friction tore the necrotic flesh loose. Dark, thick blood welled up, sliding down his forearm like oil. Talbot didn't flinch. He rubbed harder, trying to buff the rot into a shine.

"Bear a hand with the holystone," Talbot ordered the empty air, his eyes fixed on the wound. "The Admiral is coming aboard at eight bells. We must be... spotless."

Halford stared at him.

Forward of the mast, Francis and Andrews were statues. They sat with their backs against the ribs of the hull, staring at their feet. They did not blink. Their biology had shut down. Their blood had thickened to sludge, making movement impossible; the heart simply could not pump the syrup fast enough to animate their limbs. They were waiting for the gears to stop.

"Water," someone rasped.

A jagged, animal sound broke the hallucination.

Halford looked down. James Muir was curled at his feet. The seaman pushed himself up on one elbow. His eyes were not fixed on the horizon or a phantom tea set. They were fixed on the sea.

The Pacific slid past the gunwale, inches away. To a healthy man, it was a blue desert. To a man dying of dehydration, the brain inverted the data. The salt mirror effect took hold.

Muir didn't see brine. He saw a mountain spring. He saw a cool, clear cistern. The water looked heavy and sweet. It beckoned with a logic that bypassed survival instincts and spoke directly to the dying cells.

Just a sip. Just to wet the lips.

Muir's hand dipped toward the surface. It was a trance-like movement, a slow, trembling reach for the forbidden. His fingers brushed the water. He cupped his palm.

"Don't," Halford tried to shout.

The sound that came out was a hideous, dry click. His vocal cords were paralyzed, glued together by the lack of moisture.

He forced his body to move. He uncoiled his leg, the joints popping like dry twigs. He kicked out.

His boot struck Muir's wrist with a dull, sickening thud. The blow was violent, born of panic and rage.

"No," Halford croaked, the word tearing the lining of his throat. "You drink that, you die. You go mad, Jimmy. And if you go mad, I'll throw you over."

Muir recoiled. He pulled his hand back, cradling it against his chest. He looked up at Halford. There was no anger in his eyes. There was only the confused, hurt look of a child denied a kindness. His lips were white, cracked into deep fissures that did not bleed because there was no fluid left to spare.

"It's... right there," Muir whispered. "Bill. It's right there."

"It's poison," Halford hissed. "It's death."

Muir stared at the water for a moment longer, a look of profound longing, then slumped back against the thwart. The energy required to argue was gone.

Halford leaned back against the tiller. He felt the madness scratching at the back of his own eyes. He wanted to drink it too. He wanted to bury his face in the sea and gulp until the burning stopped, even if it killed him. The temptation was a psychological urge, pulling his head toward the rail.

He wrenched his eyes away from the water, seeking something solid to anchor his mind, and stared at the starboard gunwale. The heat shimmered off the wood. As he watched, the grey, salt-bleached cedar began to change. The grain softened, swelling and turning a deep, roasted gold. It wasn't timber anymore. It was bread. A massive, crusty loaf of French bread, hot from the oven, the top varnished with melted butter that dripped down the side. The smell hit him instantly, a thick, intoxicating cloud of yeast and warm flour that drowned out the metallic reek of the bilge.

He didn't think. He didn't decide. His body simply obeyed the imperative of the famine. He leaned forward, unhinging his jaw like a wolf, and bit down hard on the rail.

Crunch.

There was no yield. His teeth scraped against the rock-hard wood, driving the loose roots deep into his scurvy-softened gums. A jolt of electric agony shot through his jaw, shattering the illusion. He recoiled with a cry, spitting splinters and blood onto the thwart. He stared at the wet, jagged teeth marks marring the gunwale. The smell of bread vanished, replaced by the dry, salty scent of the Pacific.

He closed his eyes, but the darkness was worse. In the dark, he saw glasses of ice water sweating on a table. Rain falling on the tin roof of a shed. The condenser on the island dripping, *plip, plip, plip*.

He forced his eyes open. He had to stay awake. If he slept, he might drink.

He looked at the locker. It was empty. The tins of spoiled beans were gone. The desiccated potatoes were gone. The oil was gone. There was nothing left to put in their mouths to simulate eating.

His mouth needed work. It needed something to chew, something to stimulate the salivary glands, or his throat would seal shut permanently.

He reached for his waist. His fingers fumbled with the buckle of his belt. The leather was stiff, cured with salt and tannins.

He pulled the belt free. He took his knife and sawed off a two-inch strip of the tough hide.

He put the leather in his mouth.

It tasted of sweat and old animal skin. It was hard as wood. He bit down. His loose teeth shifted in his gums, screaming with pain, but he kept biting. He chewed.

The mechanical action forced a tiny trickle of moisture into his mouth. It wasn't saliva; it was just the dampness of the leather, but it was enough to lubricate the tongue.

He sawed off another piece. He kicked Muir.

"Chew," Halford rasped, dropping the strip onto Muir's chest. "Chew it."

Muir picked it up. He put it in his mouth without looking at it.

Halford cut three more pieces. He crawled forward, dragging his body over the thwarts. He forced a piece between Talbot's teeth. The Lieutenant stopped polishing his wrist and began to gnaw, his eyes still fixed on the tarnished flesh as if waiting for the Admiral to inspect it.

He gave a piece to Francis. He gave a piece to Andrews.

They chewed in the dark. It was a rhythmic, dry grinding sound, the sound of five dying men trying to eat their own clothing. *Crunch. Grind. Swallow.*

The mechanical rhythm of the chewing lulled them into a stupor, dragging them down into a darkness that lasted hours or days. When consciousness returned, the hallucinations had receded, leaving only the flat, grey reality of the horizon.

***

The sun was setting on the twenty-ninth day, and William Halford knew it was likely the last sun they would see.

He sat in the stern sheets, his body wedged into the corner of the cockpit. He was no longer steering; he was simply holding the boat upright. The wind had dropped to a light breeze, and the gig rolled in the long, oily swell.

He looked at his hands. They were wasted claws, the skin stretched tight over the knuckles, covered in sea-boils that had ulcerated and turned black. He tried to make a fist. His fingers curled slowly, trembling with the effort.

He looked at the crew.

Talbot was a bundle of rags on the floorboards. The Lieutenant hadn't moved since dawn. His eyes were half-open, showing only the whites, and his breath came in shallow, intermittent hitches.

Francis and Andrews were in the hold. Halford assumed they were dead, until a low moan from Andrews proved that the suffering was still ongoing. Muir was curled at Halford's feet, his face pressed against the wood, waiting.

"Water," Muir rasped. It wasn't a request; it was a reflex.

"None," Halford croaked.

Halford closed his eyes. He felt a strange, light-headed detachment. The pain of the hunger had faded, replaced by a floating sensation. He wasn't afraid. He was just tired. He wanted to let go of the tiller. He wanted to lie down next to Muir and sleep.

Thump.

A sound made him open his eyes.

It was a soft, heavy impact on the gunwale, just inches from his face.

Halford turned his head slowly.

A bird had landed on the rail. It was a Booby, a large, stupid sea-bird with a long beak and webbed feet. It sat there, preening its feathers, looking at the boat with a mild, unconcerned curiosity.

Halford stared. He didn't see feathers or flight. It was meat. It was blood. It was water.

He froze. His heart, which had been beating a slow, funeral rhythm, gave a violent kick.

He didn't look at the bird directly. He watched it from the corner of his eye. He knew that if he moved too fast, if he startled it, their lives would fly away with it.

He slowly, agonizingly slowly, lifted his hand from the tiller.

The bird stopped preening. It cocked its head, looking at the movement.

Halford stopped. He held his breath. His lungs burned.

The bird looked away, turning its attention to a louse in its wing.

Halford moved again. His hand hovered in the air, a trembling claw. He focused every ounce of his remaining will into his fingers. Do not shake. Do not miss.

He lunged.

His hand closed around the bird's legs.

The creature squawked, a harsh, shocked cry, and flapped its wings, beating the air frantically. It pecked at Halford's wrist, the beak tearing the thin skin.

Halford didn't feel it. He yanked the bird down, pinning it against the gunwale with his chest. He grabbed its neck with his other hand and twisted.

There was a crunch of hollow bones. The flapping stopped.

Halford fell back into the cockpit, clutching the warm, limp body to his chest. He laughed. It was a dry, hacking sound that sounded like a cough.

"Grub!" Halford yelled, his voice cracking. "Boys! Grub!"

The word penetrated the fog of the dying men. Talbot stirred. Muir lifted his head.

"What?" Talbot whispered.

"A bird," Halford gasped. "I caught a bird."

He didn't wait for a knife. He tore the feathers off with his teeth, spitting the down into the bilge. He ripped the skin open with his fingernails. The smell of the carcass hit him, a pungent, gamey reek of fish oil and warm bowels.

"Here," Halford said. He tore a strip of the dark, red breast meat from the bone. It came away with a wet tearing sound. He shoved it into Talbot's mouth.

"Eat it. Swallow it."

Talbot chewed weakly. The meat was tough, stringy, and slick with the bird's natural oils. It required effort to masticate, but the Lieutenant forced his jaw to work. He swallowed. A flush of color touched his grey cheeks almost instantly.

Halford fed them like nestlings. He gave a piece to Muir. He crawled to the hatch and pushed meat into the mouths of Francis and Andrews.

They ate the flesh raw. They ate the liver, which burst in their mouths with a metallic tang. They ate the heart.

"The blood," Halford said. "Don't waste the blood."

He held the carcass over Talbot's mouth. The reek of the warm, copper-scented fluid flooded Halford's sinuses, stinging his glands with violent salivation. *Mine.* The word wasn't a thought; it was a command from the starving animal living in his gut. His hand locked. He stared down at the Lieutenant's parted, scabbed lips and felt a surge of hatred so pure it burned like acid. Why pour this life into a corpse? Talbot was a leaking bucket; the blood would just run through him and be wasted on the floorboards. Halford wanted to shove the officer's head back against the thwart and drink until the bird was dry. It took a supreme, shuddering effort of will to break the paralysis, the discipline of the Coxswain wrestling the wolf into submission.

He squeezed the carcass. The Lieutenant drank the warm liquid. It stained his teeth dark red.

"It is... sweet," Talbot murmured, wiping a smear of gore from his chin. "It is the sweetest morsel I ever tasted."

Halford kept the legs and the wing tips for himself. He crunched the bones, sucking out the marrow. He ate the brain, digging it out of the skull with his finger. It was soft, warm, and tasted of salt and life.

He sat back against the thwart, licking the grease from his fingers. The bird was gone. It had been a large creature, but divided among five starving men, it was gone in minutes.

But it had bought them time.

The sun vanished. The twilight deepened into night, and the cold returned.

Halford resumed his post at the tiller. The initial rush of the protein faded, replaced by the heavy work of digestion. His stomach churned, unused to the solid food, cramping around the raw meat.

Hours passed. The moon rose, a sliver of white bone in the black sky.

Halford watched the stars wheel overhead. The hunger began to creep back, a dull ache behind the ribs. The bird had been a reprieve, not a cure. It was a teasing taste of life that only highlighted how close they were to death.

He wondered if it was a cruel joke. To give them just enough strength to realize they were dying, but not enough to save them.

"Is that it?" he whispered to the ocean. "Is that all you got?"

He dozed, his chin hitting his chest, then jerked awake as the boat lurched.

Slap.

Something wet hit him in the face.

Halford recoiled, his hand flying to his cheek. He thought it was a wave, or perhaps a rat from the island that had somehow stowed away and survived.

Slap. Slap-slap.

The sound echoed from the bow. It was the sound of wet flesh hitting canvas.

Halford dragged himself up to look.

On the foredeck, gleaming silver in the moonlight, lay a school of flying fish. They had leaped out of a wave, attracted by the white canvas of the new deck, and stranded themselves.

"Providence," Halford breathed. He stared at them for a moment, unable to process the sheer statistical impossibility of it. First the bird. Now this.

He wondered if it was a mercy or a malice. To feed a dying man just enough to keep his eyes open for the end seemed less like a gift from the Almighty and more like a dark joke from the deep. Was the ocean saving them, or was it simply winding the clock of their agony a few turns tighter?

He scrambled forward. There were five of them. Small, perhaps six inches long, but they were solid muscle.

The fish slapping wetly against his palms. Five fish. Five men. The arithmetic was simple, but the hunger twisted it into a hateful logic. He looked at the cockpit, judging the wreckage of his crew. Talbot was a heap of wet wool, his lips moving in silent, useless prayer while the boat drifted. Francis was a corpse that hadn't cooled yet, a husk that had forgotten how to sew a sail. Andrews lay in the bilge, moaning with a rhythm that grated on Halford's last nerve, just noise consuming air. And Muir... the man who had fought like a tiger on the beach was now a whimpering child, curled up and waiting to be fed.

Why refuel broken machines? the voice whispered. It was a cold, rational question. If he gave them this protein, it would just vanish into the hollow of their sickness. If he ate it, if he ate two, or three, he could feel the heat return to his hands. He could steer. He could live.

He stared at them, hating them for their shivering, hating them for the "gurgle" of life that refused to go out. They were parasites now, rotting ballast dragging him down. He brought a fish to his mouth, his jaw trembling, ready to bite the head off and swallow the rest before they could ask for their share. It wasn't conscience that stopped him; it was the habit of the roster. Five men. Five rations.

He gathered them up. He didn't bother bringing them back to the cockpit. He tossed one to each man.

"Eat," Halford commanded. "Bones and all. Don't leave a scale."

He bit into his own fish. It was still alive, twitching in his hand. The scales crunched between his teeth like eggshells. The flesh was firm, cold, and tasted of the clean, deep salt of the Pacific. It was the opposite of the warm, gamey bird; it was cool and refreshing.

He ate it all. He wiped his mouth.

The shivering had stopped. The boat felt steady.

Halford took the tiller. He checked the compass.

"North by East," he said.

It was a bitter course to steer. Every instinct in his gut screamed that the warm, green islands lay to the southeast, back over his right shoulder. Sailing north, deeper into the cold dark, felt like sailing off the edge of the map. But he knew the trade winds. He knew you couldn't fight them; you had to outflank them. They had spent twenty-nine days sailing the wrong way just to get a fighting chance at the right place.

He felt a strange, terrifying certainty. This was it. The bird. The fish. This was the last meal. The ocean had given them one final burst of energy, one last chance to make the turn south.

If they didn't sight the islands in twenty-four hours, they would never sight them.

He looked at the stars appearing through the breaks in the clouds. He found Polaris. He found the pointers.

He steered the gig into the night, fueled by blood and raw fish, driving her toward the invisible line where the world began again.

***

That invisible threshold solidified with the coming light, becoming hard, black, and waiting for them in the dawn.

The darkness was thinning, turning from obsidian to a bruised, dirty grey. William Halford sat at the tiller, his eyes crusted with salt, staring at the horizon line that was slowly separating itself from the water.

He was hallucinating. He had to be.

For thirty days, the horizon had been a perfect, unbroken circle. It was the definition of their prison. A man could look for a thousand years and see nothing but the curvature of the earth and the heave of the swell.

But now, there was a flaw in the circle.

A shape.

It was a dark, jagged lump, sitting low on the water off the starboard bow. It was solid. It wasn't a cloud. It didn't move. It sat there, obstinate and heavy.

Halford blinked. He rubbed his eyes with his knuckles, digging them in until he saw stars. He looked again.

The lump was still there. It had hard edges. It had mass. It was black against the grey.

"Land," Halford whispered. The word got stuck in his throat, a dry croak that sounded like tearing paper.

He cleared his throat. He swallowed the phantom taste of the flying fish. He tried again.

"Land ho!"

The scream tore out of him, raw and ragged, stripping the lining of his throat. "Land ho! Land ho!"

The bodies on the floorboards stirred. It was a slow, painful resurrection. Talbot pushed himself up on one elbow, the movement shaking the boat. Francis lifted his head from the bilge, his hair matted to his skull.

"What?" Talbot rasped. "What is it, Halford?"

"Land, sir!" Halford pointed, his hand shaking violently, the tiller vibrating against his hip. "Dead ahead! Look at it! It's solid!"

Talbot dragged himself up to the gunwale. He hooked his chin over the rail, too weak to hold his head up. He stared into the grey light.

The shape was clearer now. It was a rock. A massive, solitary sentinel rising from the sea, detached from the main island but heralding it.

"Kawaihua Rock," Talbot breathed.

The name broke him. The discipline of the officer, the rigid facade of command he had maintained through the dysentery and the starvation, shattered. Tears began to stream down his face, cutting tracks through the grime and salt on his cheeks.

"It is Kauai," Talbot wept. "We have found it."

"Kauai," Francis whispered. He didn't try to stand. He just laid his head on the gunwale and sobbed, his shoulders shaking with the force of his release. "Oh, God. Oh, God."

The hatch cover slid back. Andrews and Muir crawled out. They looked like corpses animated by a dark magic, their joints swollen, their skin hanging in folds. They pulled themselves up to look.

The sun was breaking the horizon now, washing the world in color. And the color was green.

Beyond the rock, the loom of a larger island was becoming visible. A massive, verdant mountain rose into the clouds. It wasn't just land; it was life. It was earth, trees, fresh water. It was the end of the blue purgatory.

"It's green," Andrews whispered. "I can see the green," Andrews repeated, his voice cracking with the effort of speech. Beside him, Muir stirred. The sight of the peaks rising from the sea acted as a stimulant, a jolt of electricity to a central nervous system that had been shutting down for days. Life, or the promise of it, forced focus back into his vacant eyes.

"We're saved," Muir said. His voice was a dry, wonder-filled rattle. He reached out a hand as if to touch the distant peak. "We ain't going to die, Bill. We ain't going to die."

Halford felt a sob build in his own chest, a pressure so immense it threatened to crack his ribs. It hit him in the stomach, harder than the hunger. They had done it. They had taken a twenty-two-foot boat across fifteen hundred miles of the worst ocean on earth, and they had hit the target.

He swallowed it down. He couldn't break. Not yet. The boat was still moving. The ocean was still deep.

"Trim the sheet!" Halford barked, channeling the emotion into action. "Get the canvas on her! We have to make the bay before the wind shifts!"

The men moved. They were weak, starving, and sick, but they moved with a frantic, joyous energy. They hauled on the halyards. They cleated the sheets. The gig surged forward, picking up the scent of the land.

"Pray," Talbot said. "We must give thanks."

He bowed his head. The others followed, their hands clasped over the gunwales, their faces buried in the wood.

Halford kept his eyes on the rock. He muttered the words, *Amen, Amen,* but his hands never left the tiller.

He watched the swell. The waves were changing shape as they felt the bottom. They were getting steeper, sharper. The rhythmic roll of the deep ocean was being replaced by the chaotic, nervous energy of the coast.

They were saved, yes. But they had to land. And between the boat and the green mountains lay a line of white water that was roaring like a train.

"We ain't there yet, boys," Halford whispered to himself. "We ain't there yet."

***

The day proved him right. It passed in a torturous, slow-motion unveiling of the coast. The green slopes grew distinct, turning from a painted backdrop into a rugged reality of cliffs and rain-soaked valleys. But as the sun dipped below the peaks, casting long shadows over the water, the wind that had carried them across the ocean turned traitor. It grew fitful, shifting to the head, breathing out from the land as if the island were exhaling against them.

The smell was the first thing to cross the water.

It was the scent of wet earth.

It was composed of rotting vegetation, damp soil, woodsmoke, and the sweet, heavy perfume of flowers he couldn't name. After thirty-one days of breathing nothing but sterile salt air and the reek of their own decay, the complexity of the odor was overwhelming. It made his head swim. It made his stomach cramp with a sudden, violent hunger that had nothing to do with food.

"Do you smell it?" Francis whispered from the bilge. "It smells like a garden. It smells like rain."

"Hanalei," Talbot croaked. The Lieutenant was propped up against the washboard, his eyes fixed on the dark opening of the bay ahead. "The chart... it opens to the north. We must be close."

Halford looked at the water. It was black now, the sun having dropped behind the island's spine. The massive shadow of the land loomed over them, blocking out the stars.

The gig lay dead in the water. The sails hung limp, heavy with the evening dew. The land breeze, cool and damp, was pushing gently against the bow, holding them off.

"Out oars," Halford ordered.

There was a rustle of movement. It was the sound of skeletons moving inside their clothes. Andrews and Muir dragged themselves up to the thwarts. They didn't speak. They simply reached for the heavy ash sweeps.

"Pull," Halford said.

The oars dipped. *Splash*. They bit the water.

Halford leaned into his own oar. He told his arms to pull. He sent the command down the nerves, screaming for power.

His muscles fluttered. They had no glycogen, no fiber, no mass. They were just strings. He pulled, but there was no leverage. The oar felt like it weighed a ton.

"Together," Halford gasped. "Stroke."

The men pulled. The gig moved, inching forward against the light breeze.

Stroke.

A groan escaped Andrews. The oar slipped from his hand, clattering against the gunwale.

"I... I can't," Andrews wept. "There's nothing left, Bill. My hands... they won't hold."

Halford looked at the distance. The mouth of the bay was perhaps two miles away. In a fair wind, it was twenty minutes. Rowing, in this condition, it was an eternity.

He looked at the water swirling past the hull. The current and the land breeze were pushing them back.

"Keep pulling!" Halford snarled, fear spiking in his chest. "You want to die here? You want to die smelling the dirt?"

He hauled on his oar again, ignoring the tearing sensation in his shoulders. He rowed with his bones.

"Lights," Talbot whispered.

Halford looked up.

On the shore, in the darkness of the bay, a light flickered. Then another. Orange pinpricks against the black velvet of the mountains.

Fires.

They were cooking fires. People were there. They were eating poi, or fish, or roast pork. They were sitting on dry ground, warm and safe.

"They are right there," Francis sobbed, his oar trailing uselessly in the water. "We can hail them. Shout. Maybe they'll hear us."

"Too far," Halford said. "Sound won't carry against the wind."

He stood up, bracing his knees against the thwart to keep from falling. He looked at the entrance to the bay. It was a dark maw. He couldn't see the reef. He couldn't see the surf line.

But he could hear it.

It was a low, rhythmic rumble, a bass note that vibrated in the hull planks. It wasn't the clean crash of the open ocean waves; it was the confused, angry roar of water meeting rock.

"We can't make it rowing," Halford said, sinking back down. "We don't have the beef."

Talbot slumped against the coaming. The Lieutenant was wrapped in his greatcoat, shivering violently despite the mild air. He looked at the lights, then at the dark water, then at his hands.

"We cannot risk the reef in the dark," Talbot said. His voice was faint, but the decision was firm. "We are too weak to handle the boat if she strikes. We would drown in the surf."

"We're drifting," Halford warned. "The current is setting us west."

"We will heave to," Talbot ordered. "We will wait for daylight. When the sun rises, we will run in with the sea breeze. We will be fresh."

"Fresh," Halford muttered under his breath. There was no fresh left in them. Every hour they waited was an hour the cold ate into their remaining heat.

But he knew the Lieutenant was right. Entering a strange harbor at night, in a boat that couldn't make way against the current, was suicide. The reef would chew them up before they ever felt the sand.

"Aye" Halford said. "We wait."

They brought the boat about. Halford rigged a makeshift sea anchor using the oars lashed together, hoping it would hold their head to the swell better than the lost drag.

The gig swung heavily, settling into the trough.

The silence of the ocean returned, but it was different now. It wasn't the empty silence of the deep. It was filled with the taunting noises of the land.

Halford sat in the stern, his coat pulled tight around his neck. He listened.

A dog barked.

It was a sharp, clear sound, carrying over the water. A domestic dog, guarding a house.

"Did you hear that?" Muir whispered. "A dog."

"I heard it," Halford said.

He closed his eyes. He could imagine the dog. He could imagine the house. He could imagine the people sleeping inside.

The lights on the shore winked out, one by one, as the fires died down or the people went to bed. The island went dark.

Halford checked the drift. They were moving slowly to the west, sliding along the coast.

Below them, the sound of the surf grew louder. It changed pitch. It wasn't the dull roar of a sandy beach anymore. It was a sharp, cracking thunder.

Kalihi Kai. He didn't know the name of the place, but he knew the sound of shallow water.

"The swell is picking up," Halford noted.

The boat lifted, a long, slow heave, and then dropped. The period between the waves was shortening. They were feeling the bottom.

"We're getting too close," Halford said to Talbot. "We should pull out. Get some sea room."

"We have no strength to pull," Talbot murmured without opening his eyes. "Let her drift. The current will carry us past the point."

Halford gripped the gunwale. He didn't like it. He felt the hair on his arms standing up. The ocean felt different here. It felt nervous. Agitated.

The water around the boat was black, but occasionally, a patch of foam would glow with phosphorescence, a ghostly green light that illuminated the dark shapes of the reef below.

He looked at the others. They were asleep, or unconscious. The sound of the dog barking had been a lullaby, promising that the end was near.

But Halford couldn't sleep. The sound of the breakers was a pressure in his ears. It sounded like a train coming down a track, heavy and unstoppable.

Boom.

A wave broke somewhere in the dark, close. Too close.

Halford peered into the gloom. A white line stretched across the darkness to leeward.

"Breakers," he whispered.

He looked at the makeshift sea anchor. The line was slack. They were drifting faster than he thought.

He unwrapped his legs from the thwart. He tried to flex his fingers. They were stiff, cold claws.

He needed to be ready. He didn't know what for, but the wary instinct that had kept him alive through the gales and the starvation was screaming at him now.

This wasn't a harbor. This was a trap.

Halford looked at the white line of the surf.

"Daylight," Halford whispered to the black water. "If we live that long."

He tightened his grip on the gunwale and waited for the ocean to make its move.

Part 3

THE PRICE OF RESCUE

Chapter 16

The sound changed. It ceased to be a roar and became a vibration that rattled the teeth in William Halford's jaw. It was a low, percussive thudding, the sound of millions of tons of water being arrested by solid rock.

Halford stared into the gloom. The horizon had vanished. The world had shrunk to the twenty-two feet of the gig and the patch of black water immediately surrounding her.

"We are in the draw," Halford said. His voice was flat, stripped of panic by the sheer inevitability of the moment.

Talbot did not answer. The Lieutenant sat slumped against the coaming, his head bowing with the roll of the boat.

The boat rose. It was not the rhythmic, rolling lift of the deep ocean swell. It was a sharp, jerking ascent. The water beneath them felt nervous, agitated. The gig shivered, her timbers groaning as the pressure gradients shifted around the hull.

They were in the impact zone.

Halford unshipped the rudder. It was useless now. In the surf, a rudder was a liability; the first breaker would snap it off and likely take the stern post with it. He grabbed a steering oar, a heavy ash sweep, and jammed it into the stern notch.

He stood up. His legs trembled, weak from thirty-one days of atrophy, but he locked his knees against the thwart. He needed leverage.

"Wake up!" Halford roared. "Francis! Andrews! Stand by!"

Francis stirred in the bilge. He lifted a hand, a feeble gesture of acknowledgment, but he did not rise. He couldn't. The dysentery had hollowed him out until he was little more than wet wool and bone. Andrews made no sound at all.

A wave passed under them. It was a silent, oily hummock of water, moving fast. It lifted the gig, hurried her forward for ten yards, and then dropped her into the trough behind it.

Halford watched it go. The back of the wave rear up as it hit the reef shallow ahead. It stood tall, a wall of black obsidian, and then shattered. The explosion of phosphorescent spume illuminated the night with a ghostly glare.

We are too close.

He looked astern. The dark was impenetrable, but he could feel the presence of the next set. The ocean breathes in sets. One, two, three. Then a lull.

They were in the lull.

"Mr. Talbot," Halford said, reaching down and shaking the officer's shoulder. "Sir. You must wake up. We are in the surf."

Talbot raised his head. His eyes were glassy, reflecting the starlight. He looked at Halford, then at the white turmoil to leeward.

"Keep her head to it, Coxswain," Talbot whispered.

"I'm trying."

Halford leaned on the steering oar, fighting to keep the bow pointed into the incoming darkness. The current was ripping at the keel, trying to turn them broadside. If they broached, they died.

The water around the boat began to hiss. It was the sound of air being squeezed out of the ocean.

Halford looked up.

It was coming.

A shadow blotted out the stars. A wall of water, steeper and higher than anything they had seen in the open ocean. It didn't have a slope; it had a face.

It rose out of the deep water, feeling the drag of the reef, and stood up. It grew taller, sucking the water out of the trough in front of it, dropping the gig into a hole.

Halford looked up at the crest. It was curling. A line of white foam, glowing green with bioluminescence, was beginning to feather the lip.

"Look out, Mr. Talbot!" Halford screamed. "Catch hold of the rail!"

He dropped the oar. He didn't try to steer. There was no steering this.

He grabbed the gunwale with both hands, his fingers digging into the wood until the nails tore. He braced his feet against the frame. He took a breath, sucking the damp air into his lungs, holding it.

The wave broke.

It didn't hit the boat; it fell on the boat.

A concussion that blew out Halford's eardrums. He felt the water smash into his back, a solid mass that crushed him against the thwart. The stern was kicked skyward with a violence that snapped Halford's head back. She didn't roll; she tripped. The bow buried itself deep in the trough, sticking fast in the dead water like a spade hitting rock, while the ocean heaved the tail of the boat straight up toward the stars.

Halford was no longer sitting; he was falling upward. The kick of the stern launched him forward, hurling him through the spray. For a terrible, suspended second, he was looking down into the cockpit. Francis clawing uselessly at the slick cedar planks, sliding helplessly down the vertical deck into the black throat of the forward hold. Talbot jammed against the coaming, his eyes wide and white, frozen by the crushing weight of the water pinning him to the wood.

Then the boat went over.

It was a somersault. The gig flipped backward, end over end.

Halford was underwater.

He was no longer a man; he was a piece of debris. The turbulence spun him, twisted him, hammered him against the bottom.

He felt the coral graze his shoulder, a sharp, tearing pain. Sand and grit blasted his face, scouring the skin.

He didn't know which way was up. The world was a churning washing machine of foam and noise.

He held his breath. His lungs screamed for air. The instinct to inhale was a panic in his brain, a red light flashing behind his eyes.

Not yet, he told himself. *Not yet.*

He felt a rope tangle around his leg. He kicked wildly, freeing himself. Something hard struck his hip, the boat, or a rock.

The turbulence began to fade. The wave was passing.

He clawed at the water, swimming for the surface. It felt like swimming through molasses. His sodden coat weighed fifty pounds. His boots were lead anchors dragging him down.

He broke the surface.

He gasped, sucking in a mixture of air and spray. He coughed, retching salt water.

"Talbot!" he shouted. "Francis!"

The roar of the surf swallowed his voice.

He treaded water, blinking the salt from his eyes. He was in the trough. The water was a cauldron of white foam, fizzing like champagne.

A dark shape bobbed nearby. The boat.

She was upside down, her keel pointing at the sky. The bottom was slick and wet, shining in the starlight.

Halford swam toward it. His arms felt heavy, useless. He kicked, his boots driving him forward inches at a time.

He reached the hull. He grabbed the keel strip. The wood was slippery, but he dug his fingers in. He pulled himself up, draping his torso over the bottom of the boat.

He vomited. Sea water and bile poured out of him, splashing onto the planks.

He looked around.

A dark shape was clinging to the stern, ten feet away. It was Talbot.

The Lieutenant was submerged to his chest, his arms wrapped around the rudder post. He was weighed down by his heavy officer's frock coat, the sodden wool dragging him down like a lead anchor.

"Mr. Talbot!" Halford gasped, reaching out a hand. "Hold on!"

Talbot looked at him. His face was calm, drained of all terror. He was "much exhausted," his reserves utterly spent by the thirty-one days of command. The chaos of the surf seemed to recede from the officer's face, leaving a terrifying, serene clarity. He looked at Halford's outstretched hand, scarred and claw-like, offering salvation. Then he looked down at his own chest, at the heavy, waterlogged wool buttoned to his chin. The frock coat, the very emblem of his rank and duty, had become a lead casing. To grab that hand would be to drag the Coxswain down into the dark with him. Their eyes met one last time, the rough sailor and the Christian gentleman, and in that silent exchange, the command was passed.

He neither spoke nor struggled. He simply uncurled his fingers and sank, slipping beneath the black water without a thrash or a cry, pulled down by the weight of the clothes that had been his only protection against the cold.

"No!" Halford screamed. He lunged toward the spot, but the water had already closed over the officer's head.

The trough was empty. There was only the white foam and the black water.

"Francis? Andrews?"

The silence that answered him was heavier than the roar of the breakers.

They were gone.

Francis, weak from the dysentery, hadn't stood a chance. The wave had taken him, washed him out of the bilge, and driven him into the reef. Andrews, too. They had drowned instantly, their lungs filling with the Pacific before they even knew they were underwater.

Halford felt a cold sickness in his gut. He was alone.

He looked at the shore. He could see the white line of the beach, perhaps two hundred yards away. It looked like a mile.

"Muir?" he called out, without hope.

A sound came from the other side of the hull. A cough. A splash.

"Bill?"

It was a gurgle, faint and terrified.

Halford dragged himself further up the hull. He looked over the curve of the bilge.

Muir was there. He was clinging to the gunwale, his body submerged, only his head above water. His eyes were wide, staring at nothing. He was muttering to himself, a low, frantic babble of nonsense.

"My head," Muir mumbled. "The rock. The black rock."

"Hold on, Jimmy," Halford said. "I have you."

Halford reached down. He grabbed Muir's collar. He tried to pull him up, but the man was dead weight. And the boat was unstable. It rolled in the chop, threatening to slide Halford back into the sea.

Then a low, sucking sound. The water was drawing back. The ocean was taking a breath.

Halford looked seaward.

The next wave was coming.

It was bigger than the first. It was a towering shadow, blotting out the sky. It was gathering itself, piling up on the reef, getting ready to finish the job.

"Hold on!" Halford screamed.

He jammed his fingers under the keel strip. He buried his face against the wet wood.

The wave hit.

It hit the capsized boat with the force of a sledgehammer.

The hull became a projectile. It was lifted, thrown, and spun.

Halford was ripped from his hold. He was airborne. He hit the water hard.

This time, there was no swimming. The wave owned him. It drove him down, grinding him into the sand. He felt his knee twist, a sharp pop of cartilage. He felt the sand forced into his ears, his nose, his throat.

He tumbled. He rolled. He was a rag doll in a gale.

He hit something hard. The boat.

The gunwale slammed into his chest, cracking a rib. He grabbed it. It was a reflex, a spasm of the hand. He locked his fingers onto the wood.

The wave dragged the boat and Halford together, scraping them across the coral heads. It was a grinder. A meat grinder.

Halford held on. He didn't know why. It would be easier to let go. It would be easier to open his mouth and let the water in. The pain was too much.

But his hand wouldn't open. It was a claw, fused to the wood.

The wave spent its energy. It rushed up the beach, a chaotic flood of foam and debris.

Halford felt the sand under his knees.

He was not swimming. He was crawling.

The water receded, sucking at his legs, trying to drag him back.

He dug his fingers into the sand. He hauled himself forward.

He coughed, expelling a pint of water. He couldn't breathe. His chest was on fire.

He looked up.

He was on the beach.

The sand was wet and cold. The air smelled of seaweed and death.

He rolled onto his back. He stared up at the sky. The stars were still there.

He was alive.

He sat up, groaning as his cracked rib shifted. He looked at the surf.

The boat was washing back and forth in the shallows, a broken, battered carcass.

"Muir?" Halford whispered.

He saw a dark shape in the foam. A bundle of clothes.

He stood up. His legs buckled. He fell. He crawled.

He reached the shape. It was Muir.

He was lying face down in the sand, the water washing over his head.

Halford grabbed him by the belt. He pulled. He dragged the man up the beach, away from the reach of the sea.

Muir was heavy. He was limp.

Halford collapsed next to him. He put his ear to Muir's chest.

A heartbeat. Faint. Fluttering. But there.

"You made it, Jimmy," Halford rasped. "You made it."

He looked back at the surf. He looked for the others. He scanned the white water for Talbot, for Francis, for Andrews.

There was nothing.

Just the white foam, hissing on the sand. Just the black water, rolling in, set after set.

They were gone.

Halford lay back on the sand. He closed his eyes. He felt the earth solid beneath him. It wasn't moving. It wasn't pitching. It was still.

He began to shake. Not the shivering of the cold, but the shaking of a man who has walked out of a grave.

He wept. He cried without sound, the tears mixing with the salt water on his face.

The breakers roared, a ceaseless, percussion that shook the sand beneath his cheek.

Chapter 17

Exhaustion, heavy and black as the water that had swallowed his shipmates, finally pulled Halford under. He did not sleep; he simply ceased to exist for a time, his consciousness extinguished by the overload of trauma. He lay splayed on the wet sand, a piece of wreckage among the driftwood, while the earth turned slowly toward the sun.

The sun cleared the green ridge of the mountains. It pierced William Halford's eyelids with a sharp, blinding gold, dragging him back from the void of unconsciousness not with warmth, but with an accusation.

He gasped, a sudden, jagged intake of breath that sent a spasm of agony through his chest. His ribs, cracked against the gunwale in the surf, ground together like broken crockery. He tried to sit up, but his body refused the command. He was stiff, his joints locked by the cold and the salt, his muscles seized into hard knots of cramp. He felt as though he had been beaten with iron bars and left for dead.

He blinked, forcing his eyelids apart. They were crusted shut with dried brine and sand. He rubbed them with a knuckle that was raw and bleeding.

The world flooded in. It was bright. Cruelly, impossibly bright.

He was lying on a crescent of white sand. To his left, the ocean was a flat, turquoise expanse, innocent and calm, breaking gently on the reef that had murdered them five hours ago. The water sparkled under the morning sun, hiding its violence under a veneer of tropical beauty.

To his right, the green cliffs of Kauai rose sheer and majestic, topped with mist. It was paradise. It was the vision they had dreamed of for thirty-one days in the bilge of the gig. The smell of it, the rich, rotting scent of wet earth, ironwood needles, and flowers, was thick in his throat, choking him with its richness.

Halford rolled onto his side. The movement made the world spin. The ground felt wrong. It was solid. It didn't pitch. It didn't roll. The stability was nauseating, a vertigo of stillness after a month of constant motion.

He spat out a mouthful of sand. His tongue felt like a piece of dry leather.

"Muir?"

The name was a dry croak, barely audible over the hiss of the surf.

James Muir was lying exactly where Halford had dragged him in the dark. He was ten feet away, face up, his arms flung out in a posture of total surrender. His legs were twisted in the sand, half-buried by the drift of the wind.

"Jimmy?"

Halford tried to stand, but his legs were useless dead weights. He crawled. He dug his elbows into the sand, dragging his hips forward inches at a time. The friction set fire to the sores on his knees, but he didn't stop. He was a crab scuttling across the beach, fueled by a desperate, terrifying hope.

He reached Muir. He reached out a hand, a hand that was white, puckered, and covered in the black ulcers of salt-water boils, and touched Muir's cheek.

It was cold.

It was not the surface cold of the night air or the sea water. It was the deep, clay-like cold of meat that has ceased to be life. It was the temperature of an object.

Muir's face was dark, almost purple. The blood had settled under the skin, bruising him from the inside out, a testament to the suffocation and the battering of the surf. His eyes were open, clouded with sand, staring fixedly at the blue sky he had fought so hard to see.

"No," Halford whispered. "No, Jimmy."

He put his ear to Muir's chest, pressing his head against the wet wool of the shirt. He listened for the flutter he had heard in the night, the faint bird-wing beat of a heart holding on.

Silence.

There was only the sound of the wind in the ironwood trees and the distant crash of the reef.

Muir was gone. He had made it to the land. He had touched the sand. He had breathed the air of Kauai. And then his heart, pushed beyond its limit by the thirty-one days of starvation and the final shock of the wreck, had simply stopped. He had died within feet of salvation.

Halford sat back on his heels. He looked at the dead man. A fly landed on Muir's open eye. Muir didn't blink.

"You made it, though," Halford said, his voice cracking, tears cutting fresh tracks through the salt crust on his face. "You beat the ocean, Jimmy. You died dry."

He turned his head, scanning the tide line. The wreckage of the gig was scattered along the beach like the bones of a bird picked clean by a predator. Planks of cedar, splintered and twisted, lay in heaps. The mast was snapped in two, the jagged ends pale against the dark wood. The white canvas of the sails, which Peter Francis had sewn with such care on the island, was buried in the sand, looking like shrouds waiting for bodies.

And then he saw it.

It lay near the water's edge, half-buried in a tangle of seaweed, gleaming dully in the sun.

The tin box.

It was battered, scratched by the coral, dents hammered into its sides, but it was intact. The solder held. Inside that box were the despatches. The orders from Captain Sicard. The bill of exchange. The list of the eighty-eight men waiting on the reef at Ocean Island.

Halford stared at it. It looked like a piece of trash, a discarded biscuit tin. But it was the reason they had died.

He looked at the empty beach. The sand stretched away in both directions, pristine and white, unmarked by any footprints but his own.

He scanned the surf line. He looked for a black coat. He looked for a hand raised in the swell. He looked for the grey hair of Peter Francis or the broad shoulders of John Andrews.

There were no bodies. The ocean had kept them.

Talbot. Francis. Andrews. They were gone, erased as if they had never existed. The sea had swallowed them whole, taking them down into the coral caves of the reef, leaving Halford alone on the stage.

He was the only one.

The realization hit him with more force than the wave that had capsized the boat. It was a crushing, suffocating weight that pressed the air from his lungs.

Why me?

The question rang in his head. He was the unvarnished sailor. He wasn't the pious officer like Talbot, who had prayed every morning. He wasn't the quiet, skilled professional like Francis. He was just Halford. The man who drank the oil. The man who ate the bird. The man who had bullied and cursed them into staying alive.

Why had the ocean spit him out and swallowed the rest? Was it the oil? Was it the sheer, stubborn refusal to let go of the tiller? Or was it just luck, the roll of the dice in a chaotic universe?

He looked at his own body. He was a ruin. His clothes were shredded rags, stiff with salt, hanging off a frame that was nothing but bone and sinew. His skin was a landscape of pathology. The "sea boils" on his legs and arms had ulcerated, eating deep into the flesh, turning black and gangrenous. His legs were covered in bruises that were turning purple, yellow, and green. He smelled of rot and sickness.

He felt the pain now. It came rushing in as the shock wore off, a tidal wave of agony. Every nerve ending was screaming. His cracked rib grated with every breath. His stomach, empty of the oil and the fish, was cramping violently, demanding fuel he didn't have.

But he couldn't stay here. He couldn't die on the beach next to Muir. That would make the sacrifice meaningless. The tin box was useless if it stayed in the sand.

He tried to stand. He pushed himself up. His knees buckled instantly, and he fell face forward. He grit his teeth, tasting the sand.

He tried again. He got to his knees. He swayed like a drunkard, the world tilting on its axis. He planted one foot. Then the other.

He stood.

He was unsteady, trembling like a new foal, but he was upright.

He had to move. He had to find help.

He shuffled over to the tin box. He bent down, a movement that made his head swim, and picked it up. Leaden with the weight of the lives it represented. He tucked it under his arm, pressing it against his broken rib.

He looked at Muir one last time. The flies were gathering on the dead man's face. Halford reached out and brushed them away. He closed Muir's eyes, smoothing the lids down with his thumb.

"I'll send them for you, Jimmy," Halford promised, his voice a whisper. "I won't leave you here. You're coming home."

He turned away from the sea. He turned his back on the beautiful, murderous ocean.

He looked inland. Beyond the beach, the land rose into a dense, green tangle of trees. A path, or what looked like one, cutting through the brush. And in the distance, curling up into the blue sky, was a thin wisp of grey smoke.

A morning fire. Coffee. Warmth. People.

He took a step. His leg dragged, heavy and numb. He took another, his boot scraping against the sand.

The will to walk was not enough to sustain the machinery of his legs. He managed a hundred yards, dragging his ruined knee through the drift, before the pain overcame the adrenaline. The world tilted on its axis, the green trees spinning into the blue sky. He collapsed near a clump of pandanus trees, the tin box pressed under his chest, and waited for the blackness to take him again.

Halford didn't hear them approach. The roar of the surf in his ears masked the sound of footsteps on the sand, and his consciousness had retreated to a small, dark room inside his skull.

He was lying on his side, watching a line of ants crawl over the lid of the tin box. He tried to brush them away, to protect the Captain's orders, but his hand was too heavy to lift.

"Auwe!"

The voice was soft, shocked, and distinctly human.

Halford jerked his head up. The movement sent a spike of white-hot fire through his neck.

Two figures were standing over him. A man and a woman. They were Hawaiians, dressed in simple cotton clothes against the backdrop of the rugged coast. The man was tall, with a broad, kind face and dark eyes that were currently wide with horror. The woman had her hand over her mouth, staring at Halford's ulcerated legs.

They looked like giants. They looked like angels sent to judge him.

"Help," Halford whispered. The word was a rasp of sandpaper. "Shipwreck."

The man dropped to his knees instantly. He didn't recoil from the smell of rot and sickness that clung to Halford, the stench of dysentery, old sweat, and gangrenous sores. He reached out and touched Halford's shoulder, a touch so gentle it felt like a benediction.

"You are safe," the man said in halting English. "We help."

This was Peter Nowlien. The woman was Mrs. Julia Bindt. Halford didn't know their names yet, but he knew their nature immediately.

Nowlien looked at the tin box Halford was clutching to his ribs. He gently pried Halford's fingers loose, one by one. "I take," he said. "Safe."

He handed the box to the woman. Then he turned his full attention to Halford's body. The cracked rib, the purple bruises blooming like storm clouds under the skin, the black sores eating into the wrists.

He looked at the right leg. The trousers were shredded, revealing the knee. It was swollen to the size of a melon, the skin tight and shiny, purple with pooled blood.

"Broken?" Nowlien asked, hovering his hand over the joint but careful not to touch it.

"Twisted," Halford grit out. "Surf."

Nowlien nodded. He signaled to the woman, speaking a few rapid words in Hawaiian. She nodded, her eyes filled with tears, and ran ahead toward the smoke.

Nowlien turned back. He slid his arms under Halford, one beneath the knees, avoiding the injury, and one behind the back. He lifted.

Halford braced himself for the agony, clenching his jaw until his teeth creaked, but Nowlien was strong. He lifted Halford as if he were a child, cradling him against his chest to minimize the movement.

"Julia," Nowlien said. "Water. Bed."

They carried him up the beach, away from the sound of the killing surf. The roar of the breakers began to fade, replaced by the rustle of wind in the ironwood trees and the chatter of birds that weren't scavengers.

They moved into the shade of the grove. The air here was cool and smelled of charcoal and roasting taro, a domestic scent that made Halford dizzy with memory.

They brought him to a small house. A simple structure of wood and thatch, but to Halford, the solid floorboards and the dry roof looked like the finest architecture on earth.

They laid him on a bed. A real bed. With a quilt.

Halford sank into the softness. His spine, curved against the hard wood of the gig for thirty-one days, uncoiled with a series of wet pops. The mattress absorbed his weight, holding him, comforting him.

Mrs. Bindt returned with a bowl of water and a cloth. She began to wash him. She wiped the salt crust from his face, cleaning the sand from his eyes and ears. The water was warm.

She washed the sores on his arms, dabbing them with a tenderness that made Halford want to weep again. She didn't flinch at the sight of the necrotic flesh. She cleaned it, anointed it with a salve that smelled of herbs, and bound the worst of the ulcers with clean strips of white cloth.

She bound his knee tight, stabilizing the joint.

Then came the food.

It wasn't raw bird, tearing at his loose teeth with stringy resistance. It wasn't the slick, nauseating coating of sperm oil. It wasn't the green, moldy paste of rotten beans.

It was poi. A bowl of thick, purple paste, pounded from the root of the taro. And fish. Cooked fish.

Nowlien held the bowl. He dipped his fingers into the poi, gathering a viscous dollop, and held them to Halford's cracked lips.

"Eat," Nowlien said.

Halford opened his mouth. The poi hit his tongue like a cool compress on a burn. It was smooth, dense, and possessed a faint, fermented sourness that woke his salivary glands from their month-long coma. It required no chewing, a mercy for his scurvy-loosened teeth. It simply slid down his throat, a heavy, liquid velvet that coated the raw, ulcerated lining of his stomach like a balm. It didn't taste like the sea; it tasted of the wet earth, of deep rain valleys and black mud.

Then, the fish. Nowlien fed him a piece of the white flesh. It was warm. It fell apart on his tongue, flaky and tender, releasing a savory steam that filled his sinuses. It was seasoned not with the bitter brine of the ocean, but with the deliberate, measured salt of a kitchen. It didn't taste like the struggle of the hunt; it tasted of the patience of the cook. It tasted of home.

He looked at the two faces hovering over him. They were filled with a profound, simple compassion. There was no judgment, no question of rank or duty. They didn't ask for his name or his ship. They saw a broken man, and they were fixing him.

This was the first human kindness Halford had experienced in months. On the island, everything had been a transaction of survival, rations measured, labor exchanged, discipline enforced. On the boat, it had been a shared agony, a brotherhood of suffering.

The guilt surged back, sharp and sudden. He was eating. He was warm. And Talbot was washing back and forth in the surf a mile away.

"The others," Halford whispered, grabbing Nowlien's wrist with his good hand. "On the beach. Muir. He's dead."

"We know," Nowlien said softly, covering Halford's hand with his own. "We find him. We take care."

"And the despatches," Halford said, his eyes darting to the tin box sitting on the table across the room. "The Sheriff. I must see the Sheriff. Men... waiting."

"Rest now," Mrs. Bindt said, smoothing the matted hair back from his forehead. "Sheriff come. Doctor come. You rest."

Halford let his head fall back against the pillow. The pain in his leg was a dull throb now, muffled by the bandage and the comfort of the bed.

He looked at the ceiling. It was solid. It didn't move. The shadows didn't pitch and roll.

He closed his eyes. For the first time since leaving Ocean Island, he wasn't listening for the sound of water rushing into the bilge. He wasn't waiting for the tiller to kick in his hand. He was listening to the low murmur of Hawaiian voices, and the sound of wind in the trees.

Sleep claimed him for an hour, perhaps two, a black, dreamless void that did nothing to repair the damage to his body but allowed his mind to reset. When he woke, the light in the room had changed, slanting in through the open door in long, dusty beams. The silence of the house was broken by the heavy tread of boots on the wooden floorboards. Authority had arrived.

Halford pushed himself up on his elbows. The movement cost him. His joints had seized during the nap, cementing into a rigid architecture of pain. His knee was a throbbing melon of heat beneath the bandages, and his cracked rib caught his breath with every inhalation.

A man stood in the doorway. He was white, dressed in a dark coat that seemed too heavy for the tropical air, holding a hat in his hands. He had the look of a man who was accustomed to giving orders, but his expression was softened by the sight of the wreckage in the bed.

"I am Samuel Wilcox," the man said quietly. "Sheriff of Kauai."

Halford tried to swing his legs over the edge of the bed. He needed to stand. He needed to report.

"Easy, man," Wilcox said, stepping forward and raising a hand. "Stay where you are. You have done enough moving for one lifetime."

"The despatches," Halford rasped. His voice was stronger now, lubricated by the poi and the water, but it still sounded like gravel sliding down a chute. "The tin box."

"Mrs. Bindt has given it to me," Wilcox said. He pointed to the small table where the battered biscuit tin sat. It looked absurdly mundane, a piece of rusted trash sitting on a lace doily.

"It contains the orders," Halford said, falling back into the cadence of the quarterdeck. "From Lieutenant Commander Sicard. Commanding the USS *Saginaw*. Wrecked on Ocean Island. October 29th."

Wilcox nodded slowly, absorbing the information. "Ocean Island. That is... a great distance."

"Fifteen hundred miles," Halford said. "Thirty-one days out."

"And the rest of the crew?"

"Eighty-eight men," Halford said. The number felt heavy in his mouth. "They are on the reef. They have food for two months. Maybe less. They are starving, sir. You must send a vessel. A fast vessel. A steamer."

"We will send word to Honolulu immediately," Wilcox promised. "The King is there. The American Minister. They will send a ship."

Halford let his head drop back against the pillow. The mission was done. The circuit was closed. The tin box was in the hands of the law.

"There is one more thing," Wilcox said gently. "The natives... they have been searching the beach."

Halford went still. He stared at the ceiling beams.

"They found them?"

"We found two," Wilcox said. "One washed up in the driftwood near the point."

"Talbot? The officer?"

"He is in uniform. A frock coat."

"That is him," Halford whispered. "Lieutenant Talbot."

"And the seaman," Wilcox continued gently. "Where you said you left him."

"Muir. James Muir."

"We are bringing them up. We will prepare them for burial here. In the churchyard."

"I want to see them."

"Man, you can barely lift your head."

"I want to see them," Halford repeated. It wasn't a request. It was the final duty of the Coxswain. He had brought them this far; he would see them into the ground.

It took two men to get him into the cart. The ride to the village was a blur of green trees and pain, the wooden wheels jolting over the rutted track. Halford sat propped up against the sideboards, his ruined leg stretched out before him, watching the lush, verdant world of Kauai roll by. It was too green. It was too alive. It felt indecently vibrant compared to the gray world of the gig.

They brought him to a shed near the church. The bodies were laid out on planks, covered with canvas sheets.

The air smelled of wet earth and flowers, but underneath it was the faint, unmistakable tang of the sea.

"Show me," Halford said.

Wilcox pulled back the first sheet.

It was Talbot.

The Lieutenant was unrecognizable. The ocean had not been kind to him. He had been rolled across the reef for hours, battered against the sharp coral heads. His face was bruised and blackened, a mask of purple trauma. His clothes, the heavy woolens that had dragged him down, were shredded rags clinging to a broken frame.

But his hands were folded on his chest. Someone had done that. Someone had tried to give him back his dignity.

Halford looked at the officer who had prayed every morning, who had navigated them through the gale with a toy sextant, who had drunk the oil and vomited it up. He looked small now.

"He was a good man," Halford said. The words felt inadequate, small stones dropped into a deep well. "He held on. He held on as long as he could."

Wilcox moved to the second plank.

Muir looked peaceful by comparison. He had died on the sand, not in the grinder of the surf. His face was dark with congested blood, but his features were intact. He looked like he was sleeping a heavy, dreamless sleep.

"And the others?" Halford asked. "Francis? Andrews?"

"Nothing," Wilcox said. "The current off the point is strong. It sweeps out to sea."

"They are gone, then," Halford said. "Drifting."

He looked at the two dead men. Why was his heart still beating? Why was his chest rising and falling while theirs were still? He was the roughest of them, the least educated, the hardest. Maybe that was why. The ocean couldn't digest him.

"Bury them," Halford said. "Bury them deep. So the water can't get them."

The funeral was held the next afternoon. It rained. A soft, warm tropical rain that hissed in the trees and turned the red earth to mud.

Halford sat in a chair by the open graves, unable to stand. He wore a borrowed coat that was too big for his emaciated frame. His leg was propped on a stool.

A small crowd had gathered. The Hawaiians from the village stood in respectful silence, the women wearing dark dresses, the men with their heads bowed. They didn't know the dead men, but they knew the sea. They understood the price of the voyage.

The minister read the service. The words drifted in and out of Halford's consciousness. *Ashes to ashes, dust to dust.*

He looked at the coffins. They were simple boxes of rough-hewn wood.

Inside one was the man who had commanded the expedition. Inside the other was the man who had fought for his place on the boat.

Halford remembered the wrestling match on the sand at Ocean Island. Muir pinning Dougherty. *I'm your man, Mr. Talbot.*

He had been the man. He had pulled his oar until his hands bled. He had bailed until he couldn't stand. And he had made it to the beach.

"Rest easy, Jimmy," Halford whispered.

The first clods of wet earth hit the wood with a hollow thud. *Thump. Thump.*

It sounded like the waves hitting the hull of the gig.

Halford closed his eyes. He saw the white water curling over the stern. He felt the cold weight of the ocean pressing him down.

He opened his eyes. The grave was filling up. The red earth was covering the wood.

He was alone.

He looked up at the green mountains of Kauai, disappearing into the mist. He thought of the eighty-eight men back on the sandbar, staring at the horizon, counting their tablespoons of flour.

They didn't know yet. They didn't know that Talbot was dead. They didn't know that the price of their rescue had been paid in full.

Halford gripped the arms of the chair. He felt the strength coiling deep inside him, the reserve that had kept him alive when the others faded.

He would go back. He would get on a ship, and he would go back to that cursed reef. He would see the *Saginaw* crew taken off.

Because he was the witness. He was the only one who carried the story of the thirty-one days. If he stopped, the story stopped.

"I am here," he said to the rain. "I am still here."

Wilcox put a hand on his shoulder. "Come, Mr. Halford. It is done."

Halford nodded. He let them help him up. He turned his back on the fresh mounds of earth and limped toward the waiting cart, leaving his shipmates to the eternal silence of the land.

Chapter 18

The *Wainona* rounded Diamond Head just as the sun began to bleed into the sea. To the starboard lay Honolulu, a sprawling grid of gaslight and dust nestled at the foot of the Koolau mountains. It was the metropolis of the Pacific, a city of whalers, missionaries, sugar barons, and kings.

On this particular evening, it was a city in the throes of celebration.

William Halford stood at the rail of the schooner. He wore a suit of clothes borrowed from the Sheriff of Kauai, the fabric hanging loosely on his frame. He gripped the shroud with a hand that was little more than clawed bone wrapped in parchment skin.

The harbor was a forest of masts. American whalers, their try-works scrubbed clean for the holiday, lay at anchor alongside merchant brigs from China and inter-island steamers. The air smelled of coal smoke, horse manure, roasting pork, and the sweet, cloying scent of jasmine.

It was the smell of life. It made Halford's stomach clench.

The *Wainona* ghosted toward the wharf. The sounds of the city drifted across the water, the rattle of carriage wheels, the bark of dogs, the distant, brassy notes of a band playing a carol.

Halford didn't hear music. He heard the ticking of a clock.

Every minute spent docking, every minute spent fumbling with lines, was a minute subtracted from the lives of the men on Ocean Island.

"Get me ashore," Halford rasped to the schooner's captain. "I must find the Minister."

The gangplank rattled down. Halford didn't wait for assistance. He limped down the wood, leaning heavily on a crude cane. The tin box was tucked tight under his arm, reclaimed from the Sheriff before boarding.

His ruined knee locked and popped with every step, sending a spike of nausea through his gut. He hit the dock. The ground was hard, stable, and indifferent.

He began to walk.

The streets of Honolulu were crowded. Kanakas in bright shirts, sailors in liberty blues, and American businessmen in white linen suits jostled for space on the banquettes. They were laughing. They were shouting greetings. They were drunk on the holiday spirit.

Halford moved through them like a stone moving through a stream.

He was a specter. His face was a mask of black sores and peeling skin. His eyes, sunk deep into the dark caverns of his skull, burned with a terrifying, singular intensity.

People stepped back as he passed. The laughter died in his wake. A woman in a silk dress recoiled, pulling her skirts away from him as if he were a leper.

He didn't see them. He saw only the destination. The United States Legation.

He stumbled. A hand reached out to steady him, a merchant sailor, smelling of rum.

"Easy there, mate. You look like you've seen a ghost."

"I am a ghost," Halford croaked. He shook the hand off. "Where is the Minister? Where is Pierce?"

"The Minister? It's Christmas Eve, man. He'll be at dinner."

"Where?"

"Government House, likely. Or his quarters."

Halford pushed past him. He dragged his leg over the cobblestones. The pain was a distant, white noise, drowned out by the roar of his own pulse.

He found the building. The flag of the United States hung limp from the pole in the evening calm. There were lights in the windows.

Halford climbed the steps. He didn't knock. He pushed the heavy koa-wood doors open and stumbled into the foyer.

A clerk looked up from a desk, his mouth opening in shock. "Here now! What is this? You can't..."

"Minister Pierce," Halford said. "Get him."

"The Minister is occupied. You cannot just barge in here looking like..."

Halford slammed the tin box onto the desk. The sound echoed like a gunshot in the quiet hall.

"The USS *Saginaw*," Halford said. "Wrecked. Ocean Island. October 29th."

The clerk froze. The color drained from his face. The name of the ship was known; she was overdue. Rumors had been circulating for weeks.

"God in heaven," the clerk whispered.

"Get him," Halford repeated. "Now."

The clerk scrambled out of his chair and ran down the hallway.

Halford leaned against the desk. His legs were trembling uncontrollably. The room swam. The gaslights blurred into streaks of yellow fire. He felt the floor tilting, pitching like the deck of the gig.

Hold on, he told himself. *Delivery.*

He turned his head, seeking relief from the hissing light. A stranger was standing in the alcove, watching him.

It was a scarecrow, a thing of blackened, peeling skin stretched tight over a skull that seemed too large for the neck. The beard was a matted tangle of salt and grease, stiff as wire. The eyes were gone, replaced by two feverish coals burning at the bottom of deep, shadowed sockets. The lips were drawn back from the teeth in a rictus of permanent thirst, exposing gums that were purple and swollen.

Halford flinched. He stepped back to let the savage pass. The savage stepped back. He raised a hand to ward it off, and the claw facing him rose in perfect, terrifying unison. He wasn't looking at another man; he was looking into a heavy gilt frame. The monster didn't move. The monster was him.

Door hinges creaked. Rapid footsteps.

Henry A. Peirce, the United States Minister to Hawaii, appeared. He was a man of dignity, dressed for a holiday dinner, a napkin still clutched in his hand. He stopped dead when he saw the figure in his hallway.

The emaciation. The gangrenous ulcers on the wrists. The eyes of a man who had watched his friends die.

"I am Minister Peirce," he said, his voice hushed.

Halford straightened. He tried to salute, but his arm wouldn't obey. He gestured to the tin box.

"Coxswain William Halford," he said. "Sole survivor of the gig. Captain Sicard sends his compliments. And his orders."

Peirce reached for the box. His hands shook as he fumbled with the latch. He opened it. He pulled out the packet of oilskin-wrapped papers. He tore them open.

He read the first line. Then he looked up at Halford.

"Ninety-three men?" Peirce asked.

"Eighty-eight now," Halford corrected. "Five in the gig. Four dead. One here."

"And provisions?"

"One quarter rations. Two months ago. They are starving, sir."

Peirce turned to the clerk. The shock on his face was replaced instantly by the hard mask of crisis.

"Go to the King," Peirce ordered. "Find him. Interrupt his dinner. Tell him the *Saginaw* is lost. Tell him we need a ship. Tonight."

"Yes, sir." The clerk ran.

Peirce looked back at Halford. "Sit down, man. Before you fall down."

Halford sank into a chair. The leather creaked. It was soft.

"You came from Ocean Island?" Peirce asked, scanning the letter again, as if he couldn't believe the geography. "In a boat?"

"In the gig. Thirty-one days."

"Alone?"

"With Lieutenant Talbot. And three men." Halford swallowed. The memory of the surf at Kalihi Kai rose up, a black wave in his mind. "The surf took them. At Kauai. Yesterday."

Peirce lowered the paper. He looked at Halford with a mixture of horror and reverence.

"You sailed fifteen hundred miles," Peirce murmured. "And they died at the landing?"

"Aye."

The words spilled through the Consulate's open doors and surged into the midday heat. They caught in the streets of Honolulu, jumping from mouth to mouth faster than the trade wind.

The Saginaw is lost.

A boat came.

One man alive.

They are starving on the reef.

The holiday dissolved. The music stopped in the taverns. The dinner parties paused, forks suspended halfway to mouths. The city of Honolulu, built by sailors and sustained by the sea, understood the language of the wreck.

Men poured out of the bars and the boarding houses. They gathered in the streets, a murmuring tide of humanity moving toward the waterfront and the government buildings.

They wanted to see him. They wanted to see the man who had cheated the Pacific.

Halford sat in the chair. He accepted a glass of water from the Minister. He drank it.

He felt the vibration of the city changing outside the walls. He felt the urgency building.

"They will go?" Halford asked. "A ship?"

"I have already sent word to the harbor master," Peirce promised, his voice crisp with efficiency.

"We will charter the Kona Packet. She is a stout schooner. She can sail on the tide."

"Good," Halford said.

He didn't have the strength to argue about windward beats or hull speeds. He simply closed his eyes. He saw the faces of the men on the beach at Ocean Island. He saw Read. He saw Sicard.

I did it, he told them. I told you I would.

The door to the Consulate opened again. More men entered, consuls, merchants, captains. They crowded into the hallway, staring at the skeleton in the chair.

Halford didn't look at them. He looked at the tin box. It was empty now. The burden had been transferred.

He was just a man again. A broken, starving, grieving man.

"I need to sleep," Halford whispered.

"You shall have the best bed in Honolulu," Peirce said.

"No," Halford said. "Just a place that does not move."

Halford was carried to the American Hotel, where he fell into a coma of exhaustion that mimicked death. But while the Coxswain slept, the machinery of rescue began to turn.

The news of the *Saginaw* had seeped into the coral-block foundations of the city, rising with the Christmas morning heat to reach the highest levels of the Hawaiian Kingdom.

Minister Peirce had been efficient. He had acted with the decisive speed of a diplomat facing a catastrophe. Within hours of Halford's arrival, he had secured the *Kona Packet,* a coasting schooner of good reputation. Provisions were being loaded; water casks were being rolled down the wharf.

But there was a flaw in the plan, visible only to those who looked at the weather vane on the palace roof.

The wind was blowing hard from the Northeast.

To reach Kure Atoll from Honolulu required a vessel to travel West-Northwest, a swift flight with the wind astern. But to return, to bring the eighty-eight starving men back to civilization, required a beat to windward against the full force of the winter trades. A sailing schooner like the *Kona Packet* would be forced to tack back and forth for weeks, fighting for every mile of longitude.

Weeks the men on the reef did not have.

In the Government House, a stone's throw from the bustle of the harbor, King Kamehameha V sat in his council chamber. His massive frame anchored the room, the last of the great Kamehameha line. He possessed the heavy, powerful build of the *ali'i*, a stature that commanded the room without the need for a crown. His face was grave, etched with the responsibility of a sovereign whose kingdom was being squeezed by the great powers of the world.

But today, politics were suspended.

"The report is confirmed, Your Majesty," the Minister of the Interior said, laying the paper on the koa-wood table. "The American gunboat is a total loss. She lies broken on the reef at Ocean Island."

"The men?" The King's voice rumbled, a low vibration in the quiet room.

"Ninety-three souls remain on the sand. They dispatched their gig to find relief. It reached Kauai yesterday."

"And the boat crew?"

"A single survivor, Your Majesty. The Coxswain, Halford. The surf at Hanalei claimed Lieutenant Talbot and three seamen."

The King looked out the window toward the green slopes of the Koolau range. He knew Hanalei. He knew the treacherous currents of Kalihi Kai. He could envision the tragedy clearly, the thirty-one days of suffering ending in the violent churning of the reef.

"It is a heavy price," the King said. "To come so far, and die at the door."

"Minister Peirce has chartered the *Kona Packet*," the aide continued. "She is fitting out now. She sails tomorrow."

The King turned back to the table. He looked at the chart of the archipelago spread out before him. He traced the line from Kauai to the Leeward Islands. It was a long, lonely road.

"The *Packet* is a sailing vessel," the King observed.

"Yes, Your Majesty."

"And the wind is fresh from the Northeast."

"It is."

"Then she will be too slow," the King said. "If the men on the reef are starving, as the sailor says, they cannot wait for a schooner to beat upwind. They need steam."

He looked at his ministers. The Kingdom of Hawaii was not a wealthy nation. Its navy was non-existent. But it possessed one jewel of maritime technology: the steamer *Kilauea*.

She was a screw-steamer of four hundred tons, the lifeline of the islands. She carried the mail, the sugar, and the travelers between Honolulu and the outer islands. She was the workhorse of the government, essential to the economy. To pull her off her route was to disrupt the commerce of the entire archipelago. It would cost the treasury thousands of dollars in coal and lost revenue.

The King did not hesitate.

"Order the *Kilauea* to make ready," Kamehameha commanded.

"Your Majesty?" the Minister of the Interior blinked. "The *Kilauea* is on the Hawaii run. She is full of cargo."

"Discharge the cargo," the King said. "Put the passengers ashore. Refund their money. Fill her bunkers with coal. Every inch of her."

"The expense, Your Majesty..."

"We are speaking of the lives of eighty men," the King said, his voice hardening. "We are speaking of a brother nation in distress. The United States has lost a ship in our waters. It is our duty, and our privilege, to offer the fastest aid in our power."

He stood up. The chair scraped against the floor.

"This officer... Talbot. He gave his life to bring the word. Shall we dishonor that sacrifice by sending a slow boat to save his crew? No. Send the steamer."

The order went out from the palace like a thunderclap.

Down at the harbor, the rhythm of the holiday shifted gears. The *Kilauea*, lying at the Esplanade wharf, became the center of a frenetic, coal-dust-choked cyclone.

Drays drawn by sweating horses thundered down the cobblestones, piled high with sacks of "hard coal." A human chain of Kanaka stevedores formed, passing the sacks from the carts to the bunkers.

The *Kona Packet* was still loading, her captain shouting orders to stow the salt beef, but the eyes of the waterfront had turned to the steamer.

Smoke began to curl from the *Kilauea*'s yellow funnel. First a wisp, then a thick, black plume that stained the pristine trade wind sky. The fires were being lit. The pressure was building.

Captain Thomas Long, the master of the *Kilauea*, stood on the bridge. He was a veteran of the island channels, a man who knew the reefs as well as he knew his own backyard.

"Full bunkers," Long ordered the chief engineer. "And deck loads. Fill the foredeck with sacks. We'll burn the paint off the stack if we have to, but we won't run out of dust."

The American Minister, Peirce, arrived at the wharf, looking flustered but relieved. He had done his best with the *Packet,* but the King had trumped him with royal generosity.

"You are to proceed with all dispatch, Captain Long," Peirce shouted over the roar of the escaping steam. "Spare nothing."

"We will reach them, Mr. Minister," Long replied, touching the brim of his cap. "If they are alive, we will bring them home."

By late afternoon, the *Kilauea* was deep in the water, heavy with coal and provisions. The sun was setting, casting long shadows across the harbor.

On the deck of the *Kona Packet,* the crew paused in their work. They watched the steamer.

A whistle blew, a long, mournful blast that echoed off the volcanic slopes of Punchbowl Crater.

The lines were cast off. The screw turned, churning the harbor water into a frothy white wake.

The *Kilauea* moved away from the wharf. She did not wait for the tide. She did not wait for the morning. She turned her bow toward the harbor mouth, passing the slow, sailing schooner that had been their only hope a few hours ago.

As she cleared the reef, the steamer met the first of the ocean swells. She dipped her bow, rising and falling with a heavy, powerful grace.

The black smoke from her funnel streamed out behind her, a dark banner of industrial speed. She was making eight knots, driving straight into the eye of the wind, defying the elements that had killed Talbot.

Back in the city, the church bells began to ring for evening service. But the true sermon of Christmas Day was being preached out on the water, written in coal smoke and steam.

King Kamehameha stood on the lanai of the palace, watching the lights of the ship disappear to the west. He held a report in his hand, the details of the tragedy at Hanalei.

"Godspeed," the King murmured.

The race was on. The *Kilauea* was hunting for a needle in a haystack, racing against thirst, against despair, and against the calendar that Paymaster Read kept in his tent on the sand.

Fifteen hundred miles to the west, the sun was rising on another day of heat and rats. The men of the *Saginaw* did not hear the steamer's whistle. Only the surf. But for the first time in fifty days, the silence of the horizon was being challenged by an engine that would not stop.

Chapter 19

Paymaster George Read sat on a drift-log near the water's edge, watching the sunrise. It was a beautiful, cloudless dawn, the kind that sailors usually pray for, a wash of pale violet turning to hard, brilliant blue.

It was Day 77 on the island. It was Day 57 since the gig had sailed.

The math was no longer a subject of debate in the wardroom; it was a settled verdict. A boat like the gig, provisioned for twenty-five days, could not survive fifty-seven. The variables were too stark. If the storms hadn't taken them, the thirst had. If the thirst hadn't, the starvation had.

Talbot was dead. Halford was dead. The ocean had swallowed them, and now it was waiting for the main course.

Read looked down at his hands resting on his knees, trembling with an uncontrollable palsy, the skin paper-thin and translucent enough to reveal the blue veins tracing the map of his own decay. When he touched his teeth with his tongue, they wobbled in his gums with the soft, spongy give of advanced scurvy, leaving his saliva pink when he spat.

He wasn't hungry anymore. The gnawing pangs of November and December, the sharp, cramps that had doubled him over, had faded into a dull, lethargic nausea. The body had simply stopped asking for what did not exist.

The albatross were gone. The colony had migrated, leaving the scrub silent. The monk seals, wise to the predators on the beach, had vanished into the deep water beyond the reef. The eighty-eight men of the *Saginaw* were subsisting on a few ounces of dried potato and the rats they could club in the dark.

Read stood up. The world tilted grey at the edges. He waited for the vertigo to pass, breathing through his nose, then began the long walk toward the shipyard.

The camp was quiet. There was no morning skylarking, no shouting. The men moved with the slow, underwater grace of the starving. To lift a hand was an investment; to speak was a tax. They saved their breath for the work.

Captain Sicard was already there, standing by the hull of the *"Saginaw Junior."*

The schooner was finished.

She sat on her launch rollers, a forty-foot declaration of their refusal to die quietly. She was rough, ugly, but she was a boat.

Read walked around her. She loomed high in the sand, her planks bleached white by the sun. The seams were packed with "oakum" made from picked-apart rope and sealed with boiled seal oil that had turned into a black, sticky gum.

Her masts were stepped, raked back at a sharp angle. Her sails were bent to the yards.

Read looked at the canvas. It was a patchwork quilt of misery. Pieces of sleeping hammocks, legs of trousers, and shirts had been stitched together with twine made from unraveled halyards. It looked like the laundry of a madman, but it would catch the wind.

"She looks... substantial," Read lied, coming up beside the Captain.

Sicard didn't turn. He was staring at the garboard strake, where the wood was roughest. The Captain's frock coat hung on him like a sail on a broken spar, but his posture remained rigid.

"She is a crate, Mr. Read," Sicard said softly. "She is a heavy, cumbersome crate. She will sail like a haystack and leak like a sieve."

"But she floats?"

"We pray she floats. We have no way to test her until we push her in. And once she is in, she stays in."

Sicard ran his hand along the gunwale. The gesture was tender, almost apologetic. He touched a rusted bolt-head that protruded from the wood.

"We launch on the first high tide of February," Sicard said.

"February," Read murmured.

It was three weeks away.

"We cannot wait longer," Sicard continued, his voice flat. "The men are failing. Dr. Frank tells me three more are down with the flux this morning. Private O'Neil cannot stand. If we wait for the weather to settle, we will not have the strength to push her into the water."

"Do we have the food to last three weeks?" Read asked. He knew the answer. He kept the books.

"No," Sicard said. "We do not."

The Captain turned to look at him. His eyes were sunken, rimmed with red, but they were clear.

"But we will launch anyway. We will load the sick into the hold. We will pack the rest on the deck like cordwood. And we will sail for Kauai."

"It is fifteen hundred miles, Captain."

"I know the distance, Paymaster."

"In this?" Read gestured to the boat. "Without proper caulking? Without copper sheathing? The teredo worms will eat the hull before we make the meridian."

"Then we pump," Sicard said. "And if we cannot pump, we bail. And if we cannot bail, we drown."

He looked out at the reef. The surf was pounding, a white line of violence that separated them from the world.

"Better the open sea than this sandbar," Sicard said. "I will not have my crew die here, rotting in the scrub. If we go down, we go down trying to get home."

Read looked at the boat. In November, she had been a skeleton, a symbol of hope. Now, she was a skin-covered reality, a symbol of desperation. She was their last card.

"The horizon is clear," Read observed, looking past the Captain's shoulder.

"It is always clear," Sicard replied. "We are alone, Paymaster. We have always been alone. The gig never made it. We must accept that. If Talbot were alive, he would have sent word. He would not have left us here."

"I have accepted it, sir."

"Good. Then help me check the rudder pintles. We must ensure the iron is sound. We cannot afford a failure of steering."

They worked in silence, two ghosts inspecting a coffin. The sun beat down, hot and indifferent.

Read crouched by the stern. The pintles were made from the *Saginaw's* old chain-plates, hammered flat and drilled by hand. They looked strong enough, but the wood they were bolted to was soft.

He tightened a nut with his fingers, feeling the metal bite into his skin. He tested the swing of the rudder. It groaned, a dry, wooden complaint.

He thought of his mother in Philadelphia. He wondered if she was lighting a fire in the grate right now. He wondered if she felt a chill, a sudden shadow crossing her heart.

He thought of the ledger in his tent, filled with neat columns of numbers that no one would ever read. *Expedition Concluded.*

Forty-seven days, he thought. They are long dead.

He stood up, wiping the rust from his hands. He looked at the men gathering for the morning muster. They were lined up in the sand, wavering in the heat haze. They weren't looking at the sea anymore. They were looking at their feet.

Read didn't look at the horizon. There was no point. There was nothing there but the curve of the earth and the end of the world.

"The pintles are sound, Captain," Read said.

"Very well," Sicard said. "Then we are ready. We wait for the tide."

The tide would not come for weeks, but the sun was relentless in its daily arrival. By mid-afternoon, the camp was a landscape of paralyzed exhaustion. The heat radiating from the white coral sand distorted the air, turning the horizon into a shimmering, liquid blur that danced and mocked the eye. The island held its breath, suspended in a stifling vacuum where the only movement was the heat shimmer rising from the dunes and the slow, rhythmic heave of the ocean against the reef.

Paymaster George Read sat in the opening of his tent, a piece of canvas rigged to catch the faintest breath of the trade wind. He wasn't working. There was nothing left to count. The ledgers were closed, the ink dried in the bottle. He was simply existing, his mind drifting in the dangerous, shallow waters of apathy.

He looked at his boots. The leather was cracked, split at the seams by the salt and the sun, revealing the scabs on his ankles. He tried to remember what it felt like to wear socks, to feel the constriction of a starched collar, but the memories were thin, washed out by the glare.

A ghost crab materialized from the sand near his boot, pale as bone. It scuttled three inches to the left and frozen. Read watched it. He didn't move his head; he just tracked the creature with his eyes. It sat there for ten minutes, palpitating, doing absolutely nothing. Read felt a strange kinship with the crustacean. They were both just waiting for the sun to go down or a predator to arrive. He counted the grains of sand stuck to its carapace, seven. He wondered if he should kill it. It would be an event. It would change the geometry of the afternoon. But the effort of lifting his boot seemed insurmountable, a vast expenditure of energy for a negligible result. So he just sat, and the crab sat, and the sun hammered the life out of both of them in a silence so profound he could hear the blood hissing in his ears.

"Smoke!"

The cry did not come from the masthead lookout. It came from the beach, from the sentry pacing the waterline.

It was a hoarse, tentative shout, lacking the electric conviction of a true landfall. It sounded more like a question than an alarm.

"Smoke to the northeast!"

Read did not jump. He did not cheer. He felt a spike of sudden, hot irritation. They had played this game before. A low cloud, a trick of the light, a wish projected onto the sky. He had stood on the lookout on Christmas Day and watched a schooner dissolve into vapor. He had felt that crushing weight in his chest when the "sail" turned out to be nothing but a wisp of cirrus. He would not do it again. He would not let his heart hammer against his ribs only to have it stopped by the indifference of the atmosphere.

He stayed seated. He picked at a loose thread on his cuff.

"Mr. Read?" It was Hershberger, standing outside the tent. The junior officer looked emaciated, his eyes huge in a face that had shrunk back to the bone. "Did you hear?"

"I heard," Read said. He didn't look up. He rubbed a hand over his face. The skin felt dry and brittle. "It is a cloud, Mr. Hershberger. It is always a cloud. Or a squall line. Tell the men to sit down."

"The sentry is insistent, sir. He says it is too dark for a cloud. He says it's trailing."

Read sighed. It was the duty of the officer. He couldn't just sit there. He had to go out there and look. He had to be the one to crush the hope before it spread, before it turned into the bitter poison of disappointment that would leave the men unable to work on the schooner tomorrow. False hope was more dangerous than despair; despair was stable. Hope was volatile.

He reached for his field glasses. The leather case was hot to the touch, baking in the sun. He slipped the strap over his neck. The brass binoculars felt heavy, a dead weight against his chest.

He stood up.

The movement was too fast. The blood rushed from his head, pooling in his legs. The world spotted with black dots, spinning lazily. He grabbed the tent pole, waiting for the vertigo to pass, breathing through his nose. *Steady*, he told himself. *It's just the heat.*

He stepped out into the glare.

The men were gathering on the beach. A slow shuffle migration of jointed bones and sunburned skin moving toward the water. They shielded their eyes, pointing at the horizon. They were silent. They knew the cost of a false alarm.

Read walked past them. He felt their eyes on him. They wanted him to confirm it, or they wanted him to deny it. They wanted authority.

He walked to the water's edge, where the wet sand offered a firmer footing. He looked to the northeast.

Blue. White caps. The hard line of the sea.

The glare was blinding. The sun was reflecting off the water with a ferocity that made his eyes water.

He found the bearing.

There was a mark.

It was faint, a smudge of charcoal against the lower sky, right on the water's edge. It looked like a bruise on the horizon.

Read lifted the glasses.

His hands shook. It was the palsy of starvation, a fine, rhythmic tremor that he couldn't control. He braced his elbows against his ribs, jamming them into his body to create a tripod. He held his breath.

He brought the lenses up.

The circle of magnification danced. Sea. Sky. Sea. Sky.

He found the smudge.

He focused. He adjusted the screw with thumb and forefinger, fighting the stiffness of the brass. The image sharpened, then blurred, then sharpened again.

It was low. It was dense. It had a dark, slate-grey core that thinned out at the edges.

"It is a squall," Read muttered to himself. "Just a rain squall coming down the wind."

He lowered the glasses. He wanted to turn away. He wanted to tell Hershberger to secure the lookout and get the men out of the sun.

But he looked again with his naked eye.

The trade wind was blowing briskly from the northeast. He watched the clouds above the smudge. Cumulus puffs, white and fluffy, drifting steadily to the southwest. They changed shape as they moved, dissolving and reforming.

The stain on the water was stationary.

Or if it moved, it was moving *against* the wind.

A cold prickle danced on the back of his neck. A rain squall moved with the weather. A cloud drifted with the breeze.

This thing was fighting the trades.

He raised the glasses again. He jammed the eyepieces against his sockets, ignoring the pain. He forced himself to breathe, to slow his heart rate, to become a recording instrument. He needed to be sure. He needed to be scientifically, nautically sure.

He watched the base of the smudge.

It wasn't rising from the water like evaporation. It was trailing. It was a long, flat ribbon of darkness, streaming backward from a point source that was still hull-down below the curve of the earth.

He analyzed the color.

It wasn't the grey of rain.

It was the greasy, heavy, unnatural black of bituminous coal. It was a smudge of pure pollution, an ugly, man-made scar against the pristine horizon that promised heat, friction, and speed. Unlike the ghostly, perfect white sail that had taunted him on Christmas, this was dirty, mechanical.

A steamer.

There was no other explanation in physics or nature. It was a column of coal smoke generated by a furnace.

His mind raced, trying to find a reason, trying to find a trap.

Steamers did not ply these waters. The trade route to Japan lay far to the north, a thousand miles away. The route to Australia lay far to the south. The ocean between Midway and Kauai was a desert. A merchant steamer would never burn precious coal to fight a headwind in this desolate latitude unless she had a specific destination.

Unless she was hunting.

Read lowered the glasses. His mouth was dry, tasting of dust and sudden, terrifying fear. The implications were too big to process. If it was a steamer, and it was heading here...

"It is smoke," he whispered.

"Sir?" Hershberger was at his elbow, his face a mask of anxiety, his eyes pleading. "Is it... is it a ship?"

Read turned to look at him. The desperation in the young man's face. The eighty-eight men standing on the beach, holding their breath, waiting for a word that would either kill them or save them.

He had to be right. If he said it, and he was wrong, he would destroy them.

He looked back at the horizon. The line was thicker now, darker. It was elongating. It was a finger of soot pointing straight at the reef.

It wasn't a passing ship. It wasn't a chance encounter.

It was the answer to a question they had stopped asking forty days ago.

"It is smoke," Read said, his voice rising, cracking with the strain. "It is a well-defined line. It is not a cloud."

He took a breath. He shouted it.

"Steam! It is a steamer!"

The word hung in the hot air, suspended for a second of absolute silence.

A steamer meant intent. A sailing ship might wander off course, blown by a gale. A steamer came because it was sent. It meant the gig.

It meant Halford. It meant Talbot.

It meant they weren't dead.

It meant that somewhere, weeks ago, a boat had landed. It meant that someone knew they were here.

Read raised the glasses one last time. He could see the source now, a tiny, hard speck of black rising above the blue curve of the world. The funnel.

"She is standing in," Read choked out. "She is bearing for the anchorage."

Read's knees finally gave way, and he sat hard in the wet sand, the field glasses banging against his hollow ribs. He didn't feel like a rescued officer; he felt like a piece of salt-bleached driftwood that had suddenly, inexplicably, begun to pulse with a heartbeat again.

He sat there for a moment, his breath coming in jagged hitches. He looked at the men.

"They are coming," Read whispered. "They are coming for us."

The discipline of the United States Navy, drilled into them by the lash and the Articles of War, evaporated in a single second.

"Steamer! Steamer ho!"

For a heartbeat, there was paralysis.

The men stood frozen, their mouths open, staring at Read as if he were a madman. They looked at the horizon. They saw the smoke.

Then, the camp exploded.

A primal, collective scream tore from their throats, it was the sound of eighty-eight men simultaneously releasing a breath they had been holding since October.

Men fell to their knees in the sand, weeping openly, their hands covering their faces. Others ran into the surf, splashing water at the sky, laughing with a hysteria that bordered on delirium.

Private O'Neil, who that morning had been unable to stand for muster, crawled out of the hospital tent. He dragged himself across the sand, tears streaming down his face.

"She's here! She's here!"

Read stood in the center of the bedlam. He felt numb. He watched a fireman grab the Boatswain's Mate and spin him around in a clumsy, stumbling waltz. The exertion of happiness was instantly punishing. The coal-heaver collapsed mid-step, his legs folding under the sudden expenditure, retching dry bile onto the sand. Around him, the cheering shredded throats, turning shouts into jagged, hacking coughs that rattled in fluid-filled lungs. Men hugging each other, their bony frames clattering together, patting backs that were nothing but vertebrae and sunburned skin.

Captain Sicard stood by the flagpole. He was gripping the halyard, looking out at the ship through his own glass. His shoulders were shaking.

The *Kilauea* was hull-up now. She was turning, presenting her broadside to the reef as she searched for the anchorage. She was a beautiful, ugly, black-smoking angel of the industrial age.

She blew her whistle.

Whooooooo.

The sound rolled over the breakers, deep and resonant. It was the voice of the world. It was the sound of commerce, of mail, of news, of life.

The men screamed back. They waved their shirts. They waved their hats. They waved their arms until they were dizzy.

"The signals!" O'Connell roared, suddenly remembering his duty through the haze of joy. "Light the fires! Let them see us!"

The order gave them a focal point. The manic energy needed a target.

They ran to the dunes.

Weeks ago, in the first flush of their exile, they had built signal piles, great mounds of dried naupaka brush, driftwood, and tar-soaked rags, spaced along the beach for this exact moment. For months, those piles had sat cold and gray, inhabited only by rats and spiders.

Now, they were the altars of their deliverance.

"Matches!"

A marine fumbled with a waterproof tin. His hands shook so badly he dropped it in the sand. Another man snatched it up. He struck a lucifer. The sulfur flared blue, then yellow.

He touched it to the oil-soaked rags at the base of the pile.

Whoosh.

The fire caught instantly. The flames leaped up, orange and greasy, hungry for the dry wood. Black smoke billowed into the sky, joining the smoke of the steamer.

A second pile was lit further down the beach. Then a third.

The heat hit them. It was intense, searing their faces, but they didn't back away. They danced around it. They were pagans worshipping the god of rescue.

Read turned away from the fire. He looked toward the shipyard.

The "Saginaw Junior."

The schooner stood on her rollers, forty feet of seasoned oak and desperate labor. She was the product of their sweat. She was the vessel that was supposed to save them when the world forgot them.

She was finished. Her seams were caulked. Her masts were stepped. Her sails, the patchwork hammocks they had stitched with bleeding fingers, were bent to the yards, ready for the voyage to Kauai.

Now, she was a ghost. The tools lay where they had been dropped. An adze, its blade biting into a log, abandoned mid-swing. A mallet lying in the sawdust. A plane resting on a half-smoothed plank.

Only Mr. Butterfield hesitated. Amidst the stampede for the water, the Carpenter stopped and laid a trembling hand on the scarf joint of the keel.

He ran his palm over the sheer strake. The wood was warm, holding the heat of the day. To his eye, it wasn't just oak; it was a vessel stored with the last vital spark of eighty-eight men. Every adze stroke had cost a heartbeat. Every copper drift-bolt driven home had cost a day of life. Leaving her felt like an amputation, a severance of the limb that had kept them afloat in the void. He laid his cheek against the rough grain, inhaling the scent of seal oil and oakum one last time, whispering a quiet apology to the thing that would never swim.

He patted the rough timber once, a craftsman's benediction for a failure that had served its purpose, then wiped his nose and ran toward the surf.

Read walked over to the boat. He touched the rough wood of the hull. An hour ago, this wood was more precious than gold. It was the only thing that had kept them sane.

Now, it was just driftwood again.

He looked at the empty saw-pit. He looked at the pile of copper bolts they had straightened by hand. He looked at the sails that would never catch the wind.

It was a strange, melancholy sight. The boat seemed to know it had been discarded. It sat heavy and silent in the sand, a monument to a fear that had just evaporated.

"We are spared," Read whispered.

He felt a sudden lightness. They didn't have to squeeze into that open hull. They didn't have to brave the winter storms in a boat held together by rust. They didn't have to decide who would drink the water and who would die.

He turned his back on the *"Saginaw Junior."* He left her there, a silent, wooden hulk on the beach and walked toward the water.

The sun began to set. The signal fires roared against the twilight, casting long, dancing shadows on the sand.

The *Kilauea* had anchored. She lay just off the reef, her riding lights twinkling in the dusk. A boat was being lowered.

Read walked down to the water's edge. The sand was cool under his boots. The roar of the surf, which had been a sound of imprisonment for sixty-eight days, now sounded like a gateway.

He looked at the men gathered by the fire. They were singing now. A ragged, off-key chorus of "Home, Sweet Home."

Their voices were thin, reedy with starvation, but they carried over the water.

Mid pleasures and palaces though we may roam...
Read felt the tears start. He let them fall. He didn't wipe them away.
He looked at the dark shape of the steamer.
"Talbot," he whispered. "You did it."

He imagined the Lieutenant on the bridge of the ship, guiding her in. He imagined Halford at the wheel. He imagined Francis and Andrews waving from the deck.

They had made it. They had beaten the ocean. They had sailed the gig to Hawaii and sent the ship.

The boat from the *Kilauea* was pulling for the channel. The oars dipped in the phosphorescent water.

Read waited. He straightened his frock coat. He buttoned it, his fingers fumbling with the buttons. He wanted to look like an officer. He wanted to welcome them with dignity.

But inside, he was just a boy waiting for his father to come home.

The fires crackled behind him, consuming the brush of the island. The *"Saginaw Junior"* sat in the dark, abandoned. The ledgers were closed.

The long wait was over.

Chapter 20

Captain Montgomery Sicard stood alone at the waterline. The tide was washing over his boots, burying his heels in the wet sand.

He had spent the last hour watching his command dissolve into a mob of dancing, weeping specters, and he had permitted it. He had watched them pile the brush and the scrap timber. He had watched the flames rise, illuminating the gaunt, hollowed faces of men he had kept alive by the sheer force of his will.

But now, the fire was just a glow in the background. The reality was the boat pulling toward him.

He buttoned his frock coat.

The wool was stiff with salt and mildew, the gold lace tarnished to a dull, greenish brown. It hung on his frame loosely, hiding the ribs that pressed against his skin like barrel hoops, but he smoothed the front with a trembling hand. He was the commanding officer of the USS *Saginaw*. He would meet the relief expedition with the dignity of his rank.

The whaleboat grounded.

The keel hissed against the sand. The men at the oars shipped them with a clatter that sounded obscenely loud in the sudden quiet.

A man in the stern sheets stood up. He was dressed in a clean dark coat and a white shirt. He wore a cap with a gold band. He looked healthy. His face was full, his skin clear of sores, his movements vigorous and easy.

It was Captain Thomas Long, master of the *Kilauea*.

Sicard walked forward. He tried to stride, but his legs were weak, and he found himself shuffling through the sand. The vertigo of starvation spun the world at the edges of his vision.

Long stepped out of the boat. He splashed into the shallows and walked up the beach, his eyes widening as he took in the scene. The emaciated scarecrows standing in the firelight. The abandoned hull of the schooner. The man approaching him, a bearded, ragged figure with the eyes of a haunted ascetic.

Long stopped. He took off his cap.

"Captain Sicard?" Long asked. His voice was gentle, respectful, the tone one uses in a hospital or a morgue.

"I am he," Sicard said. His voice rasped. He cleared his throat and tried again, forcing the tone of command. "I am Lieutenant Commander Sicard. You are welcome here, sir."

"I am Thomas Long. His Majesty's Steamer *Kilauea*."

They shook hands.

The contact was jarring. Long's hand was warm, fleshy, and strong. Sicard's hand was a collection of bones.

"We saw your smoke," Sicard said. "We... we are grateful."

"We came as fast as the boilers would allow," Long said. He looked over Sicard's shoulder at the silent, staring crew. "You have had a hard time of it, Captain."

"We have survived," Sicard replied.

He paused.

The question was a obstruction in his throat. It had been sitting there for forty-eight days, growing heavier with every sunset. It blocked his airway.

He looked at the boat. He looked for a familiar face among the rowers. He looked for the flash of a lieutenant's uniform, or the broad shoulders of a coxswain.

The rowers were strangers. Kanaka sailors, looking back at him with pity.

Sicard looked back at Long. He saw the answer in the man's eyes before the words were spoken. The flinch.

"My boat," Sicard whispered. "The gig."

Long looked down at the sand. He twisted his cap in his hands.

"They made it, Captain," Long said.

A surge of hope, hot and blinding, flared in Sicard's chest. They made it. They had crossed the void. Talbot had done it.

"They reached Kauai," Long continued, his voice low. "Thirty-one days. A remarkable passage, sir. One of the greatest in the history of the ocean."

"Where are they?" Sicard asked. He looked at the steamer's lights twinkling in the darkness. "Are they aboard? Are they well?"

Long took a breath. He looked up, meeting Sicard's gaze with a steady, sorrowful solemnity.

"Only one, sir."

The world stopped. The roar of the surf, the crackle of the fire, the beating of his own heart, it all ceased.

"One?" Sicard breathed.

"Coxswain Halford," Long said. "He is alive. He is in Honolulu, recovering."

"And... Mr. Talbot?"

"Dead, sir."

It struck Sicard between the eyes, shattering the fragile composure he had maintained since October.

"Drowned," Long said gently. "In the surf at Hanalei. They were too weak to pull the oars. The boat capsized in the breakers. Mr. Talbot... Halford says he was washed off. He sank immediately."

"And the others?"

"Quartermaster Francis. Seaman Andrews. Dead in the water. Seaman Muir... he made the beach, sir. Halford dragged him up. But he died of exhaustion before the natives found them."

Sicard stared at the man. The words, they didn't make sense.

They had made it. They had sailed fifteen hundred miles. They had survived the gales, the starvation, the thirst. They had reached the land.

And they had died in the surf?

"Talbot," Sicard whispered.

He saw the young officer's face as he had stood in the tent, clean-shaven, his eyes bright with that calm, spiritual fervor. *I believe I can navigate her, sir.*

The hand outstretched. *Goodbye, Captain.*

He had sent him. He had written the orders. He had inspected the boat. He had allowed them to go.

"He is buried at Hanalei," Long offered. "With military honors."

Sicard nodded dumbly. He felt a sudden, violent need to sit down. His legs were dissolving. The sand seemed to be rushing up to meet him.

He caught himself. He grabbed the gunwale of the whaleboat to steady himself. The wood was cold.

"I sent them," Sicard said. "I sent them to die."

"You sent them to save these men," Long corrected him firmly. "And they did. Halford delivered the despatches. The King sent me because of them. Your men are saved, Captain. Because of Mr. Talbot."

"Saved," Sicard repeated.

He looked up the beach. The fire was still burning, casting long, grotesque shadows. The eighty-eight survivors were watching him. They were huddled together, silent, waiting for the news.

They were alive. They would go home. They would see their wives, their mothers, their children. They would eat fresh bread and sleep in dry beds.

Because John Talbot had drowned in the dark.

The transaction was complete. The ocean had accepted the trade. Five men for eighty-eight.

It was a good bargain, mathematically. It was the kind of calculation the Navy approved of.

But Sicard felt a hole open in his chest, a void as cold and deep as the trench where the *Saginaw's* bow lay.

He thought of the *"Saginaw Junior,"* abandoned on the beach. They hadn't needed it. They could have waited. If they had waited one more week...

No. That was madness. They were dying. Talbot had to go.

"Halford," Sicard said, latching onto the name. "Halford lives?"

"He does. He is a man of iron, sir. He walked to the village with a broken rib and a ruined leg to deliver your box."

"Good," Sicard said. "That is... good."

He straightened up. He adjusted his coat again.

He was the Captain. He could not collapse. He could not weep. Not here. Not in front of the stranger who had saved them.

He had a duty to perform. He had to tell the men.

He had to walk up that beach, into the light of the victory fire, and turn it into a funeral pyre.

"Thank you, Captain Long," Sicard said. His voice was hollow, a wooden reproduction of speech. "For your speed. And for the news."

"My orders are to evacuate you immediately," Long said. "We have food on board. Medical supplies."

"Yes," Sicard said. "But first... I must speak to my crew."

He turned his back on the water. He looked at the waiting men.

They knew.

They could see it in his posture. They could see it in the way his head hung low, in the slow, dragging trudging of his walk.

The cheering had stopped completely. The dancing had stopped. The only sound was the crackle of the signal fires, consuming the brush.

Sicard walked toward them. It was the longest walk of his life. Every step was a penance.

He walked past Read, who was standing by the water's edge, his face pale in the moonlight. Read met his eyes. Sicard gave a barely perceptible shake of his head.

Read closed his eyes.

Sicard reached the flagpole. He stopped. He looked at the eighty-eight faces. They were gaunt, dirty, beautiful faces. They were alive.

He opened his mouth to speak, to deliver the announcement that would end the expedition.

He thought of the Homeward Bound pennant, streaming in the wind at Midway. He thought of the laughter.

He thought of Talbot's hand in his.

Sicard took a breath. The air tasted of smoke and salt and ashes.

"Men".

His voice broke. He cleared his throat, forcing the iron back into his spine. "I have the great sorrow to announce to you that we have been saved at a great sacrifice."

He paused. He looked at the sand. He looked at the rows of expectant eyes that were currently illuminated by the joy of rescue.

"Lieutenant Talbot," Sicard whispered, then louder, "Lieutenant Talb ot... is dead."

The sentence hung in the air. It didn't land immediately. It floated, absurd and impossible, against the backdrop of the steamer's lights. Talbot was the golden boy. Talbot was the navigator. Talbot was the reason the ship was there.

"He was drowned," Sicard continued, the words tumbling out now, heavy and dull stones. "In the surf at Kauai. He reached the land, but the sea took him."

Read felt the blood drain from his face. The world narrowed down to the Captain's mouth.

"And Quartermaster Francis," Sicard said. "And Seaman Andrews. And Seaman Muir."

Read closed his eyes. Peter Francis, who had sewn the sails with such care. James Muir, who had wrestled for his seat in the boat.

"Only Halford lives," Sicard finished. "He alone has brought us relief."

In the sudden void of human noise, the bonfire took over.

A pocket of sap boiled and burst, crack, a sharp, percussive report that made the front rank flinch. The sound echoed off the dunes like a pistol shot. A log shifted, groaning in the white-hot center of the pile, sending a fountain of orange sparks spiraling up into the dark. They drifted down, hissing as they hit the black water of the lagoon.

The heat pressed against their sunburned faces with a dry, blistering intensity. The smell of burning ironwood, usually sweet, suddenly clogged the air with the thick, choking scent of carbon.

O'Connell, the Boatswain's Mate, took off his cap. He crumpled it in his hands. He looked at the fire they had built, the signal beacon burning brightly in the night.

"Dead?" O'Connell whispered. "Mr. Talbot?"

It didn't seem possible. They were supposed to be the victims. They were the ones rotting on a sandbar, counting the days until starvation. Talbot was supposed to be the hero sailing into the sunset.

To learn that the rescuers had died so the rescued could live was a twisting of the moral universe that the mind refused to accept.

"He gave his life," Sicard said, his voice regaining a measure of strength, "that we might go home."

Read turned away. He couldn't look at the Captain anymore. He looked at the *Kilauea*.

The steamer sat offshore, her riding lights reflecting on the water. A few minutes ago, she had looked like a chariot of fire. Now, she looked like a hearse.

It was a cold, sick feeling in the pit of his stomach. He was breathing. He was standing on dry sand. He was going to eat fresh bread. He was going to see Philadelphia again.

Because John Talbot had drowned in the dark.

Because Peter Francis had been crushed on a reef.

It felt like a theft. Read felt as though he had stolen the air from Talbot's lungs.

He looked at the fire. The flames were consuming the brush and the scrap timber. The wood popped and hissed.

Nobody moved to stoke it. The manic energy to build the beacon was gone. The fire seemed suddenly obscene, a garish celebration of a tragedy.

A heavy shape crumpled near the edge of the light. It was Dougherty. Two months ago, on this same beach, he had tried to choke James Muir for a seat in that boat. He had used his bulk, his rage, and his broad coal-heaver's hands to fight for a ticket out, and he had lost. He had cursed that failure every day since, hating the lack of leverage that kept him prisoner here.

Now, he looked at his palms, trembling in the firelight. The strength he had prayed for would have killed him. If he had pinned Muir, if he had won, he would be the one washing in the surf at Kauai. His defeat was the only reason he was breathing.

"I fought him for it," Dougherty choked out, rocking back and forth, his fingers digging into his knees. "I fought him for the grave."

"Silence," O'Connell snapped, but there was no heat in it. It was a reflex of rank, nothing more.

Sicard walked over to Read. The Captain's face was wet. He didn't bother to wipe the tears away.

"We must embark, Paymaster," Sicard said. "The steamer cannot lay off the reef all night. The weather may turn."

"Yes, sir," Read said.

"Get the men moving. Personal effects only. The logbooks. The instruments."

"And the rest?"

"Leave it," Sicard said. "Leave it all. Let the sand have it."

Read nodded. He turned to the men.

"Prepare to embark," Read ordered. His voice sounded thin, reedy. "Form a line at the water's edge."

They moved. But it was not the stampede of an hour ago. It was a funeral procession.

They walked slowly, dragging their feet. They went to their tents and retrieved their few pitiful possessions, a carved piece of coral, a diary, a ragged bible.

They left the tools where they lay. They left the cooking pots. They left the rat-gnawed blankets.

Read walked to his own tent. He picked up his ledger.

He looked around the small canvas space that had been his home for sixty-eight days. He hated it. He hated the smell of the guano. He hated the sound of the wind.

But leaving it now felt like a betrayal.

Leaving meant accepting the trade. It meant saying, *Yes, I will take this life you bought for me.*

He walked back to the beach.

The whaleboat from the *Kilauea* was waiting. Captain Long stood by the bow, his hat in his hand, watching the men approach. He understood. The way they walked, heads down, shoulders slumped. He didn't rush them.

The first group of men climbed into the boat. They didn't scramble. They stepped in carefully, avoiding each other's eyes.

The oars dipped. The boat pulled away.

Read stood on the sand, waiting for the next turn. He watched the fire dying down. The abandoned *"Saginaw Junior"* loomed in the darkness nearby, a silent witness.

It was fitting. They had built a boat to save themselves, and they had abandoned it to celebrate their salvation, and now it was just trash. Like the tents. Like the tools.

Everything they had done, every plank they had ripped, every nail they had straightened, it was all secondary. The real work had been done by five men in a twenty-two-foot boat.

"Paymaster," Sicard called from the water. "Your boat."

Read walked down the slope. The water was warm around his ankles. He climbed into the whaleboat.

He sat on the thwart. He looked back at the island one last time.

The firelight flickered on the white sand. The scrub brush was dark and silent. The rats would be coming out soon, reclaiming their kingdom.

They were going back to the world of the living.

But as the oars bit the water and the boat surged toward the waiting steamer, George Read knew that a part of them would stay here forever. They were leaving their ghosts behind, not just the men who had died, but the men they had been before the reef took them.

The whaleboat cut through the lagoon, the oars creaking in the locks.

The Kanaka rowers pulled with a nervous, hurried rhythm, their eyes darting toward the white line of the breakers. They muttered to one another in low, rapid Hawaiian, keeping their backs to the dark water of the reef. They knew this place not as Ocean Island, but as *Hōlanikū*, the gateway to the *Pō*. They rowed like men who were trespassing in a graveyard, anxious to carry the living away before the spirits of the dead could claim them back.

They crossed the bar, feeling the swell lift them one last time, and pulled toward the lights of the steamer. As they drew alongside, the black hull of the *Kilauea* loomed above them like a cliff face of iron and rivets. Nets were lowered. Hands reached down. They were hauled up, one by one, out of the darkness of the sea and onto the vibrating, coal-stained deck of the modern world.

The deck was solid. It hummed with a low, mechanical thrumming that felt entirely different from the organic groan of a wooden ship. It was the vibration of contained power.

Paymaster George Read stood at the rail of the poop deck. He held a mug of hot coffee in his hands, the ceramic thick and heavy, warming his palms. The steam rising from the cup smelled of roasted beans and condensed milk, a luxury so intense it made his head swim.

Below him, on the main deck, the evacuation was complete. The eighty-eight survivors were huddled under blankets, eating bread and soup, tended to by the Kanaka crew. They were silent, stunned by the sudden warmth and the lack of fear.

The anchor chain rumbled.

It was a harsh, metallic roar that echoed off the water. The steam winch hissed. The ship swung, her bow turning away from the reef, seeking the open ocean.

Read looked back. Kure Atoll lay low in the water, a black streak separating the sea from the stars. The fires they had lit on the beach were still burning, lonely eyes blinking in the dark.

It illuminated the white line of the surf, the barrier they had stared at for sixty-eight days.

As the *Kilauea* gathered way, the island began to recede.

The fires grew smaller. The roar of the breakers faded, swallowed by the rhythmic *thump-thump-thump* of the steamer's screw.

Read watched the darkness reclaim the land.

The rats would be coming out now. They would be swarming the campsite, sniffing at the abandoned tents, reclaiming their kingdom of guano and sand. The monk seals would return to the beach, hauling their bulk onto the warm coral, undisturbed by the clubs of starving men. The albatross would wheel overhead, their cries unanswered.

The island was returning to its ancient, implacable silence.

It was a graveyard. The bones of the *Gledstanes* were there, buried in the scrub. The bones of the *Parker* were there. The iron bones of the *Saginaw*, her cannons, her anchors, her bell, slowly rusting into the limestone.

And now, the ghosts of the gig crew were there too.

Read took a sip of the coffee. It scalded his tongue, a sharp, necessary pain.

He thought of *Hōlanikū*. They had lived on the knife-edge between the living and the dead. They had tipped over, fallen into the abyss, and then, by the grace of a twenty-two-foot boat and five men, they had been pulled back.

But they had left something behind.

The boy who had cried over his doughboy. The man who had wrestled in the sand. The officer who had prayed. Those versions of themselves were gone, bleached out by the sun and the salt.

The steamer turned east. The trade wind, the same wind that had killed Talbot, now pushed the smoke from the funnel ahead of them, a dark banner leading them home.

Read watched the orange glow of the fires until they were just pinpricks. Then they blinked out.

The horizon was empty. There was only the black ocean, the stars, and the rhythmic beating of the engine, driving them back to the world of gaslights, and paved streets, and forgetting.

Read turned his back on the night. He didn't wait to see the reef fade from view. He drained the last dregs of the coffee, handed the cup to a passing steward, and went below to find his bunk.

Chapter 21

The first thing was the green.

Paymaster George Read stood on the hurricane deck of the *Kilauea*, his hands gripping the rail with a force that turned his knuckles white. He stared at the island of Oahu rising from the sea.

It was an assault on the eyes.

After seventy days of staring at the blinding whiteness of Kure Atoll, a landscape composed entirely of coral grit, blue water, and bleached driftwood, the lushness of Honolulu was almost repulsive in its vitality. The slopes of Diamond Head were furred with vegetation. The valleys behind the city were deep, shadowy gashes of emerald and jade, dripping with rain.

It looked swollen. It looked rich. It looked alive.

Read adjusted his collar. It was starched, and uncomfortable. He was wearing a borrowed coat, a size too large, provided by the generous officers of the steamer. He was shaved. His face, reflected in the mirror of his stateroom that morning, was a stranger's face, gaunt, hollow-cheeked, the skin burned to a dark mahogany that made his blue eyes look startlingly pale.

He felt like an impostor in the uniform. Underneath the clean wool, his body was still the body of a castaway. His ribs counted themselves against the fabric. His gums ached. His stomach, confused by three days of full rations, churned with a low, constant nausea.

The *Kilauea* rounded the point. The harbor opened up.

Noise.

It rolled across the water like a wave.

The roar of humanity.

The wharves were black with people. It looked as if the entire population of the Sandwich Islands had descended on the waterfront. There were thousands of them. Kanakas in bright shirts, American merchants in white linen, women in calico dresses, sailors climbing the rigging of the anchored whalers to get a better view.

They were cheering.

It was a wall of sound. A chaotic, screaming, joyous din that drowned out the *thump-thump* of the steamer's screw.

To ears attuned only to the wind and the surf, the noise was overwhelming. The brass notes of the band felt like needles driven into the eardrum. The scent of the flowers was a sweet, suffocating perfume that masked the honest smell of the sea, triggering an additional wave of nausea. Even his feet rebelled; his toes, spread wide by months of barefoot walking on sand, were crushed inside the borrowed leather boots, screaming for the freedom of the dirt.

Read flinched. He wanted to cover his ears. He wanted to run back to the silence of the ocean.

"God in heaven," Captain Sicard murmured, standing beside him.

Sicard looked old. The beard he had trimmed for the arrival could not hide the deep lines etched into his face by the last two months. He stood rigid, bracing himself against the rail as if facing a gale.

"They have turned out the city, Captain," Read said.

"They are cheering," Sicard said, his voice flat. "Do they not know?"

"They know we are alive, sir. That is enough for them."

The *Kilauea* slowed. The steam winch hissed. Lines were thrown. The ship nudged against the pilings of the Esplanade Wharf with a gentle shudder.

The crowd surged forward. The police held them back, forming a thin blue line against the press of bodies. Faces were upturned, shouting names, waving handkerchiefs.

Read looked down at the men of the *Saginaw* gathered on the main deck.

They were a motley regiment. They wore a mixture of their own rags and clothes donated by the steamer's crew. They looked shell-shocked. They stood in clusters, holding onto each other, staring at the mob with wide, frightened eyes.

They were the survivors. They were the heroes.

But they didn't look like heroes. They looked like men who had seen the bottom of the world and were terrified of the light.

"Lower the gangway," Captain Long ordered from the bridge.

The wood rattled down.

The band began to play. *Hail, Columbia.* The brass notes cut through the humid air, bright and sharp.

"We must go down," Sicard said. He straightened his shoulders. He pulled his cap low over his eyes.

Read followed the Captain down the ladder. He stepped onto the wharf. It was paved with cobblestones that smelled of horse manure and dust.

The crowd erupted. The cheering intensified, a deafening, percussive force. Hands reached out to touch them. Flowers were thrown, leis of plumeria and jasmine raining down on their heads, their heavy scent masking the smell of the coal smoke.

Read felt a hand on his arm. A woman, weeping, thrust a wreath of flowers around his neck.

"God bless you," she sobbed. "God bless you."

Read nodded, mute. He couldn't speak. He felt a terrible, crushing sadness welling up in his throat.

He looked for Sicard. The Captain was surrounded by dignitaries. Men in top hats were pumping his hand. The American Minister, Mr. Peirce, was there, beaming, shouting something that was lost in the noise.

And then, the crowd parted.

A path opened up on the wharf. A silence traveled down the line, quieting the cheers.

A carriage had pulled up. A man was being helped down.

He moved slowly. He leaned heavily on a cane. His right leg was stiff, dragging slightly. He wore a clean blue suit that hung on him like a shroud.

William Halford.

The Coxswain.

He looked terrible. He looked magnificent.

His face was a skull. The skin was scarred with the pink marks of healing ulcers. His eyes were deep pits of shadow. But he was standing.

Sicard stopped. The Captain broke away from the Minister. He walked toward his coxswain.

The crowd watched. The band stopped playing.

Halford straightened up. He tried to come to attention. He winced as his weight shifted onto his bad leg, but he held the pose. He brought his hand up in a slow, trembling salute.

"Captain," Halford rasped. His voice was a wreck. "Reporting for duty, sir."

Sicard stopped three feet away. He looked at the man who had sailed the gig. He looked at the man who had watched Talbot drown.

Sicard didn't return the salute. He reached out. He took Halford's hand in both of his own.

"Halford," Sicard whispered.

Read saw the Captain's shoulders shake. He saw the facade of the naval commander crack, just for a second.

"You saved us," Sicard said. "You saved us all."

"I delivered the box, sir," Halford said simply. "That was the order."

"The others?" Sicard asked, though he knew. He had to ask. He had to hear it from the witness.

"Gone, sir," Halford said. He didn't look away. "Mr. Talbot. Francis. Andrews. Muir. All gone. At the landing."

"I know," Sicard said. "I know."

Read stepped forward. He stood beside the Captain. He looked at Halford.

"Mr. Read," Halford nodded to him.

"Halford," Read said. "You look... you look alive."

"Barely, sir," Halford said. A ghost of a smile touched his lips, grim and humorless. "But the food is better here."

The crowd began to cheer again, unable to hold their silence. They surged around the survivors, a tide of goodwill and curiosity.

But in the center of the noise, in the small circle of space occupied by the three officers and the coxswain, there was a quiet zone. A vacuum.

They were the only ones who knew.

They knew the price of the flowers. They knew the cost of the music.

Read looked at the harbor. He looked at the *Kilauea*. He looked at the horizon beyond the harbor mouth.

"Come," Sicard said, his voice returning to the steel of command. "We have a report to make to the Admiral. And we have men to feed."

He offered his arm to Halford.

"Lean on me, Coxswain," Sicard said.

Halford hesitated. The reflex of subordination flared in his eyes, warring with the necessity of pain, a lifetime of deck discipline recoiling at the touch of an officer. Then his knee buckled, a sharp, mechanical failure, and he grabbed the forearm.

Sicard took the weight. It was heavy, a dead drag of bone and exhaustion that pulled at his own starved shoulder, but it was bearable compared to the small, dense rectangle pressing against the ribs beneath his borrowed frock coat.

The letter.

Talbot had pressed it into his palm fifty-seven days ago. *If I do not make the islands, you will see that she gets it?* The paper was thin, dry, and sealed with a blob of red wax that had softened in the heat of the Captain's body. It was addressed to a woman in Kentucky who was likely sleeping at this very hour, unaware that her son was washing back and forth in the surf at Hanalei, his commission cancelled by the reef.

Sicard pressed his elbow tight against his side, trapping the packet against his beating heart. The contact with the paper induced a wave of vertigo that nearly buckled his knees. He had won the strategic gamble; he had traded five men to save eighty-eight. But the man inside the uniform felt the cold, terrifying certainty that he was a fraud. He was standing in the sun, breathing the scent of jasmine and coal smoke, while the better man moted in the cold Kauai dirt.

He tightened his grip on Halford's hand, his fingers digging into the Coxswain's calluses, anchoring himself against the vertigo of his own guilt. He would have to deliver it. He would not just report a casualty to the Department; he would have to break the seal of a mother's grief.

They walked down the wharf together, the Captain and the sailor, limping through the flowers and the cheers.

Read followed. He touched the ledger in his pocket. The final entry.

Honolulu. January 14. Arrived.

It was just a few words. It didn't explain anything. It didn't explain the hunger. It didn't explain the silence. It didn't explain why they were here and Talbot was not.

He looked up at the green mountains of Oahu. They were beautiful.

He took a breath of the heavy, scented air. It smelled of life. It smelled of forgetting.

Two hours later, bathed, shaved, and poured into a dress uniform that smelled faintly of camphor and another man's cologne, Captain Montgomery Sicard stood at the center of the room. The air in the reception hall was still. It hung heavy with the scent of polished koa wood, beeswax, and the cloying perfume of jasmine flowers arranged in silver bowls. The smell was aggressive. The jasmine hit the back of his throat like syrup, triggering a gag reflex he barely suppressed. It was too rich, too cloying compared to the sterile, salt-scoured air of the reef.

He felt encased in plaster. The uniform he wore, a dress coat provided by an officer of the Kilauea, fitted him poorly. The collar chafed his neck, which was still raw from the salt boils. The wool felt intolerably heavy, a suffocating layer of civilization that trapped the heat of his body.

He stared at the table in front of the King. It was a massive slab of polished koa, dark and lustrous. Sicard's mind detached. He didn't see furniture; he saw scantlings. *I could get three garboard strakes out of that,* the voice in his head whispered. *It's straight grain. It would hold a screw.*

He looked at his hands. They were clean. The grime of the coral, the grease of the seal meat, the soot of the signal fires, it had all been scrubbed away with hot water and soap. But they still felt dirty. They felt like the hands of a man who had buried his friends in the sand.

He kept them clasped behind his back to hide the tremor.

Across the room, sitting on a chair of velvet and gilt, was His Majesty, King Kamehameha V.

The King was a mountain of a man. He wore a black frock coat with the star of the Order of Kamehameha pinned to his breast. His face was grave, his eyes dark and unreadable. He watched Sicard with a gaze that seemed to strip away the uniform and see the starving man underneath.

Surrounding the King were his ministers, the American Minister Mr. Peirce, and the dignitaries of Honolulu. They were silent. They were watching the survivor.

Sicard cleared his throat. The sound was too loud in the high-ceilinged room.

He had written the speech that morning, sitting at a desk in the American Consulate, his pen scratching against the paper while the sounds of the city drifted in through the window. He had agonized over the words. How do you thank a King for saving your life when the price of that life was five men? How do you balance the ledger of gratitude and grief?

He unfolded the paper. His fingers were stiff.

"Your Majesty," Sicard began.

His voice was thin. It lacked the resonance of the quarterdeck. It was the voice of a man who had shouted against the wind for seventy days and had nothing left. He paused, forcing himself to breathe as the words on the paper swam before his eyes, and looked up to meet the gaze of the King.

"I appear before Your Majesty," Sicard said, finding the steel in his chest, "to offer, on behalf of the government of the United States, and of the officers and crew of the USS *Saginaw*, our heartfelt thanks."

The words felt hollow. *Thanks*. It was too small a word.

"We stood on the threshold of eternity," Sicard continued. "We were cast upon a desolate reef, stripped of our ship, our resources, and our hope. We watched the horizon for a sail that never came."

He saw the faces of the men in the saw-pit. Lynch, covered in sawdust, coughing. O'Neil collapsing in the sand.

"We were saved not by chance, but by the prompt and generous action of Your Majesty."

Sicard bowed his head slightly.

"When the news of our distress reached your ears, you did not hesitate. You did not count the cost. You sent your own steamer, the *Kilauea*, stripping her of her cargo and dispatching her with a speed that saved us from the slow death of starvation."

He swallowed. The memory of the *Kilauea*'s smoke on the horizon rose up in his mind, that black smear that had looked like a bruise and then like a miracle.

"For this act of humanity, for this kindness and hospitality, we are your debtors forever."

The King nodded slowly. His expression did not change, but there was a softening in his eyes. He understood. He was a man of the sea; he knew what it meant to wait for a ship.

Sicard gripped the paper tighter. Now came the hard part.

"But our deliverance was bought with a price."

The room seemed to grow colder.

"I must speak of the men who made this rescue possible. I must speak of the gig."

Sicard closed his eyes for a second. He saw the boat pulling away from the lagoon. The white canvas of the sails. Talbot's hand raised in farewell.

"Lieutenant John G. Talbot," Sicard said. The name was a stone in his mouth. "A young officer of rare promise. A Christian gentleman. He volunteered for the forlorn hope when others held back. He navigated a small boat across fifteen hundred miles of the most tempestuous ocean on the globe."

He looked at the American Minister. Peirce was weeping silently, a handkerchief pressed to his eyes.

"He did his duty," Sicard said, his voice trembling with a sudden, sharp anger that he quickly suppressed. "He did more than his duty. He gave his life to save ours."

He thought of Talbot drowning in the dark. He thought of the heavy coat dragging him down. He thought of the silence of the soil.

"And with him, three noble seamen. Peter Francis. John Andrews. James Muir."

He listed them like a roll call.

"They were men of iron. They suffered thirst, hunger, and exposure that would have broken lesser spirits. They endured thirty-one days of hell in a cockleshell boat."

Sicard looked down at his boots. The polished leather seemed obscene.

"They reached the land. They saw the green hills of Kauai. And in the moment of their triumph, the sea claimed them."

He paused. He couldn't go on. The image of the bodies washing in the surf, bruised and blackened, blocked his throat.

He took a breath. He looked at the King again.

"Only one remains," Sicard whispered. "Coxswain William Halford."

The name hung in the air. Halford was not in the room. He was in the hospital, recovering from his wounds. But his presence was there, a ghost standing at Sicard's shoulder.

"To him, and to the memory of his dead comrades, we owe our lives. Their devotion and gallantry will never be forgotten by the Navy, or by the men they saved."

Sicard folded the paper. He put it in his pocket.

He touched the packet containing the bill of exchange, the two hundred pounds sterling meant to charter a rescue. He hesitated, then withdrew his hand empty. To offer money now, in the face of such royal grace, would be an insult. The King had not sent a ship for profit; he had sent it for brotherhood.

"Your Majesty," Sicard said, his voice steady now, quiet and final. "We are eighty-eight men who have walked out of the grave. We thank you for opening the door."

He bowed low.

The King stood up. The movement was massive, a displacement of air.

"Captain Sicard," the King said. His voice was deep, rolling like the surf at Hanalei. "The Kingdom of Hawaii mourns with you. The sacrifice of Lieutenant Talbot and his men is a sorrow to us all. But their bravery is a light that honors both our nations."

The King stepped down from the dais. He walked over to Sicard. He extended his hand.

Sicard took it. The King's grip was warm and solid.

"You are welcome in my islands, Captain," the King said softly. "Rest. You have carried a heavy load."

"Thank you, sir," Sicard whispered.

The audience was over.

Sicard turned. He walked out of the hall. He walked past the ministers, past the weeping diplomat, past the guards in their dress uniforms.

He walked out of the palace and into the bright, blinding sun of Honolulu.

It was the same sun that had baked the sand of Ocean Island. It was the same sun that had blistered their skin and boiled their brains.

But here, it shone on manicured lawns and carriage paths.

Sicard stopped on the steps. He put his hat on. He pulled the brim low.

The adrenaline that had sustained him for seventy days, the manic energy of command, was gone. It had drained out of him in the reception hall, leaving a hollow shell.

He was a captain without a ship. He was a commander who had lost his executive officer.

He looked at the harbor. He could see the masts of the ships rising above the rooftops.

He thought of the *Saginaw*. She was still there, impaled on the reef, being slowly ground to dust by the Pacific. She was the only thing that really understood.

She had stayed behind.

Sicard walked down the steps. He didn't know where he was going. He just needed to walk.

He pulled his hat brim lower and stepped off the curb, disappearing into the dust and the bustle of the Honolulu street. He sought the distraction of the city, the rattle of carriage wheels and the peal of church bells. Beneath the laughter and the commerce, he could still hear it. It vibrated in the cobblestones; it echoed in the hollow of his chest. The ceaseless, grinding thunder of surf. The roar of the reef.

Epilogue
THE ECHO

The career of the USS *Saginaw* ended on the coral teeth of Kure Atoll, but the careers of the men who survived her continued, shaped and shadowed by the sixty-eight days they spent on the boundary of existence.

For William Halford, the sole survivor of the gig, the ordeal did not end with the healing of his leg or the mending of his ribs. He carried the map of the voyage on his skin for the rest of his life, a topography of scars left by the salt boils and the sun. But the Navy, an institution that values survival against odds, recognized the magnitude of his feat.

Halford was promoted to the rank of Gunner, a warrant officer position that lifted him out of the enlisted mess and gave him the authority he had so clearly demonstrated in the cockpit of the gig. He was awarded the Medal of Honor.

The citation was brief, a bureaucratic distillation of thirty-one days of agony into a single sentence of recognition. It spoke of his "gallant and heroic conduct" as the sole survivor of the boat crew. He wore the medal not as a decoration, but as a witness. He remained in the service for decades, a living legend among younger sailors who looked at the grim, unvarnished man and whispered about the price of a quart of sperm oil and the taste of raw albatross. He lived until 1919, outliving the age of sail and steam, a walking monument to the indomitable will of the common seaman.

For Montgomery Sicard, the path was different. The loss of a ship is a stain that often ends a commander's ascent, regardless of the cause. A Court of Inquiry was held, as was mandatory, to investigate the wrecking of the *Saginaw*. Sicard stood before his peers, armed with his charts and his logs, and gave his account of the currents and the darkness.

He was exonerated. The Navy recognized that the decision to check Ocean Island was made in the direct line of his duty. His career did not founder on the reef. He rose through the ranks with the steady, inexorable precision that had defined his command on the island. He became a bureau chief, overseeing the construction of the new steel navy that would replace the wooden paddle-wheelers of his youth.

He eventually attained the rank of Rear Admiral. He commanded the North Atlantic Squadron, a fleet of steel battleships that possessed firepower the *Saginaw* could never have imagined. Yet, those who served with him noted a certain gravity, a permanent shadow behind the eyes of the Admiral. The burden of the five men he sent into the surf at Kauai never fully lifted.

But the most enduring legacy of the wreck was not found in the service records of the living. It was found in the stone and brass dedicated to the dead.

In the chapel of the United States Naval Academy in Annapolis, far from the roar of the Pacific surf, a memorial tablet was commissioned. It was placed there to instruct future generations of officers on the definition of duty.

The tablet is made of marble, cold and permanent. It does not list the rations or the navigation. It lists the names.

Lieutenant John G. Talbot.

Peter Francis, Quartermaster.

John Andrews, Coxswain.

James Muir, Captain of Hold.

The inscription reads: "*In memory of the men of the USS SAGINAW who were drowned, 19 December 1870. While attempting to land on the Island of Kauai.*"

It stands as a silent lecture to the midshipmen who pass it every day. It reminds them that the sea is not merely a theater of war, but a crucible of character. It reminds them that the highest tradition of the naval service is not victory in battle, but the willingness to lay down one's life for one's crew.

Talbot and his men did not vanish into the black water of Kalihi Kai. They were transmuted. They ceased to be flesh and blood and became an ideal. They became the standard against which every act of sacrifice in the Navy would be measured for a century.

PRESENT DAY

The roar is the same, a ceaseless, grinding thunder that has not paused for a single second in one hundred and thirty years.

Kure Atoll. *Hōlanikū.*

It is a place of blinding light and deafening sound. The albatross still wheel overhead, their wings spanning the trade winds, casting fleeting shadows on the white sand. The monk seals still haul their heavy, grey bodies onto the beach to sleep in the sun, indifferent to the history beneath their flippers. The rats are gone, eradicated by conservationists to save the birds, but the island remains a wild, hostile, beautiful speck in the void.

Beneath the surface of the lagoon, where the water shifts from electric turquoise to deep indigo, the silence returns.

In the high-energy surf zone, where the swell trips over the limestone barrier, the reef is a chaotic topography of spur and groove. The water is choked with particulates, a swirling fog of crushed shell and sand.

Through the gloom, the shapes appear.

They are not natural. They are hard, linear, industrial.

The paddlewheel shaft lies fractured on the bottom, a broken limb of the Industrial Revolution cast into a wilderness of living coral. It is thick, heavily concreted, crusted with pink coralline algae, yet unmistakable. It is the spine of the ship, snapped by a force that the engineers in California could not calculate.

Nearby, the weapons sleep.

The two Parrott rifled pivot guns loom against the pale reef. They are dark, heavy shapes, distinctly lethal. They lie on their sides, half-buried, sleeping giants that once roared in the Gulf of Mexico, now silent in the Central Pacific. The iron is corroding, bleeding rust into the water, slowly returning to the mineral state from which it was forged. But it endures. It resists the ocean.

The ocean does not keep organic matter in the surf zone; it grinds it to dust and scatters it into the current. The flesh of the *Saginaw*, the oak planks, the pine decks, the hemp ropes, has long since disintegrated.

But the iron remains.

It is a forensic map of catastrophe. It is a physical proof that ninety-three men once stood here, shivering in the dark, watching their world break apart.

The "*Saginaw Junior*" is gone, washed away by a century of tides. The ship's bell is gone, lifted from the reef in 2008 to stand its watch in a museum in Hilo. The gig survives, a relic of cedar and salt, housed in a Navy collection in Virginia, outlasting the men who pulled her oars.

But the reef remains.

It is the gatekeeper. It is the threshold between the *Ao* and the *Pō*, the realm of the living and the realm of the gods.

The waves roll in from the north, heavy with the momentum of the Aleutians. They rise up, dark and glossy walls of water. They feel the drag of the bottom. They stand tall.

They break.

They crash down on the iron bones of the gunboat with a violence that shakes the seabed. The water boils white. The foam hisses.

And then the wave recedes, pulling back into the deep, leaving the iron to rust in the suspended animation of the blue.

The violence is temporary; the geology is eternal. The reef stands as it stood before the *Saginaw*, and before the *Gledstanes*, a jagged gatekeeper between the world of men and the world of gods.

The currents shift. The sand settles. The view clears.

There is nothing here but the iron, the coral, and the light. *Hōlanikū* has swallowed the intruders, and the boundary of existence is sealed once more.

THE END

Historical Image

USS Saginaw at Mare Island *Illustration, circa 1860.* The side-wheel steamer as she appeared at the Mare Island Naval Yard shortly after construction. The image documents the transitional paddle-box design and the wooden hull that would later be lost on the reef at Ocean Island. *The Last Cruise of the Saginaw (Boston: Houghton Mifflin Company, 1912).*

The Midway Islands as We Left Them *Sketch by Montgomery Sicard, 1870.* A rendering of the shore camp at Midway. The image documents the improvised huts and the pervasive albatross population of the atoll. This sketch represents the final survey of the terrestrial landscape before the *Saginaw* departed for Ocean Island.
The Last Cruise of the Saginaw (Boston: Houghton Mifflin Company, 1912).

The Landing at Midway Islands *Sketch by Montgomery Sicard, 1870.* A rendering of the sandbanks during the seven-month dredging operation. The foreground documents the local seals and albatross that shared the atoll with the blasting parties.
The Last Cruise of the Saginaw (Boston: Houghton Mifflin Company, 1912).

The Wreck of the Saginaw *Sketch by Montgomery Sicard, 1870.* The Captain's depiction of Saginaw's fate.
The Last Cruise of the Saginaw (Boston: Houghton Mifflin Company, 1912).

Gathering Timbers from the Wreck *Sketch by Montgomery Sicard, November 1870.* Crew members salvaging lumber from the surf zone following the ship's disintegration on the reef. These planks and timbers provided the raw materials for the construction of the rescue schooner. *The Last Cruise of the Saginaw (Boston: Houghton Mifflin Company, 1912).*

The Storehouse *Sketch by Montgomery Sicard, 1870.* The camp's primary supply depot. The structure was elevated on stilts to protect the remaining stores of hardtack and salt pork from the island's pervasive rat population.

The Last Cruise of the Saginaw (Boston: Houghton Mifflin Company, 1912).

The Condenser *Sketch by Montgomery Sicard, 1870.* A technical rendering of the improvised distilling apparatus. Engineered from a salvaged boiler and copper speaking-tubes, this machine provided the camp with fresh water.

The Last Cruise of the Saginaw (Boston: Houghton Mifflin Company, 1912).

The Captain's Tent *Sketch by Montgomery Sicard, 1870.* The commanding officer's quarters at "Camp Saginaw." Fashioned from salvaged canvas and rigging, this structure served as the administrative hub for the ninety-three survivors.

The Last Cruise of the Saginaw (Boston: Houghton Mifflin Company, 1912).

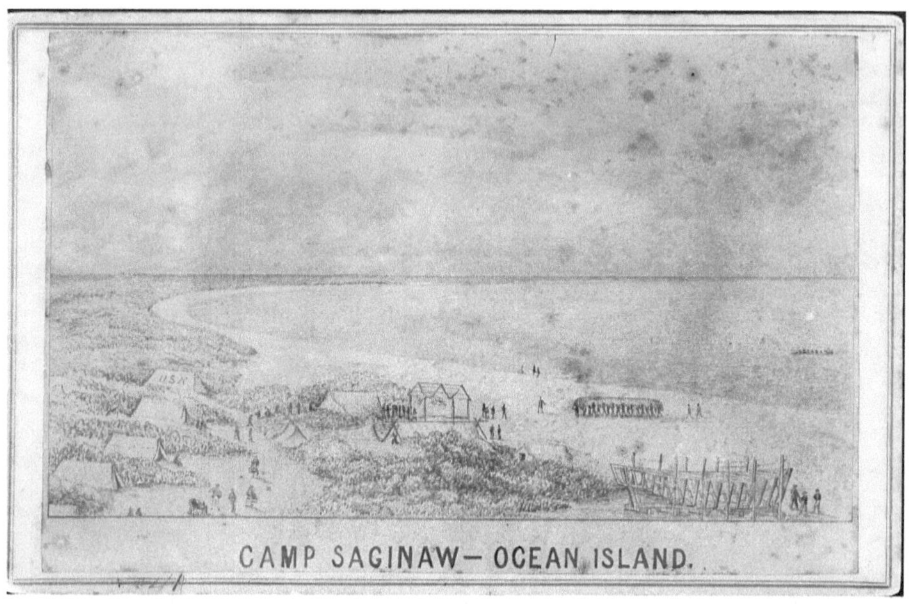

The Camp *Sketch by Montgomery Sicard, 1870.* The camp from survivors of Saginaw. The image documents the stark, low-profile environment of the atoll and the improvised shelters constructed from salvaged canvas and wreckage.

The Last Cruise of the Saginaw (Boston: Houghton Mifflin Company, 1912).

The Gig Before Launching *Sketch by Montgomery Sicard, 1870.* The 22-foot captain's gig prepared for its 1,500-mile voyage. The sketch highlights the improvised sails and modified hull designed to endure the open-ocean passage to Hawaii.
The Last Cruise of the Saginaw (Boston: Houghton Mifflin Company, 1912).

Ripping Timbers for the Schooner *Sketch by Montgomery Sicard, 1870.* Survivors using hand saws to rip salvaged oak and pine into workable planks.
The Last Cruise of the Saginaw (Boston: Houghton Mifflin Company, 1912).

The Frame of the Schooner *Sketch by Montgomery Sicard, 1870.* The skeletal ribs and keel of the *Saginaw Junior* on its stocks at Ocean Island. *The Last Cruise of the Saginaw (Boston: Houghton Mifflin Company, 1912).*

The Starboard Side of the Gig *Contemporary Photograph, 1871.* A profile of the 22-foot captain's gig following its recovery. The image shows the modifications made to the hull on the island, including the raised washboards designed to keep the boat afloat in heavy seas.
The Last Cruise of the Saginaw (Boston: Houghton Mifflin Company, 1912).

Deck View of the Gig *Contemporary Photograph, 1871.* Deck view perspective of the boat after its arrival in Hawaii. The cramped interior reflects the physical constraints endured by the five men during their thirty-one-day passage.

The Last Cruise of the Saginaw (Boston: Houghton Mifflin Company, 1912).

Rear Admiral Montgomery Sicard *Portrait Photograph, circa 1890s.* A later portrait of the *Saginaw's* commanding officer. Sicard (1836–1900) survived the subsequent court of inquiry and eventually rose to command the North Atlantic Squadron.

The Last Cruise of the Saginaw (Boston: Houghton Mifflin Company, 1912).

Coxswain William Halford *Portrait Photograph, circa 1870.* A studio portrait of the only survivor of the relief expedition. Halford was awarded the Medal of Honor for his "distinguished gallantry" in reaching Hawaii to seek help.

U.S. Naval History and Heritage Command (NH 930).

Lieutenant John G. Talbot *Portrait Photograph, circa 1870.* The ship's Executive Officer and leader of the relief expedition. Talbot drowned in the surf at Kalihi Kai on December 19, 1870, after navigating the gig 1,500 miles across the Pacific.

The Last Cruise of the Saginaw (Boston: Houghton Mifflin Company, 1912).

Passed Assistant Engineer James Butterworth *Portrait Photograph, circa 1870.* The officer responsible for the ship's machinery. On Ocean Island, Butterworth utilized his expertise to construct the improvised condenser that provided the crew with fresh water.
The Last Cruise of the Saginaw (Boston: Houghton Mifflin Company, 1912).

Captain Thomas Long *Contemporary Photograph, 1871.* Master of the Hawaiian government steamer *Kilauea.* Long navigated the relief vessel to Ocean Island in January 1871 to embark the ninety-three survivors. *The Last Cruise of the Saginaw (Boston: Houghton Mifflin Company, 1912).*

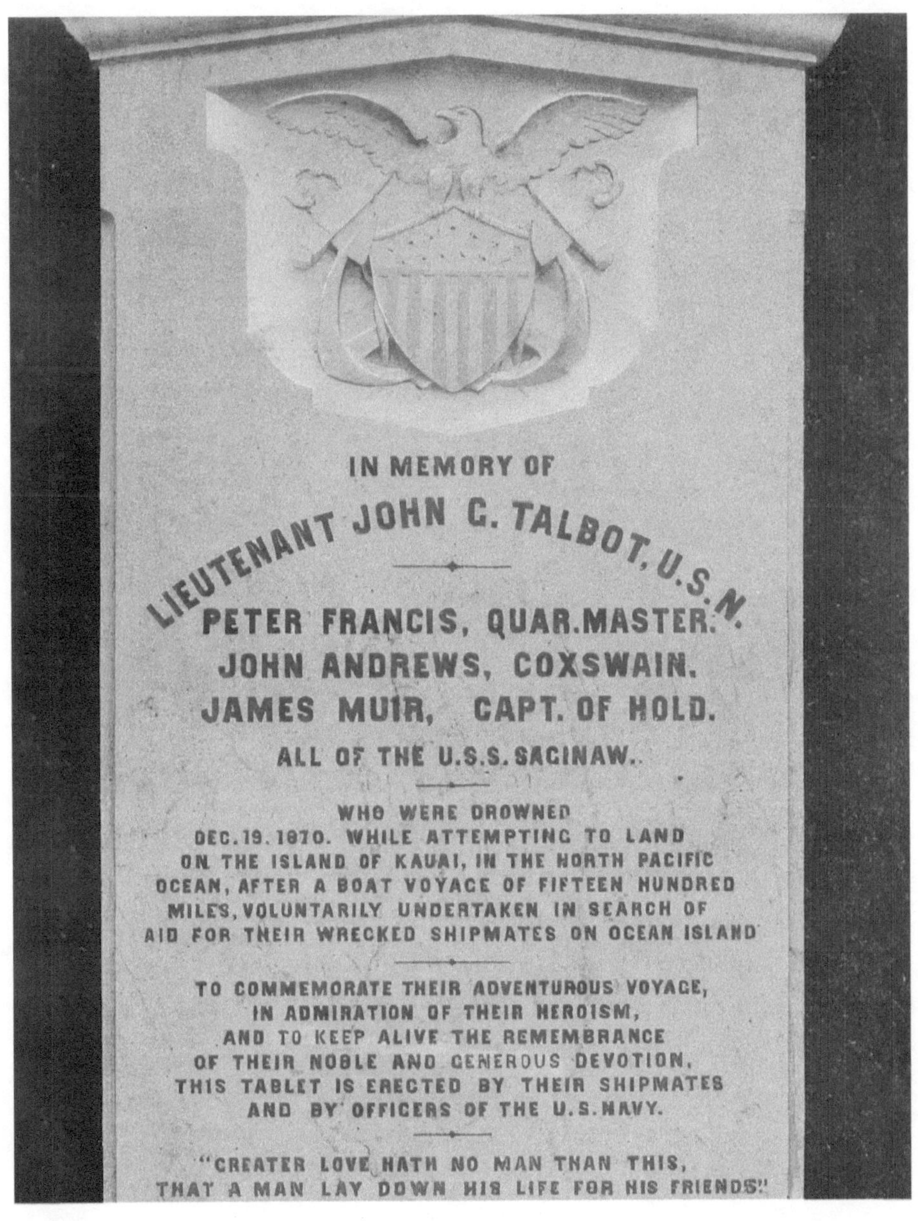

The Memorial Tablet *Contemporary Photograph.* The tablet dedicated to the memory of Lieutenant Talbot and the volunteers of the *Saginaw's* gig. It stands as a permanent witness to the sacrifice made to secure the rescue of the crew.
National Museum of the U.S. Navy.

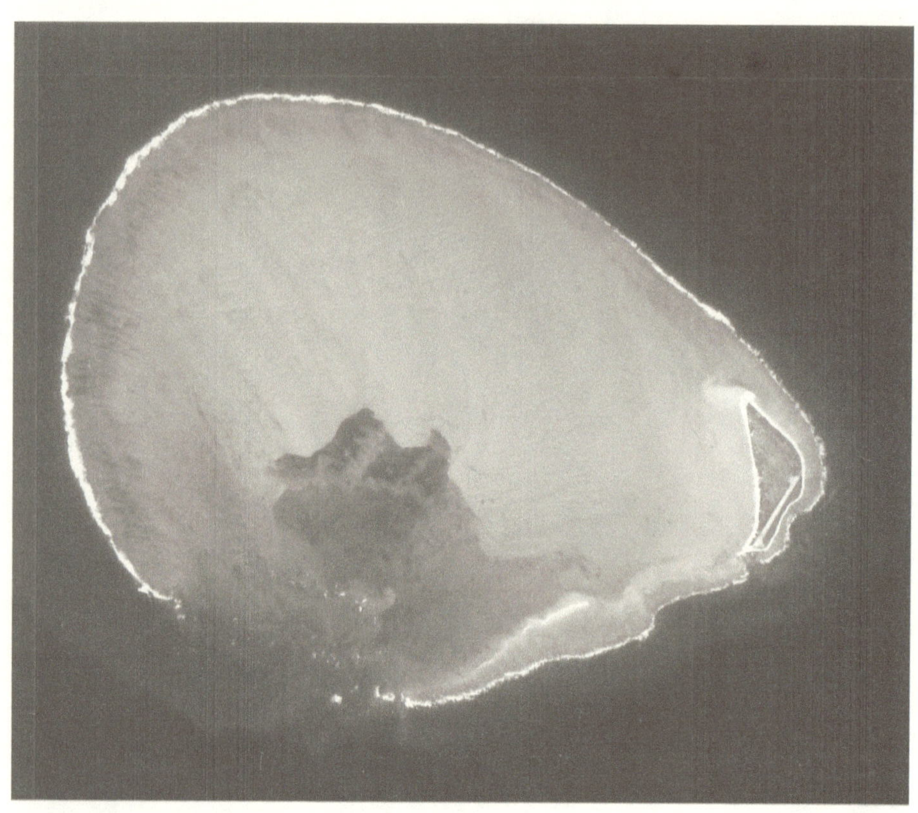

Satellite View of Kure Atoll (Hōlanikū) *NASA/International Space Station (ISS) Expedition 6.* An orbital view of the remote atoll. The white line of the seaward reef marks the site where the *Saginaw* struck. The tiny speck of Green Island is visible within the turquoise lagoon.
Image Science and Analysis Laboratory, NASA-Johnson Space Center.

Green Island in October 1959 *Official U.S. Navy Photograph.* A ground-level view of the island as it appeared nearly ninety years after the wreck. The low-profile scrub and shifting sands reflect the desolate environment faced by the survivors.
National Museum of the U.S. Navy.

Aerial Survey of Green Island *Photograph by Chandler S. Robbins, 1959.*
An aerial perspective showing the island after the clearing of landing strips
for albatross research. This view illustrates the precarious isolation of the
sandbank within the surrounding reef.
U.S. Geological Survey (USGS).

Endnotes

Sources and Select Bibliography

Primary Eyewitness Accounts & Archival Records

Halford, William. c. 1871. *Account of the Cruise of the Saginaw's Gig.*
Note: Halford's narrative records the mechanics of the boat's handling, the severe rationing, the physical degradation of the five volunteers, and the final capsizing at Kalihi Kai.

Read, George H. 1912. *The Last Cruise of the Saginaw.* Boston and New York: Houghton Mifflin Company.
Note: The foundational published memoir. Read provides micro-textures of daily survival on the sandbank, the construction of the rescue vessel from salvaged timber, and the psychological weight of isolation.

Sicard, Montgomery. 1870–1871. *Official Reports and Correspondence of Lieutenant Commander Montgomery Sicard.* > *Note:* Documents Sicard's command decisions, his recommendation to abandon salvage on the reef, his address to King Kamehameha V, and his formal recommendation of Halford for the Medal of Honor.

United States Navy Department. 1870–1871. *The Deck Log-Book of the U.S.S. Saginaw.* Record Group 24, National Archives and Records Administration (NARA).
Note: Captures weather observations, navigation computations, and the impact with the reef crest on October 29, 1870. Related artifacts (boathook and sextant) reside in the Castle Museum of Saginaw County, Michigan.

United States Navy Department. 1871. *Annual Report of the Secretary of the Navy for the Year 1871.* Washington, DC: Government Printing Office.

Note: Records the disaster from the strategic viewpoint of the Pacific Fleet.

Academic & Modern Historical Works

DeArmond, R. N. 1997. *The USS Saginaw in Alaska Waters, 1867–1868.* Fairbanks: Limestone Press.

Note: Tracks the earlier operational life of the gunboat, pulling from the journals of Peveril Meigs and Richard Worsam Meade.

Hawaii Board on Geographic Names (HBGN). 2023. *Meeting Materials regarding Kure Atoll (Hōlanikū).* Meeting of June 7, 2023.

Note: Administrative records tracking the cartographic and cultural naming history of the atoll.

Raupp, Jason Thomas. 2015. *"And So Ends this Day's Work": Industrial Perspectives on Early Nineteenth-century American Whaleships Wrecked in the Northwestern Hawaiian Islands.* Doctoral Thesis, Flinders University, South Australia.

Note: Provides historical and industrial context for the Pacific shipwrecks preceding the *Saginaw.* Maps the physical debris of nineteenth-century maritime disasters.

Van Tilburg, Hans Konrad. 2010. *A Civil War Gunboat in Pacific Waters: Life on Board USS Saginaw.* Honolulu: University of Hawaii Press.

Note: The definitive modern study. Van Tilburg bridges the gap between historical documents and underwater archaeology.

Periodical & Archaeological Reports

McCleary, J. R. 2000. "Nineteenth Century Building Instructions, U.S.S. Saginaw." *Nautical Research Journal* 45, no. 3.

Note: Technical analysis of construction details and inclined oscillating steam engines.

National Oceanic and Atmospheric Administration (NOAA). 2003, 2006. *Maritime Heritage Expeditions at Kure and Midway Atolls.* Office of National Marine Sanctuaries.

Note: Survey files mapping the debris field, including boiler tubes, paddlewheel shafts, and Parrott rifled pivot guns.

Sea History. 2008. "Whaling Shipwrecks in the Northwest Hawaiian Islands: The 2008 Maritime Heritage Archaeological Expedition." *Sea History*, 2008.

Note: Detailed underwater archaeological survey of the *Saginaw* and the whaler *Parker*.

The Final Muster

The following is the roll of the officers and crew of the U.S.S. Saginaw as it appeared on the pay-roll at the time of her loss on the reef of Ocean Island, October 29, 1870.

Officers
Montgomery Sicard, Lieutenant Commander
John G. Talbot, Lieutenant
J.K. Cogswell, Ensign
Perry Garst, Ensign
A.H. Parsons, Ensign
George H. Read, Passed Assistant Paymaster
James Butterworth, Passed Assistant Engineer
H.C. Blye, Passed Assistant Engineer (In charge of contractor's party)
John J. Ryan, Second Assistant Engineer
C.D. Foss, Second Assistant Engineer
Herschel Main, Second Assistant Engineer
Jones Godfrey, Second Assistant Engineer
George H. Robinson, Master's Mate

Petty Officers
Peter Francis, Quartermaster
Nicholas Barton, Quartermaster
Thomas Hayes, Sailmaker's Mate
John Lane, Boatswain's Mate
James Foschack, Gunner's Mate
J.M. Logan, Yeoman

William Halford, Coxswain
Samuel A. Thompson, Master at Arms
Charles Hale, Paymaster's Yeoman
A.E. Myfinger, Cabin Steward
Solomon Graves, Cabin Cook
Joseph Ross, Wardroom Steward
George D. Wauchoss, Wardroom Cook
Henry B. Clark, Third-class Apothecary
William Edman, Ship's Cook
Henry Wallace, Steerage Steward
L. McCabe, Steerage Cook

Engine Room Force
Francis Scott, First-class Fireman
Lorenzo Coburg, First-class Fireman
George White, First-class Fireman
George Hubert, Second-class Fireman

Seamen
William Cairns, Seaman
Michael Lynch, Seaman
Henry D. Vivian, Seaman
Daniel Collins, Seaman
Joseph A. Bailey, Ordinary Seaman
John H. Wallace, Ordinary Seaman
Dennis A. Fitzgerald, Ordinary Seaman
John Daley, Ordinary Seaman
Charles Brown, Ordinary Seaman
Dennis M. Hayes, Ordinary Seaman
Michael Jordan, Ordinary Seaman
Edward James, Ordinary Seaman

Landsmen
James Nichols

W.J. Evans
Edward O'Brien
Thomas Kearney
J.R. Miller
Martin Doran
William Fallon
Thomas Larkin
Joseph McLaughlin
George Saunders
William Combs
Joseph A. Agarrie
Michael Garvey
John Murphy
John Downs
James McNamara
John Riley
Thomas Melody
James M. Nolan

Marine Guard
Charles A. Martin, Orderly Sergeant
John G. Moore, Corporal
Phillip Morris, Corporal
D.G. Brennan, Private
Thomas Wiseman, Private
David Muir, Private
James Sarsfield, Private
Thomas Jones, Private
John McGrath, Private
Lewis Peck, Private

About The Author

R.J.Jones

R.J. Jones is an Australian author with a background in digital media spanning more than two decades. His work focuses on reconstructing real events through detailed research and clear, immersive narrative.

Drawing on primary historical sources, including logbooks, journals, and firsthand accounts, Jones writes narrative non-fiction that emphasizes accuracy, structure, and the physical realities of survival. His approach combines careful documentation with a strong sense of place, bringing historical events to life in a direct and accessible style.

His interest in history, science, and the natural world informs his exploration of events shaped by extreme environments and human decision under pressure. His background in film, photography, and digital production continues to influence his work, with a focus on clarity, pacing, and narrative cohesion.